"The recent revival of interest in Huldrych [illegible] in life and after his death, Zwingli's career and beliefs have been much misunderstood. In this succinct introduction, Dr. Eccher opens up the world of this neglected Reformer with sympathy and understanding alongside criticism and disagreement at different points. This is a much-needed guide to a complex man, whose influence on the Reformation has yet to be fully appreciated."

—**Gerald Bray,** research professor of divinity, Beeson Divinity School

"Stephen Eccher has provided a helpful work of historical retrieval for ecclesial renewal with this book. Not only does it inform and clarify a complicated Reformation life for modern readers, it also instructs as to the value of remembering the complex. Such work requires the care of a pastor as well as a historian in order to bring a right understanding of Zwingli's place and contribution—and in that shepherding care Eccher has excelled."

—**Jason G. Duesing,** provost and professor of historical theology,
Midwestern Baptist Theological Seminary

"Often pushed to the sidelines in studies of the mainline Reformers, Huldrych Zwingli is making a comeback. This book, well-written and carefully researched, makes an important contribution to that effort. Zwingli the pastor shines forth as the shepherd of the church in Zurich and the pioneer of the Reformed tradition. Highly recommended!"

—**Timothy George,** distinguished professor of divinity,
Beeson Divinity School, Samford University

"In the best tradition of writing on the Reformation, Stephen Eccher weaves together theology and history, biography and context, and past and present in a book on Zwingli that is both profound and a joy to read. Moving easily between the sixteenth century and our time, this is the ideal book for those who think the Reformation is a distant, forgotten time as well as for those who know it is not. A compelling read."

—**F. Bruce Gordon,** Titus Street Professor of Ecclesiastical History,
Yale Divinity School; author of *Zwingli: God's Armed Prophet*

"Eccher blends the rich storytelling of a good historian with keen theological insights into the pastoral ministry of Zwingli. This book unveils Zwingli as pastor just as the Swiss Reformer 'unveiled' the gospel from his Zurich pulpit in spite of a life filled with conflicts."

—**Jason K. Lee,** professor of theological studies, Cedarville University

"Stephen Eccher's book, *Zwingli the Pastor*, deftly tackles the complexity of Zwingli's history and legacy in order to draw to light a side of Zwingli all too rarely observed and easily overshadowed by the politics of his time. Rather than sidestep that conflict, Eccher's book invites the reader to explore the enigma that surrounds Zwingli through the conflicts he navigated during his pastoral ministry. Eccher's insightful contribution will no doubt become a mainstay for any Reformation bookshelf."

—**Jennifer Powell McNutt,** Franklin S. Dyrness Chair in Biblical and Theological Studies and associate professor of theology and history of Christianity, Wheaton College Graduate School

"With engaging clarity and authority, Eccher unwraps the enigmatic figure who set the Swiss Confederation on the road to Reformation. This excellent and compelling book does full justice to the theological vision of this unabashed radical who took Zurich by storm and died defending the cause."

—**Andrew Pettegree,** Bishop Wardlaw Professor, University of St. Andrews; author of *Brand Luther*

"With engaging style yet subtle precision, Stephen Eccher reveals the biblical grounding, difficult context, and pastoral wisdom which shaped the transformative ministry of Ulrich Zwingli. The recent renaissance in Zwinglian literature has long been needed, for the Zurich Reformer was the first major Reformed theologian, preceding Calvin and challenging Luther in the Reformation rediscovery of the gospel. Due to Eccher's academic credentials and popular voice, *Zwingli the Pastor: A Life in Conflict* will doubtless become the introductory text for those who want to discover the foundational thinker of the Reformed movement."

—**Malcolm B. Yarnell III,** research professor of theology, Southwestern Baptist Theological Seminary; teaching pastor, Lakeside Baptist Church, Granbury, Texas

ZWINGLI *the* PASTOR

A Life in Conflict

ZWINGLI *the* PASTOR

A Life in Conflict

STEPHEN BRETT ECCHER

Zwingli the Pastor: A Life in Conflict

Lexham Press, 1313 Commercial St., Bellingham, WA 98225
LexhamPress.com

Print ISBN 9781683597353
Digital ISBN 9781683597360
Library of Congress Control Number 2023942787

Lexham Editorial: Todd Hains, Andrew Sheffield, Mandi Newell
Cover Design: Jim LePage
Typesetting: Abigail Stocker

For my mom and dad,
with all my love and my deepest affection

Ulrich Zwingli statue outside the Wasserkirche (Water Church) erected in 1885 to commemorate the quadricentennial anniversary of the Reformer's birth

Contents

Acknowledgments

IT IS HARD FOR ME to imagine this work coming to fruition without the thousands of students I have been blessed to meet and teach at Southeastern Baptist Theological Seminary over the course of my career. Each of my students, both past and present, has always sharpened, challenged, and inspired me in my work. They have collectively steered me away from the esoteric aspects of the past and continually grounded me in the "so what" questions of history. As inquisitive students eager to prepare for ministry, they have helped me frame my academic labors for the benefit of Christ's bride, the church. Of those students, a special thanks to Drew Dickerson, Chandler McClean, Justin Myers, Joshua Pegram, Samuel Santiago-Bullington, and those students in my "History and Theology of the Reformation" and "Calvin and the Reformed Tradition" classes who read and critiqued chapter drafts of this book. Drew and Sam in particular served this project well as research assistants, and I am thankful for their contributions.

As a professor and author, I am inevitably a confluence of the teachers who taught me. And mine were some of the best. Former teachers and friends like David Allen Black, the late Dan Goodman, John Hammett, Perry Hildreth, Jason Lee, Steve McKinion, Gary Poe, and David Rayburn were those who first instilled in me a love for history, theology, and the Reformation.

My deepest gratitude to my friends at the University of St. Andrews and its Reformation Studies Institute. Bruce Gordon, Bridget Heal, Roger Mason, and Andrew Pettegree in particular stoked my love for the Reformers and helped turn a young, naïve Southern Baptist into a

Reformation historian. Your care for and investment in me were gifts that I will cherish for life. Jennifer Powell McNutt walked alongside me as a student in my doctoral studies at St. Andrews and now serves as one of the most valued of encouragers in my work.

Many thanks to the good people at Lexham Press for their work on this project. My editor Todd Hains played an essential role, helping to envision what this book might be long before the first word was ever written. Todd's recommendations, alongside his Lutheran convictions, also helped bring out the rich, though admittedly paradoxical and complex, narrative of Zwingli's life.

Special appreciation to Danny Akin, the administration, and the trustees at Southeastern Baptist Theological Seminary for providing me the space and resources to complete this book. Their support for this project has been a blessing. Also, a gracious research grant awarded through Southeastern and a sabbatical in spring 2019 were crucial in bringing this book to publication.

Writing about Zwingli's network of humanist friends throughout this book frequently left me reflecting on the cherished group of scholars and friends that surround me. I am ever grateful for my textual community at Southeastern: Seth Bible, Miguel Echevarria, Chip Hardy, Scott Hildreth, Ross Inman, Dave Jones, Ken Keathley, Jerry Lassetter, Tracy McKenzie, Ben Merkle, Adrianne Miles, Mark Liederbach, Matthew Mullins, Jake Pratt, Benjamin Quinn, George Robinson, Walter Strickland, and Steven Wade. Each has walked alongside me on this journey in unique and valuable ways. I am not the teacher or writer that I am today without their friendships, which are a cherished grace. Steve McKinion and Matt Mullins in particular read nearly the entirety of this book and offered invaluable suggestions. Certain others read and contributed to individual chapters. Scholars outside of Wake Forest, including Jonathan Arnold, Jason Duesing, Madison Grace, Jason Lee, Greg Mathias, Stephen Presley, Heath Thomas, Mike Wilkinson, Joshua Waggener, and Malcolm Yarnell, have supported me greatly in my work. Madison has been a constant support during the peaks and valleys of my writing process. My crew at Southeastern was instrumental to the completion of this work. Chip, Matt,

Scott, Steve and Steve, Trac, and Walter have been unwavering supporters, encouraging my daily 5:30 a.m. arrivals to the office and keeping track of my writing as they pushed me to get this project to print.

As one might imagine, any presentation about the pastoral ministry of a historic figure will inevitably be colored by the impressions of pastors from the author's own life. And I have had two of the best to draw inspiration from. First, my deepest gratitude goes to the late Reverend George Anderson, who served as the initial model of what a minister of God's word looked like for me. To an inquisitive, wide-eyed child first experiencing Christianity, his soft but authoritative voice helped me make sense of my world. His regular calls to repentance, alongside instructions about Christ's love and of a heavenly Father always awaiting the return of His prodigal children, profoundly ministered to me. He was the first to sow the seeds of the gospel in my life. Nothing greater could be asked of a faithful shepherd, and for that I am ever thankful. Second, to Dwayne Milioni, my heartfelt appreciation for the way that he has shepherded and cared for my soul over two-plus decades. D-Mil treated me like a son from the very beginning and loved me well during a season when I was hard to love. He has been a mentor, father in the faith, friend, and co-laborer. But I am most grateful for the weekly gospel drip that he provided my family through his preaching. That was a ministry to me as much as it was to them.

To say that this work would never have happened without Bruce Gordon is not hyperbole. More than any one person, Bruce stirred my love for the Reformers and my passion for the Swiss Reformation in particular. He provided excellent supervision during my master's and doctoral studies at St. Andrews, always instilling in me care for a sound historical methodology while also bestowing wisdom regarding how to navigate the challenges of the academy. That he spent countless hours of his own time to help me understand and read early modern Swiss German during my doctoral studies, for instance, speaks as much to his love for his students as it does his passion for the Reformation. His continued support and enthusiasm for my ongoing work remains a kindness beyond words.

To my wife, Cara, and my four amazing daughters: you are my life. I am grateful that you provided me the space and time to complete this work. But my heart was and always will be with you all. No amount of lauding for any book can compare with the cherished love I receive from my girls. And to my parents, Steve and Bev, what could be said? From the instruction you afforded me as a child, to your unwavering support of my academic pursuits across the pond, and now through my writing and teaching, you have both been a steadying anchor. The blustery winds and crashing waves that are life's challenges never stood a chance because of your love and support.

Author's Clarification

WRITING IN THE TWENTY-FIRST CENTURY about the distant and disparate world of the sixteenth century is fraught with difficulty. This is particularly true for translations of primary texts and in relation to the use of words and phrases from the early modern period. Words have meaning but not always the same meaning to different people. Therefore, I made certain editorial decisions to follow a few guidelines for the sake of consistency and contextualization.

Where English translations of Zwingli's writings are available, those have been retained and checked against the original Swiss German and Latin. Given the age of some of those translations, the English was updated in places following the originals for better readability to modern audiences. Where no English translations are available, the German and Latin were directly translated from the original sources by the author. When original Latin or German terms were purposefully employed in the prose, these were provided an accompanying definition in parentheses.

To remain true to the historical context of Zwingli's world, early modern verbiage was employed in favor of the more common modern parlance. This means that modern terms like Switzerland were jettisoned in favor of Swiss Confederation, cantons were defined as Swiss States, and so on. However, German terms were adapted to their English forms.

The phrase "evangelical gospel" is contextually situated and is used to distinguish between those Reformers who contended that justification was by grace through faith, as opposed to the sacramental theology of late medieval Catholicism. The capitalized word Reformed corresponds to the covenantal theology that emanated from the Swiss theologians of the early sixteenth century. The terms "Anabaptist" and "Radicals" are pregnant with meaning and are especially difficult to define given their polyvalent application in the historiography. However, "Anabaptist" is used here to refer to those Swiss Anabaptists, commonly known as the Swiss Brethren, whose theology birthed from the Grebel and Manz group and was eventually codified in the *Schleitheim Confession* of 1527. "Radicals" was employed as an umbrella category, including these Swiss Anabaptists, but was also applied to other figures who labored for reform outside of the governance of the civil magistrates.

Masculine pronouns corresponding to God have been retained and capitalized. To maintain the language of the early modern world, masculine pronouns have also been retained in the primary source translations. However, gender-inclusive language has been employed in the prose of this book to emphasize the theological importance of humanity as a broad designation.

Introduction

Visitors to the capacious Grossmunster ("Great Minster") Church in the city center of Zurich are greeted within a few feet of the main entrance by a relief of Heinrich Bullinger. Bullinger was a Swiss Reformer who pastored there from 1531 until his death in 1575. The carving on the northern façade of the building presents a bearded Bullinger adorned in common clerical robes and clinging to a Bible. This prominent display is a fitting tribute to a man who not only helped oversee the Grossmunster chapter at Zurich for forty-four years but also led the Swiss church through the tumultuous season following Reformation. The portico where this representation of Bullinger resides serves as the primary entrance and exit to the building, so the Reformer figuratively greets and bids farewell to all who visit the historic site.

Strikingly absent from this arresting tribute is Bullinger's friend, mentor, and predecessor at Zurich, Huldrych Zwingli. Visitors to the Grossmunster may still find vestiges of Zwingli today. However, one must almost know where to look to find them. For instance, on the building's southern side there is an obscure rear portal displaying the chi-rho and alpha-omega symbols often associated with Christ. Carved just above this archway in German are the words "Huldrych Zwingli started the Reformation in this house of God." This entry is sealed off by a closed pair of bronzed doors comprised of twenty-four pictorial panels, many of which depict Zwingli's life. The location of this door on the end opposite from the tourist traffic leaves this evidence of Zwingli's work at Zurich off the beaten path and thus largely ignored even by the city's local foot traffic. Apart from this entry and a few scant postcards of Zwingli in the gift shop, the Reformer is conspicuously absent from the famous church.

If you stray from the Grossmunster, a short winding walk westward brings you to the Wasser ("Water") Church, a small chapel located on the banks of the Limmat River. On the back side of that chapel is a bronze memorial to Zwingli that was unveiled in 1885 to commemorate his birth. The green-patinaed statue presents a larger-than-life Zwingli standing atop a pillar. Such a scale offers an apt depiction of Zwingli, given his importance and centrality to the narrative of the Swiss Reformation.[1] Much like the Bullinger memorial, the Zwingli of this statue is clad in a simple clerical robe and clutching a Bible with his right hand. However, unlike his successor's likeness, this effigy has the Reformer's left hang gripping a sword that points downward, resting calmly on the ground in front him. The statue faces due south, Zwingli's eyes ever affixed on Swiss lands like Zug and Schwyz, which stubbornly remained Catholic during his lifetime.

Today, this representation is a controversial landmark for the Swiss, given their modern sensibilities and the country's penchant for political neutrality. That secularism is now the dominant ideology for this once deeply religious people only adds to the disdain and oddity of this monument in the twenty-first century. Still, for a Reformer whose theology envisioned Zurich governed as a theocracy, with a divinely appointed role for both the prophet and the king, this statue is appropriate.

The statue's endurance in our modern world embodies many paradoxes and ironies essential to better understanding Zwingli's life and work. The Reformer served as a military chaplain in his younger years but later was an outspoken critic of Swiss mercenaries dying for the wars of foreign powers. He also suffered a horrific death on a battlefield in 1531. Thus, his grip on a blade offers both a powerful reminder and grim symbolism regarding his relationship with religious war. As a Reformer, he passionately spoke against the use of images in Christian worship, fearing that they would lead the Swiss to worship the creation rather than the Creator. So, a bronze likeness of him offers an enduring twist to this effort to remember him. But perhaps the most striking aspect of this memorial is its location. There is a sense of geographic irony to a representation of Zwingli so far displaced from the Grossmunster Church where he headquartered his reform efforts. It depicts a shepherd removed from his principal field of labor, a pastor distanced from his parishioners, a preacher separated from his pulpit.

This towering figure of the Reformation era remains mostly an afterthought to the people of Zurich today. His life and work are largely forgotten, even though he is the Reformer most associated with the idea of remembrance. The gifted preacher arrived at Zurich in 1518, tasked with shepherding the people primarily through the pulpit. Along the way he brought a revolution to the Zurich church, one that allowed its people to realize Reformation.

Zwingli's Reformation ambitions proved challenging. His desires for reform also required great sacrifice. From start to finish, discord, strife, and war marred Zwingli's story.[2] Every inch of Reformation ground gained at Zurich came steeped in conflict, every battle burdened by cost. This reality is one of the primary reasons for his marginalization today. It is true that conflict colored all the various manifestations of Reformation. The early modern period was an era of deep division. A fractured Christendom characterized the preceding medieval world, which many mistakenly assume was unified prior to the Reformation.[3] Nevertheless, in an era known for its religious and theological wars, conflict plagued Zwingli's ministry uniquely. Whether related to his ongoing battles with Catholicism, the civil magistrate's hesitancy to embrace his social vision, or radical factions within his own camp, unrest and contention marked Zwingli's pastoral tenure at Zurich.

For a man who sought to follow in his Savior's footsteps, there is a symmetry to Zwingli's biography based on John 1:11. Like Jesus, Zwingli came to shepherd his own Swiss people. He served diligently for twelve years at Zurich. Yet following his death in 1531, the Zurich people refused to count him as their own and worked to distance themselves from their former shepherd. At times they even tried to blot him from memory. To understand the modern Swiss concerns about Zwingli, and to recognize the minimization of his life both then and now, is to know his story.

It is not the purpose of this book to tell the entirety of Huldrych Zwingli's complex and layered life. This work is not a traditional biography. Regrettably, there is a dearth of Zwingli sketches from the mid-twentieth century until now. Thankfully, the works of historians like Luca Baschera, Bruce Gordon, Christian Moser, Jim West, and others are reengaging with this important figure and correcting the lack of Zwingli scholarship in the English-speaking world. We are indebted to these scholars. However, this project directs attention elsewhere. This book will consider Zwingli's pastoral ministry at Zurich, especially how conflict shaped and informed his pastorate, while also providing the context for his developing theology. Two earlier seasons of ministry and the affairs of the Zurich church in the years immediately following his death in 1531 will frame his decade-plus ministry at Zurich. But this book focuses mostly on the preacher's fascinating, extraordinary, and volatile time shepherding the Zurich people in both their faith and their embrace of the Reformation. Staking its claim at the intersection of history, theology, and ministry, this project aims to explore the unique ideas and reforms Zwingli mediated to the Swiss people, ideas born from, embodied by, and steeped in war.

The Reformer John Calvin famously spoke of our world as a "dazzling" or "glorious theatre" where each person experiences the works of God while playing a bit role in the unfolding of God's divine will.[4] For his part, Zwingli was a central character in the Swiss Reformation, his ministry at Zurich serving as a crucial transitional act in God's divine play. As one might expect, he made friendships, found love, and realized great achievements along the way. But all good dramas also include tense moments and unforeseen struggles that make life's blessings even sweeter. In Zwingli's case, strife uniquely characterized the drama of his life from start to finish. Conflict and division seemingly mired every act of his adventure. Before undertaking a journey into the drama of Zwingli's pastoral endeavors at Zurich, it will benefit us to consider a brief historical overview of his life and ministry. This will help identify the experiences and influences that shaped the embattled pastor who later emerged at Zurich.

ZWINGLI THE STUDENT

Zwingli was born on January 1, 1484, in the rural town of Wildhaus. One can still visit his birth house, a fantastic rustic home with its late medieval construction preserved. His given name was Ulrich, but early in his ministry he modified that to Huldrych, which means "rich in grace."[5] This change should come as no surprise, especially for a man who grew to know the power behind words and as a sense of prophetic obligation increasingly guided him. The dating of Zwingli's birth situated him as a contemporary of the German Reformer Martin Luther, who was a few months his senior. These two figures shared convictions and similarities, as one might expect. However, they were also two very different men who worked in unique contexts with disparate visions for reformation based on distinct theological frames.

Little is known of Zwingli's early childhood, with only a few meager details about this period available to us. Zwingli's father, also named Ulrich, was a prosperous farmer who served as a local magistrate at Wildhaus, a small rural community in the shadows of the Toggenburg Mountains. Early memories of his father's work undoubtedly shaped the future Reformer, likely informing his later views on the importance of community and guiding his understanding of the relationship between church and state.[6] At age five, Ulrich was sent to nearby Weesen for his education. He found accommodation with his Uncle Bartholomew, who helped direct his ministerial path in the coming years. At ten, Zwingli moved to Basel for his secondary education before spending a brief stint at Bern, a community he later helped reform.

In 1498, Zwingli enrolled at the University of Vienna. Little is known of this formative time of study, though some suggest his failure to mention any of his instructors at Vienna during later reflections indicates a lack of influence.[7] In 1502, he returned to the University of Basel, where he was immersed into the wondrous world of Renaissance humanism. The famed humanist Thomas Wyttenbach tutored him and helped ingrain in Zwingli a passion for studying primary sources. Swimming alongside others in the waters of humanism is also how he encountered Florentine Neoplatonism, a movement that elevated the place of the spiritual over the material.[8] As we will later see, this focus, much like his emphasis on original sources, profoundly guided the Reformer during his later pastorate at Zurich.

THE RENAISSANCE HUMANIST

Before he became a Reformer, Zwingli was a committed humanist. While it is difficult to discern when the shift from the latter to the former took place, many of the beliefs forged during his immersion into humanism remained throughout his life. These convictions guided his vision for reformation at Zurich. They also shaped his reading of the Bible, which informed the sermons he lovingly fed his flock. Understanding Renaissance humanism is crucial to considering Zwingli's pastoral ministry. Defining terms at this point is necessary. Sixteenth-century humanism must not be confused with modern usages of the term. To do so would grossly misrepresent Zwingli. The humanism of modernity is a philosophical system based upon a series of epistemological and anthropological suppositions. Modern humanist convictions are rooted in the belief that one cannot know anything for certain about the metaphysical. This belief frequently results in a wholesale rejection of God as a foundational premise. Modern humanism is also focused upon human reason and stresses things like the inherent goodness of humanity, the agency of individual persons, and an assumed ethic based upon the common good for society.

Other than a shared name, Renaissance humanism has almost nothing to do with the later, modern form. The humanism that Zwingli embraced was a late medieval cultural movement driven by education. Renaissance humanism drew from the literary fount of antiquity for its inspiration, exploring primary texts from the past as a means of contemporary renewal in the present. The humanists' desire to return *ad fontes* ("to the sources") drove their educational program. Those sources might include Greek philosophers, such as Plato and Aristotle, or a Roman orator like Cicero. Early church fathers and especially the Bible also drew humanists' attention. Regardless of the source, for the humanist, truth was not contained in past works in propositional form alone. More importantly, engaging with the myriad of literary and argumentative expressions from writings of bygone eras also provided a gateway toward truth. In other words, humanists sought not to directly embrace and imitate ideas or beliefs from antiquity but to explore and utilize the forms of argumentation from those ancient writings as a means of advancing human learning.[9]

Modern-day humanism is an ideology. Renaissance humanism was a pedagogy, an educational means or way of finding wisdom—not necessarily the wisdom itself. As a pedagogy, it was a deeply communal endeavor, conversing with voices from the past alongside those in the present to make sense of the human experience. Committed humanists shared ongoing discussions about their studies, pushing one another toward a renewal of society in a network of teachers, clerics, and writers.[10] Once figures like Zwingli employed their humanist training in the study of Scripture, the ends of inquiry became a means of discovering what they believed was biblical truth.[11] As this occurred, the Protestant Reformers began enacting change, tearing down what they considered the extrabiblical practices and beliefs of Catholicism before subsequently reconstructing both their theologies and their communities based upon earlier ideas from antiquity.[12]

Tapping into the rising wave of the Renaissance, this form of humanism also sought both beauty and eloquence in its educational program. Wisdom was inextricably and symbiotically interconnected with the ancient form in which it was embodied.[13] Aesthetic became an important component of the ideas conveyed. Moreover, this literary journey was experiential, tapping into the use of human imagination. The humanist yearned to experience the past as a means of self-realization or finding one's own potential as a person.[14] An equation of virtue was constructed: "good letters lead, under God's guidance, to good men."[15] In this way, Renaissance humanism always had a goal of transforming the person through studies of the past. Once Zwingli experienced this radical transformation, primarily through the Holy Scriptures, this became a guiding didactic premise directing his ministry in the years to come at Zurich.

FIRST MINISTERIAL POSTS

Zwingli's studies led to his ordination as a priest at Constance in 1506. This was the consummation of years preparing to serve God and His church. Following his ordination, Zwingli made his way to the rural community of Glarus, where his ministerial career began. His well-connected uncle, who had helped direct the young student's path since his childhood, secured for him this clerical post. Such an opportunity, a rarity for a twenty-three-year-old minister like Zwingli, would have heightened the expectations he carried with him to the small town.

During his thirteen years at Glarus, the newly minted priest cut his teeth on pastoral ministry. Although this remains a veiled period of Zwingli's life, one can assume he administrated the typical practices of the priesthood, most notably overseeing the observance of the Mass. Beyond this assumption, the sources reveal the deeply political and paradoxical nature of his work at Glarus. During this time, various Swiss communities established political alliances with external foreign entities. Glarus and its priest eventually cast their lot with the Pope, rather than with the Hapsburgs or the French. For his part, a handsome pension was awarded to Zwingli for his loyalty to the papacy.

Ironically, Zwingli received this money while penning the first of his literary works, *The Fable of the Ox*.[16] This was a satire that attacked the popular practice of exporting Swiss soldiers to fight for foreign entities, like the papacy. As the fable demonstrated, the thought of young Swiss men fighting for the ambitions of others was abhorrent. Thus, the political and personal tensions that Zwingli felt during his time at Glarus must have been excruciating. As we will see, these contradictions, along with the devastations of war he experienced as a military chaplain, set in motion a series of events that shaped Zwingli's pastoral ministry for years to come. Zwingli said in the latter days of his life, "Next to my concern for the Word of God ... the interests of the [Swiss] Confederacy lie nearest my heart."[17] As this statement reveals, church matters were not the only burden for the Reformer. His concerns also intersected with and extended into political and social affairs.

Despite the demands of his post at Glarus, there was still opportunity for the young Zwingli to grow personally. At Basel he had learned the importance of study and began to cultivate early commitments to humanism. An insatiable appetite to consume wisdom from the past drove him. Erasmus of Rotterdam, "the prince of the humanists," nurtured this disposition in him from a distance.[18] Zwingli was enamored with the Dutch humanist, who mediated an ancient literary world to him that reshaped the young priest with every historic work encountered. The exploration of ancient writers connected him with the traditions of the past, while also projecting patterns of thought and a commitment to the Scriptures that grew in him daily. During this time, Zwingli even founded and tutored at a school that trained Swiss boys in Latin as preparation for future university studies. This work kept him connected with his community beyond the typical labors of a priest. The instruction also afforded him the chance to further hone his intellectual gifts, which were beginning to blossom.

However, Zwingli's waning days at Glarus were frustrating and disappointing. Glarus continued to support the mercenary industry despite his opposition. Watching his countrymen slaughtered on an Italian countryside at Marignano during a war campaign in 1515 further stoked Zwingli's fury. Seething with anger, he vented his frustrations by publishing *The Labyrinth*.[19] This satirical myth expressed outrage that the Swiss were being deceived, sacrificing their own countrymen on the altar of foreign interests. His frustrations went unheeded, and he took leave of his post at Glarus for nearby Einsiedeln.

Zwingli spent two years at Einsiedeln. Once again, a dearth of sources leaves us with an opaque picture of the Reformer at this time. The preacher continued his humanist immersion into the past and even began mastering the biblical languages. The fantastic library at Einsiedeln aided in his intellectual and spiritual growth as he continued to voraciously consume the Bible alongside the early church fathers and other sources.

Much like with Glarus, this time was not without turmoil. Zwingli's sexual proclivities were well known and not altogether uncommon for priests of the day. However, his frequent promiscuity, along with a particularly scandalous affair with the daughter of a well-known figure at Einsiedeln, did great damage to his ministerial reputation.[20] These scandalous rumors abounded to the point that his later appointment at Zurich was nearly derailed by them. Some historians have tried to gloss over this account. However, such attempts would be a mistake. All too often during this era, it was commonplace for priests to have sexual relations with women. So, the scandal speaks to the state of the church at the time. Perhaps more importantly, to remove this account would be to minimize the dramatic change in Zwingli's life that was to come. This transgression, which he later acknowledged, and the repentance that followed offer evidence of the gospel's transformative work in Zwingli's life. It also colored the Reformer's understanding of grace and forgiveness while shaping his later argumentation for clerical marriage.

Despite this bad repute, Zwingli's gift of preaching first surfaced during this season of ministry. His reputation for eloquence grew with every homily. This talent led his friend and fellow Reformer Oswald Myconius to secure an invitation for Zwingli to fill a vacant preaching post at Zurich.[21] Opposition due to his sexual scandal notwithstanding, Zwingli was eventually appointed as the peoples' priest at Zurich in late 1518. A life-altering move was in short order, one that changed not only Zwingli but the Zurich community to which he was entrusted.

THE SHEPHERD MEETS HIS FLOCK

On December 27, 1518, Zwingli began the day-long trek from the rolling countryside of Einsiedeln to Zurich's bustling city center. With every passing hour of that cold, fifty-mile march, skirting Lake Zurich for much of the way, the stark reality of his new life undoubtedly set in. The confluence of emotions expected of any new pastor, ranging from fear to excitement, must have been overwhelming and grown as the spires of the Zurich churches came more sharply into focus.

As Zwingli entered the city, the unique dual spires of the Grossmunster, which still tower over the Zurich skyline today, served as a visual marker guiding him toward his new home. This church was founded in the eighth century, its original structure first built atop the graves of two Christian martyrs, Felix and Regula, whose bones were supposedly housed there.[22] The current iteration is a massive twelfth-century building constructed in a distinct Romanesque architecture, which adds to its allure. For a man who grew up in the rural farming community of Wildhaus, the visually imposing building was surely overwhelming, offering a tangible illustration of the magnitude of the pastoral task that lay before him.

The august gaze of the famous Holy Roman Emperor, Charlemagne, welcomed Zwingli to his new parish. A larger-than-life carved stone likeness of the medieval emperor rested on the south wall of the building. The imperial dignitary who once founded the church was honored by this sculpture, which was set aloft in the tower overlooking Lake Zurich. From his lofty perch, this stone Charlemagne watched over the people of Zurich for years. But on this day, the statue welcomed the community's new preacher. This dramatic picture foreshadowed in a very real sense the nature of the ministry set before Zwingli. The new preacher would shepherd the people of Zurich. That was the duty entrusted to him. Yet he would labor under the watchful eye of the civil magistrates, which Charlemagne signified. Zwingli's future ministry would find success only to the degree to which he was able to successfully navigate the tenuous relationship between church and state.

THE START OF A REVOLUTION

Only months before Zwingli arrived at Zurich, Erasmus had stated to a friend, "What else, I ask you, is a city than a great monastery?"[23] This was a sentiment Zwingli could have easily shared with the humanist he admired so dearly. The young preacher believed Zurich was ripe for renewal, a city ready to serve the Lord as a community set apart to uniquely display God's glory and goodness. And he believed his preaching ministry would serve as a catalyst of a *christianismus renascens* ("Christian rebirth") not only for individual Zurichers but for all of society as well. The community just needed to be rightly ordered in its spiritual affairs and set on the proper religious course.

To accomplish this task, Zwingli moved away from familiar liturgical norms, promising during his first sermon to preach in a manner unfamiliar to the community. This departure included shedding the standard lectionary rotation, which assigned certain preaching texts for each week's worship. As a replacement, he began preaching entire books of the Bible based upon canonical pericopes. At first, Zwingli's preaching maintained the political themes that had characterized earlier ministries, such as his criticism of the mercenary practice. Yet with each passing week, he more clearly proclaimed an evangelical gospel message. This stirred the hearts of many who were eager to imbibe the hope of the gospel. It also aroused the anger of those staunchly opposed to him. Some at Zurich clung tightly to their customary traditions, reticent to move away from what was familiar. Others wholeheartedly supported the authority and dogma of Catholicism. This was the diverse flock Zwingli shepherded.

Just as the new preacher was getting established at Zurich, he faced a challenge far greater than a divided congregation or opposition to his cause. Before his first year of ministry concluded, the preacher contracted plague. Exposure to deadly diseases was a commonplace work hazard for early modern ministers serving as the primary caregivers of the soul in an era devoid of modern medicine. This near-death encounter stunted Zwingli's reform efforts. It also profoundly shaped his theology. As we will discover, this occasion provided him an experiential lesson regarding God's sovereign hand. It was a lesson never forgotten. The encounter helped characterize the God the preacher mediated to his Zurich flock in the coming years.

Zwingli's persistent gospel proclamation in the early 1520s soon engendered a faithful following, as people from different sectors of society became active participants in his Reformation work. From the outset of his ministry, the Swiss preacher began mentoring a cadre of young priests and lay humanists. Zwingli's instruction dazzled these enthusiastic followers, as did his charisma and biblical knowledge. The preacher's sermons also enthralled and enfranchised magistrates and merchants from Zurich's influential upper class. Perhaps nothing illustrates the outworking of Zwingli's Reformation vision via community more than a breaking of the Lenten fast in 1522. This visible, social response to the gospel was deeply scandalous. Zwingli defended the violation from the pulpit in one of his most famous sermons, "Concerning Choice and Liberty of Foods."[24] As this incident demonstrated, Zwingli established a web of gospel partners who were willing to undertake a Reformation journey with their preacher. None of these partners knew where this journey would take them. And they had no idea what it might cost them along the way. But the wave of Reformation excitement and their preacher's gospel-laden messages refused to keep them sidelined from the work.

The ire of Rome, especially from Hugo the Bishop of Constance, whose diocese oversaw Zurich, came because of Zwingli's bold gospel proclamation. Like Luther before him, the Swiss preacher also faced formal charges of heresy. The Zurich Council adjudicated these accusations in January 1523 at the First Zurich Disputation. This event provided Zwingli the chance to formally outline his convictions, which he did through sixty-seven theological articles.[25] His statements at the disputation demonstrated his deft intellect, sound reasoning skills, and strong reliance on the biblical text. All of these traits helped him stave off pastoral ruin at that crucial juncture of his ministry. In the end, the magistrates sided with their pastor. The evangelical gospel, they concluded, would continue to be proclaimed.

REALIZING REFORMATION

The mid-1520s were perhaps the most profitable years of Zwingli's ministry. However, they were equally volatile. Reforms advanced at a heightened pace but not without consequences, some of which were painful to the Zurich shepherd. One of the most important and life-altering of these changes went well beyond the church. In spring 1524, Zwingli publicly celebrated his marriage to Anna Reinhart, a widow who brought several children with her to Zwingli's home. It was Anna's own son, Gerold, who played matchmaker for the two. Beyond the changes to his family life, something more subtle took place for Zurich. Though the couple had formally wed in 1522, the publicizing of their nuptials was a key step toward realizing reformation. The importance of this moment cannot be overstated. The church forbade clerical marriage for centuries. Therefore, reform was formally enacted via this defiant act, the establishment of a new religious and social order at Zurich serving as a powerful, visible reminder of Zurich's departure from the papacy's governance.[26] The preacher now had a wife. Anna became an important co-laborer to her husband, a trusted partner in his pastoral work.

The new father had more concerns in the coming days beyond his own children. His spiritual sons in the faith soon diverted his attention. Just as most parents can relate to the frustrations of watching their children stray from a prescribed path, many of Zwingli's spiritual children began in the mid-1520s to color outside of the lines of his instruction. Thus, while Zwingli saw the forming of new relationships, like with his beloved Anna, dissolving partnerships within his own reform camp tempered those additions. As early as 1523, some of those closest to Zwingli began pressing him to move further and faster than he believed prudent. The more they pushed him, the more their vision for reform appeared to threaten his gospel work. A painful schism loomed on the horizon. Much of the debate between Zwingli and these radical factions centered on hermeneutics and biblical authority. Zwingli taught these students to love and believe the Bible. However, his emerging covenantal theology and enduring commitment to a magisterial Reformation left him at odds with his disciples. Once they embraced a regenerate church with believers' baptism as its doorway, the divide was sealed.

Even before the formal rise of Anabaptism, many of those committed to reform at Zurich began taking their preacher's exhortations regarding the Bible's rejection of icons to heart. Beginning in 1524, a wave of violent iconoclasm swept through the community, threatening to spiral Zwingli's reform efforts into social chaos. Once again, as with the Anabaptists, Zwingli was placed in the tenuous position of sharing convictions with Radicals on certain theological matters. However, he rejected their means of destruction as a viable way to realize their desired ends. The iconoclasts' road of destruction was not a pathway he could follow them down. Instead, the Zurich pastor led a tempered, organized purging of the city's church buildings. This mainly meant the removal of images and whitewashing of walls to remove the temptation of idolatry he believed was inherent in their usage. These actions further distanced the Zurich church from the traditions of Catholicism. A formal break with Rome was imminent.

Though the mid-1520s saw fracturing within Zwingli's camp along different theological and social fault lines, this was also a season of consolidating support from the Zurich Council for his Reformation vision. Zwingli's work with and submission to the civil magistrates burned bridges with former gospel partners. However, these valuable relationships with the governing body became the key to unlocking the preacher's vision for Zurich. For half a decade, the Swiss pastor played his political part, slowly sowing gospel seeds while casting a vision for reformation to the city's power brokers. Those political moves eventually paid religious dividends in 1525. The Zurich church abandoned the Roman Mass and replaced it with a new Reformed liturgy, the first of its kind for Protestantism. Zwingli's gospel preaching six years earlier began this work, which now came full circle. This inaugurated the Reformation at Zurich.

EXPANDING REFORMATION

The institution of a new Zurich liturgy was a monumental ministry success for Zwingli. But there was still gospel work to accomplish. The preacher soon set his eyes on other prizes. In the waning years of the 1520s, the Reformer expanded his ambitions, widening his efforts into neighboring Swiss states to help others taste the fruits of Reformation. Given his growing notoriety as a Reformer, his influence often came implicitly through his writings. In the lands of Graubunden, for instance, the preacher's *Exposition of the Sixty-Seven Articles* served as the basis for the theological argumentation of those seeking change in the mountainous region east of Zurich.[27]

Zwingli also interacted with other Swiss people in tangible ways. Sometimes this meant preaching itinerantly in nearby towns like Stein am Rhein. Other times it meant lengthier and more involved work such as his influence upon the Bernese Reformation. In that instance, Zwingli advised the Bernese Reformer Berchthold Haller regarding strategies for renewal. His influence was so strong that one scholar said of Bern, "What the Reformers [at Bern] in fact did was simply to substitute their own church of largely Zwinglian and Bucerian inspiration for the Church of Rome."[28] Zwingli even attended the Bern Disputation at 1528 as a show of support when reformation was formally unfurled.

Zwingli's work also extended beyond Swiss borders. His participation at the Marburg Colloquy in 1529 afforded him the chance to exert theological influence in German lands and beyond. That fateful encounter also provided a lone opportunity for a face-to-face meeting with Martin Luther. But instead of bringing the Swiss and German churches together, Marburg demonstrated how theologically distant the two were. Any hope for an accord was thwarted by irreconcilable theological differences. This painful failure highlighted one of Rome's concerns regarding the Reformation. Casting aside papal authority meant the proliferation of multiple "popes" and an endless parade of schism to come. Marburg became yet another instance of conflict and division coloring the narrative of Zwingli's life.

VIOLENT DEMISE

Zwingli's expanded work in the late 1520s and early 1530s also reengaged him with Catholic foes. The Zurich preacher had a long history of conflicts with Rome going back to his days as a priest. Now that he was a Reformer committed to preserving "true religion," his criticism and rejection of the papacy became unyielding. Mounting political tensions facing the Swiss Confederation only further exacerbated Zwingli's religious intolerance. As the Reformation spread to other towns, religious fragmentation threatened Swiss unity. The Switzerland of today is politically dissimilar to the makeup of those same lands five hundred years ago. During the sixteenth century, loose affiliations between separate and distinct communities established the cooperative foundation for the Swiss Confederation. The various states held tenuous alliances based mostly on economic trade and military alliance. That some territories remained Catholic while others embraced the Reformation created an untenable political climate.

The Confederation quickly devolved into a powder keg of controversy. Religious and political discord threatened to spark war. Though it may seem unthinkable in our modern age of tolerance and religious liberty, in the sixteenth century, Catholics and Protestants alike were ready to spill blood for their beliefs. One biographer aptly summarized the sentiments of the Swiss at the time: "Long spears and good halberds were ready to defend the faith."[29] The two sides eventually faced off in 1529 because of their opposing convictions. Zwingli was eager to eradicate the Catholics, whom the Protestant forces outmatched militarily. This hope went unfulfilled though. What became known as the First Kappel War was anything but a war. The two armies met on the battlefield for tense saber-rattling. But the conflict ended before it even began, as the bloodless war concluded in an awkward peace that permitted each land its own faith.

The compromise at Kappel did not last. By mid-1531, tensions threatened to spill over into another war based on a host of economic, political, and religious factors. Catholic refusal to allow the preaching of the evangelical gospel in certain areas of the Confederation outraged Zwingli. The Reformer's binary beliefs about true and false religion compelled him to push for war. Many Zurichers maintained a strong reticence toward the notion of religious war. Indifference to the religious divisions characterized some people, while others believed their prophet was needlessly shredding key alliances holding the Confederation together. The Reformer, however, persisted in his convictions. He believed a consolidation of power for the sake of the gospel was required. Eventually, Zurich agreed, and the preacher led the Zurich army out from the city to face the Catholic forces in fall 1531.

The army that Zurich fielded at Kappel this time around was much smaller than two years earlier. Their forces now stood depleted, ironically a consequence of Zwingli's own preaching against the mercenary practice. For years, Zwingli had criticized the Swiss-on-Swiss bloodshed facilitated by that hated industry. Now he was ready to raise arms against his Swiss brothers. However, he believed the motivation for this fight was just and worthy. Foreign ambitions were not directing the Swiss fighting. Protestants were standing against Catholics. God's people were defending the gospel against the purveyors of idolatry and the Pope's false religion.

Zwingli accompanied the Zurich battery into war believing God would sustain them. This proved a devastating miscalculation. Outnumbered and ill-prepared, the Zurich forces were routed by the Catholics at Kappel on October 11, 1531. Zwingli died that day on the battlefield, the prophet's demise bound up in his own mistaken prophecy. The economic and political consequences of the loss for Zurich were staggering. The long shadow cast by this defeat also proved challenging for the Zurich church. The Swiss Reformation was thrust into flux as the Zurich church proceeded without the man most credited with establishing the new religious ethos they now enjoyed.

Kappel abruptly and awkwardly drew the curtain closed on Zwingli's life. In one sense, for a gifted figure who accomplished much in ministry, this may seem a drama without a proper ending. Yet some may contend this was a fitting conclusion to the Reformer's story. The many experiences of his ministry at Zurich were fascinating and eventful, though always mired in conflict. But these same challenges also helped shape the trajectory of the Swiss Reformation, which ultimately led to a Reformed Zurich church. These struggles also influenced and informed the embattled preacher's theology as it developed into a unique Zwinglian form that many still draw from today. Perhaps it should not be surprising that the battles that once proved serendipitous to the proclamation of the gospel and the promotion of reform eventually culminated in a war that threatened to undo all Zwingli's previous Reformation advances. The Reformer died as he ministered: amid war and conflict. This reality leaves us with the conflicted remembrance that lingers today and a statue that many long to remove of a Reformation preacher separated from his pulpit.

Chapter 1

The Swiss Preacher

"This is the seed I have sown. Matthew, Luke, Paul, and Peter have watered it, and God has given it wonderful increase, but this I will not trumpet forth, lest I seem to be soliciting my own glory and not Christ's."[1]

TOURISTS TRAVELING TO SWITZERLAND OFTEN frequent the tranquil cities of Bern, Geneva, Lucerne, or Zurich on their journeys. These destinations offer some of the country's most beautiful locales and best experiences of the uniqueness of Swiss culture. However, nestled alongside the winding banks of the Rhine River and tucked between Schaffhausen and Constance is a hidden gem called Stein am Rhein. This quaint town, whose name means "stone on the Rhine," affords visitors a chance to step back in time by walking through an old town almost entirely untainted by modern construction. The *Rathaus* ("town hall") serves as the town's geographic center and is surrounded by a wondrous array of preserved medieval wooden homes with painted fresco facades. The endless parade of colorful medieval depictions is overwhelming to the eyes and allows visitors to envision life as it was hundreds of years ago.

The town is also home to an impressive mural of Huldrych Zwingli painted by Carl von Haeberlin on the side of a building at the close of the eighteenth century. Haeberlin completed this piece to commemorate the Reformer who had spread his Reformation ideas to the town through his preaching two hundred years earlier. The painting, titled *Zwingli Preaching in Stein*, depicts the Zurich preacher proclaiming the Word of God to the people of Stein in their parish church.

In Haeberlin's rendering, Zwingli is situated atop a small flight of stairs in front of an altar, itself framed by a wooden panel of Jesus and His twelve disciples. Zwingli stands cloaked in a common black ministerial robe rather than the ornate brilliance of a clerical vestment. His head is covered by a flat black cap. Both fashion selections signify Zwingli's departure from the pomp and traditionalism he perceived as wrong with Catholicism. His left hand reaches back, resting comfortably on an open Bible. This positioning reminds audiences of Zwingli's unwavering dependence on the Scriptures as the authority for his proclamation. That the Bible replaced the bread and cup on the altar table signified Zwingli's shift away from the Eucharist toward the Word of God as the focal point of Swiss worship. The Bible, which sits in front of a single candle, serves as the lone, normative authority for the Christian community, radiating the very words of God to His people and lighting their pathway toward redemption.

Although this mural of Zwingli is situated today in Stein am Rhein, it beautifully captures the heart of the preacher's ministry to the people of Zurich as well. Zwingli first arrived at Zurich a seasoned and talented preacher. He came prepared to install an innovative preaching plan encountered through his studies in the church fathers during his previous years at Einsiedeln. This lectionary choice demonstrated his ongoing appropriation of a humanist pedagogy. More importantly, it helped unveil his growing commitment to the Bible. Writing to the Swiss people years later, Zwingli exhorted, "Do not put yourself at odds with the Word of God. For truly, it will persist as surely as the Rhine follows its course. One can perhaps dam it up for a while, but it is impossible to stop it."[2] This commitment to the power of the Scriptures was a foundational premise for his ministry at Zurich. In his mind, if reformation was to be realized, then the Bible would be the catalyst to change.

Zwingli based his commitment to Scripture on the belief that the Bible was literally God's Word. And the Zurich people needed to hear their Lord's voice more than ever. Only God's Word would bring life, renewal, and transformation to the people. Zwingli used this elevation of the Bible's authority to show Jesus to the Zurich people. He still offered commentary on the political affairs of the day, as was the case during his previous ministries. Yet more and more, Jesus and His atoning work took center stage in the Reformer's preaching. Focusing on Christ's salvific work enabled the preacher to highlight the freedom that was found only through the gospel. This was a liberty many people were eager to embrace, while others were more skeptical of what was being offered. This amplification of Scripture also resulted in concerns regarding the Zurich church's worship patterns. A battle between what Zwingli framed as the Bible's prescriptions and Catholic religious norms more familiar to the community pervaded much of his ministry. Such concerns seasoned his gospel proclamation.

These homiletical decisions placed him at odds with those at Zurich committed to the traditional practices, rhythms, and authority of the Catholic Church. They also created an unforeseen problem amid Zwingli's reform efforts. Although the Scriptures became an agent of change at Zurich, not everyone agreed on the interpretation of the text. Nor was there agreement regarding what reforms should be undertaken or how quickly those proposed changes should be made. Schisms within Zwingli's own camp became the net result of this reality. The unrest that ensued demanded that the Swiss preacher carefully labor to win the people to his vision for reformation amid a chorus of other voices. And there was no more powerful means of garnering support for his proposed changes than through the pulpit to which he had been entrusted.

PREACHING AT GLARUS AND EINSIEDELN

Zwingli was thrust into a prominent and high-profile clerical position when he came to Zurich as one of the city's main preachers. Yet he ascended to that post not as a novice unfamiliar with the rigors of preaching. For over a decade, Zwingli had labored as a Catholic priest in the

Swiss towns of Glarus and Einsiedeln. These years proved formative as he learned preaching patterns, oratory techniques, and hermeneutical tools that traveled with him to Zurich. In fact, reading church fathers like John Chrysostom during this time nurtured in him the radical expositional style of preaching he later employed as the foundation for his ministry at Zurich. He also encountered things during these years, especially while serving as a chaplain in the Swiss army, that profoundly shaped his later preaching. These years of ministry cast a long shadow over his later time at Zurich.

Though Zwingli was known for his preaching at Zurich, that was largely an ancillary task for him during his time at Glarus. Instead, he diverted his attention elsewhere, as was customary for a clerical priest in the years prior to the Reformation. Attending to his parish meant regular oversight of the Roman Mass. This was central to his ministry at Glarus. The newly minted priest mediated God's salvation to his flock through the church's liturgy, especially via the Eucharist. Given the importance of the Eucharist, other intercessory activities built on that religious rite. He welcomed newborns into the church via baptism, married the betrothed, anointed the dying, and heard confessions of those burdened by sin. He was conversant with each of these common priestly tasks.

Zwingli's post at Glarus immersed him in the lives of the rural town's people, yet it did not isolate the budding humanist from Europe's intellectual community. He continued to share correspondence with other thinkers, many of whom he met during his time at Basel. In a 1510 letter, the humanist and musical theorist Heinrich Loriti (known as Glarean) addressed Zwingli as *humanissimus* ("cultured" or "refined"), ascribing to the Swiss priest a level of learning scarcely found in his profession at the time.[3] Zwingli continued to drink deeply from ancient writers while dialoguing with his contemporaries about intellectual gems unearthed from the past. Though none of his sermons from this period survive, these influences must have played a role in his preaching. The dissonance between the flock's rustic sensibilities and their shepherd's cerebral studies must have been striking. Still, the challenges of this divide were likely bridged by the preacher, who never lost sight of his rural roots at Wildhaus. This legacy proved an important trait for the preacher. Though he ascended in his intellectual pursuits, he was never far removed from his humble origin.

Zwingli's connection with his congregation at Glarus also ran along nationalistic lines. This important reality shaped his preaching, as he seamlessly weaved contemporary political concerns into his proclamation. Much like with Luther and his native Germany, Zwingli's preaching was always situated in and shaped by his immediate Swiss context. This was especially true given the political climate of the early sixteenth century. While political neutrality dominates modern perceptions about Switzerland, such was not the case in Zwingli's time. During the late medieval period, the Swiss Confederation had a long-standing tradition of sending its own to fight as mercenaries for other countries. Thus, it was not surprising that Zwingli accompanied other young Swiss soldiers into battle in June 1513.

Serving as a chaplain in the papal armies alongside his countrymen, Zwingli ministered to the dead and the dying. He had overseen similar clerical duties in preceding years, but something was different about those war-torn moments. His heart was now divided in his work. Earlier criticisms of the mercenary profession, most notably in his 1510 fable *The Ox*, expressed his vehement opposition to a theater in which he now found himself a key actor.[4] His disdain for the mercenary industry grew with each passing day and each Swiss soldier killed in battle. He loved his brothers-in-arms, so his preaching to them during those military campaigns must have been authentic and raw, given the brutality of war and the imminent threat of death. But that exuberance to serve this military flock must have been accompanied by a grueling internal struggle. Zwingli was a preacher not totally committed to his own message. Imploring the troops to battle valiantly with God on their side did not square with his personal outrage over the mercenary practice. Once again, without extant sourcing, we are left imagining Zwingli doing his patriotic duty by rallying the Swiss soldiers with impassioned sermons. But his personal belief that the battles they waged were in vain, through a war not their own, had to temper his preaching.

These experiences forever changed Zwingli. He witnessed immeasurable horrors during these military campaigns. The internal conflicts of his preaching traveled home with him. Swiss commitments to the mercenary trade also remained and were not easily broken. The issue resurfaced two years later, in 1515. Zwingli was forced once again to preach on the battlefield to his countrymen, this time on a military campaign in northern Italy. He later recounted exhorting the Swiss soldiers to hold fast in their obligation to support Pope Leo X's papal army as it pushed back the surging French.[5] However, this public support for the war effort among the soldiers betrayed his true feelings. Despite any public veneer of support shown through sermons encouraging soldiers to support the Pope, his personal opposition to Swiss entanglements in foreign affairs did not wane. The papal army's catastrophic defeat at Marignano in September 1515 further heightened his disdain for the mercenary practice. Approximately eight thousand Swiss lives were lost. Images of the stinging loss would haunt Zwingli. This was especially true given that the mercenary service left his countrymen pitted against one another, fighting on behalf of competing forces. The tragedy of Swiss-on-Swiss bloodshed traumatized Zwingli to his core.[6]

The cruelty of combat left Zwingli a hardened war veteran once he returned to Glarus. The internal struggle that characterized his battlefield preaching could not be held at bay. In his mind, the town continued to financially prostitute its young men for the political appetites of foreigners even after the Marignano tragedy. Glarus's obstinance eventually forced his departure. He transferred to the nearby town of Einsiedeln, which proved a pivotal season of growth for the preacher.

Einsiedeln is where Zwingli first established his reputation as a captivating preacher. Some of this success came through his years of invaluable experience in the previous decade. Yet it was more than just the seasoning of ministry that secured him preaching acclaim. Years of study as a Renaissance humanist now began to pay ministerial dividends. Even while Zwingli elevated the importance of God's Word, a winsome use of words characterized his preaching. Zwingli became adept in the biblical languages through rigorous studies in Greek and Hebrew. The publication of

Erasmus's *Novum Instrumentum* in 1516 only added to his immersion into the Scriptures. In the preface to that famous critical edition of the New Testament, the Dutch humanist declared, "But happy is the man whom death takes as he meditates upon this literature [the New Testament] ... let us die in its embrace, let us be transformed by it, since indeed studies are transmuted into mortals."[7] Through Erasmus, Zwingli believed that one could meet Christ in the text of Holy Writ. To encounter Jesus in the Bible was to be transformed by Him. Therefore, such language studies had a pedagogical and spiritual purpose. Zwingli embarked upon Scriptural studies "so that I might learn the teaching of Christ from its original source."[8] The Christ of Scripture became the One offered to the Einsiedeln community.

This approach to reading and preaching the Bible was not without its detractors. Years later, Luther not only once questioned Zwingli's proficiency in Greek but also believed the Reformer was pridefully dependent upon his own intellect when reading the Bible. Commenting on Zwingli's insistence that the Greek text provided him insight into the sacramental controversy of the late 1520s, Luther rebutted, "There's more to it than reading the New Testament; the thirst for glory entirely blinds people [like Zwingli]."[9] Despite such criticism, Zwingli's passion for words and use of language never waned. He now had both the textual means and the humanist medium to explore the Bible more deeply. He believed this combination granted him access to God's divine voice. Zwingli's focus on words eventually allowed his preaching to highlight a striking disconnect between the prescriptions of Scripture and Rome's blatant deviation from them in doctrine and practice. This disconnect was so striking that once the English humanist Thomas Linacre contrasted Erasmus's original Greek text with Catholic beliefs and practices, he exclaimed, "Either this [the Greek New Testament] is not the gospel, or we are not Christians."[10] A renewed access to God's voice ushered in a new way of considering what was Christian. And such truths could not be unseen once Zwingli became aware of this biblical reality.

Much like Erasmus's, Zwingli's preaching took on anti-clerical tones. He highlighted the gulf that existed between worship prescriptions and patterns of piety found in Scripture and those manifested in the Catholic tradition he was growing to distrust.[11] This dissonance was perhaps nowhere more evident than in relation to Zwingli's preaching at Einsiedeln against the backdrop of the town's Black Virgin shrine. Throngs of pilgrims ventured each year to this religious destination. Travelers came seeking absolution of sin through sacramental acts of penance. Zwingli's preaching stood out sharply against the church's reliance on image worship, which many believed facilitated spiritual vitality. One biographer has argued that the Reformer's criticism was mostly moral in nature at this time and did not attend to doctrinal concerns surrounding things like pilgrimages and indulgences.[12] However, according to Zwingli's recollections, Christ's mediating work on the cross and the need to worship the Creator, not the creation, was already prominent in his preaching during this season.[13] The distinction here is not to be understated. Christ's provision as the sole means of finding a right standing before God dominated Zwingli's argumentation at this juncture of his preaching ministry. No amount of human effort or pious action, like penance or pilgrimage, could offer that.

Zwingli started committing the Scriptures to memory through his own language studies while at Einsiedeln. The Reformer conveyed that he "copied with my own hands" much of the New Testament using Erasmus's famous critical edition of the text.[14] A reversal of Babel's curse became a gateway to Zwingli's own literary paradise, as he engaged with multiple biblical languages. And the flock at Einsiedeln reaped the harvest of his work. None of his sermons from this period are extant. However, some insights regarding this season of his preaching may be found in this pedagogical method, along with the growth in notoriety he gained as a preacher.

Words quickly became the preacher's color wheel from which his sermons painted vibrant depictions of the Bible's message. Clever wordplays and the use of imagination, both hallmarks of humanism, undoubtedly helped transport parishioners into the biblical text itself.[15] Once there, the people of Einsiedeln could celebrate freedom alongside the Hebrews during their exodus from Egypt, walk with Jesus on the shores of the Sea of Galilee, or witness the beauty of their Savior during His passion. Yet Zwingli not only displayed the Bible's brilliance in his sermons. He shaped the text's meaning as well. His use of hermeneutical literary tools like allegory, synecdoche, tropology, and hyperbole informed the preacher's biblical interpretation. Zwingli wielded these humanist tools like a skilled craftsman, dazzling his audiences along the way.

Zwingli became more dependent upon the text of Scripture than the routines of Catholic tradition during this season at Einsiedeln. His elevation of the Bible as the church's normative authority established a pattern of biblicism that he not only carried into his ministry at Zurich but also bestowed upon his later disciples, men like Heinrich Bullinger and those who later became the Swiss Anabaptists. This time also saw the rise of a biblical exegete who interpreted the text through a humanist frame. Erasmus's influence was crucial here.[16] However, Zwingli's own unique concerns, one of which was to make Christ known among his people, and his engagement with humanism also flavored his preaching. Again, we are without Zwingli's sermons from this period, but we are not left without a sense of his preaching. The German humanist Beatus Rhenanus glowingly exhorted Zwingli in late 1518, "But you in preaching to your congregation show the whole doctrine of Christ briefly displayed in a picture; how Christ was sent down from earth by God to teach us the will of the Father."[17] Zwingli showed the people of Einsiedeln Christ and what it looked like to follow Him. Soon the preacher was ready for his new parish, eventually arriving at Zurich on December 27, 1518.

A HISTORIC PROMISE

Despite the excitement of his recent move to Zurich, Zwingli did not have the time to be swept up in the ceremonial trappings commonly associated with a preacher's arrival to a new parish. The Reformer refused to be distracted by matters ancillary to his pastoral duties. He came to Zurich primarily for the purpose of proclaiming God's Word. Five days after arriving, on Saturday, January 1, 1519, also his thirty-fifth birthday, Zwingli stood behind the pulpit at the Grossmunster eager to address his flock for the first time. While he preached many sermons in his career, and the Zurich people heard countless exhortations from that pulpit, something stunning took place on that day. Although this sermon is not extant, Heinrich Bullinger characterized the event as follows:

> On Saturday, New Year's Day 1519, Huldrych Zwingli preached his first sermon and announced that on the following Sunday morning he would begin to expound the holy gospel of Matthew, through and with divine truth and not with human hands. Soon there was a remarkable flocking of all kinds of people, especially of the common person, to these evangelical sermons.[18]

Zwingli made a promise to his new flock while introducing himself. From the beginning of his Zurich ministry, he committed himself to preaching *lectio continua*. This was a verse-by-verse, expositional type of preaching, which deviated from the traditional pericope.[19] This preaching strategy allowed Zwingli to focus on the text itself and connected him stylistically with the golden-tongued patristic preacher John Chrysostom. Zwingli received a copy of Chrysostom's *lectio continua* sermons from the Basel printer Johann Froben and was enamored by the prospects of this preaching model.[20] By taking such an approach into the pulpit, Zwingli intentionally placed himself in a historic stream. It also helped him work around both the liturgical forms and scholastic interpretations of the medieval era. The preacher believed God's people needed to hear directly from their Lord.

This pledge was a risky proposition. But it was one that Zwingli felt was necessary if he was going to be true to his humanist training and the Scriptures. Much like Luther at Wittenberg, Zwingli believed the Word of God was the key to reformation.[21] His ministry at Zurich had to be based upon the Bible if he was going to be a success. According to Bullinger's recollection, Zwingli's unfamiliar preaching style enamored the people who soon began descending upon Zurich in droves.

EARLY ZURICH SERMONS

Zwingli was a master rhetorician by the time he began his ministry at Zurich. He knew Scripture intimately through years of study. He also made the text leap from the pages of Scripture through his eloquent prose. Zwingli believed that these abilities, coupled with his plan to preach *lectio continua*, were the perfect recipe for transforming the Zurich community. Reformation was a distinct possibility. And if this possibility were to be realized, the preached Word would be the catalyst to change.

As promised, Zwingli began preaching verse by verse through Matthew's Gospel, including what some considered the superfluous genealogies. Every word of Scripture mattered to Zwingli. So, he considered, mined for truth, and proclaimed each text. Recalling this early season of preaching at Zurich in his apologetic work *Archeteles*, the preacher outlined how the exposition of more New Testament books followed:

> I immediately added the Acts of the Apostles to the gospel, so the Zurich Church might see in what way and to whom the gospel was carried forth and spread abroad ... [then] came the First Epistle of Paul to Timothy, which seemed to be admirably adapted to my excellent flock. For there are contained in it certain standards, as it were, of the character worthy of a Christian."[22]

His preaching plan had a purpose. The flock first met Jesus alongside the disciples. Then they recounted how the gospel spread missionally through early church planting efforts. The people were subsequently guided toward a renewed ecclesial form, only to be instructed about Christian virtue by the Apostle Paul. This was a recasting of what it meant to be a Christian. It was also meant to reshape the nature of the Zurich State through a reforming people.

Little is known about the content of Zwingli's first sermons at Zurich. He did not preach from a manuscript, nor were there any secondary recordings.[23] Taking sermon notes was not nearly as familiar to his audiences as it is to modern ones. Also, his preaching was not published at this early juncture. Thus, there are no records of his sermons into the early 1520s. What can be said about Zwingli's preaching during those first few years at Zurich must be pieced together from later reflections, including his own reminiscences and accounts offered by co-laborers like Heinrich Bullinger, Leo Jud, and Caspar Megander.[24]

According to Zwingli, his preaching of the gospel extended back to 1516 and was independent of the Reformation at Wittenberg. In his *Exposition of the Sixty-Seven Articles* from 1523, Zwingli declared, "Before anyone in this area had even heard of Luther, I began to preach the gospel of Christ in 1516."[25] This was likely a marker referencing the year that he began reading the Bible in the original languages with the help of Erasmus's critical edition of the New Testament. A confluence of what he later identified as his calling and gifting also shaped his preaching. Defending his preaching in 1522, Zwingli declared, "For about six years I have labored to the best of my ability with the talent entrusted to me, so when the Lord came and demanded His increase, I might not slothfully bring forward with fear and shame one idle talent wrapped in a handkerchief!"[26] Therefore, an evangelical understanding of the gospel always framed his preaching at Zurich.[27]

From the outset of his Zurich ministry, Zwingli's preaching was appreciably different from what it had been at Glarus. He diligently worked to bypass the scholastic glosses of medieval thinkers that once shaped his exegesis, opting instead to hear directly from the biblical authors. While the Apostles Peter and Paul were men like Thomas Aquinas and Johannes Duns Scotus, only the former "spoke under the inspiration of the same Spirit."[28] The latter simply did not speak with the same authority. Divine inspiration was a crucial qualifier linking the words of Scripture with God's voice. Thus, his preaching sought to allow the Lord's voice to speak directly through the biblical text to a Swiss people he believed were thirsting to drink from the wellspring of the river of life. To capture the nature and urgency of this important shift, Zwingli qualified his preaching as offered "without any human agenda and without any hesitancy or wavering."[29] God's Word was not to be weaponized for selfish human ends or overshadowed by human concerns. Biblical truths were also not to be veiled or sheepishly shied away from while preaching. Too much was at stake to do otherwise.

This dramatic change in Zwingli's preaching continued to highlight his growing elevation of the Bible. As a Renaissance humanist, Zwingli was committed to reading ancient sources like the Greek philosophers and early church fathers. But his elevation of the Scriptures as the normative source of authority revealed the Reformer's commitment to the doctrine of *sola Scriptura* at an early juncture of his ministry at Zurich. While extrabiblical sources had value, he reminded his hearers that even Catholic canon law recognized that "the fathers should give way to the Word of God and not God's Word to the fathers."[30] Linking this re-elevation of

Scriptural authority to his calling as a pastor, Zwingli contended, "I must rescue the sacred writings [the Bible] so wickedly tortured, and I feel by that achievement I shall restore the spoils of highest honor to our Great Melchizedek."[31] The Reformer's preaching methodology recalibrated the Swiss church's understanding of religious authority. The Swiss could rightly hear the voice of the Lord only after they stopped listening to Rome's.

The motifs of politics and war dominated his preaching in those first few years.[32] Drawing on earlier works like *The Ox* and *The Labyrinth*, Zwingli frequently decried the Zurich people's willingness to become entangled in political concerns external to the Confederation.[33] He could not forget the lingering trauma of having witnessed Swiss bloodshed for external ambitions.[34] Memories from the battlefield undoubtedly added a fiery intensity to his preaching. Those reflections also connected Zwingli with his audience, many of whom shared related frustrations. Zwingli quickly became the people's advocate, with concerns that extended to both individuals and the whole of society.

Zwingli's preaching resonated with many people from the outset of his ministry at Zurich. By now, he was a master of words. He regularly invited his audiences to participate in an invigorating journey, replete with experiential encounters from the Scriptures. These powerful sermons helped rally support from his audiences and stirred people toward action. Thomas Platter, a young humanist who heard several of these early sermons, said of Zwingli's preaching, "He explained so pointedly [Jesus as the Good Shepherd], that I felt as if someone had pulled me up into the air by the hair of my head."[35] The preacher's immersion into the literary forms, illustrations, and arguments found in antiquity made him a master wordsmith. Much like Erasmus, whom he sought to emulate, Zwingli made words work for him. He could powerfully turn a phrase, craft clever contrasts, or paint vivid word pictures to his own desired ends. His eloquence was so profound it left one observer declaring him "a new Moses that had arisen to save his people from spiritual bondage."[36] The people of Zurich quickly began seeing in their young preacher a prophetic quality.

Zwingli's argumentation was not the only thing that made his preaching so powerful. His gifts of persuasion and relatability also aided him.

The preacher connected with his people by drawing on shared experiences common to both parties. For instance, encounters from his childhood in rural Wildhaus provided the Reformer a familiarity with the agrarian, parabolic language from the Gospels. Zwingli subsequently framed those biblical stories in winsome prose that not only brought the text to life but also echoed encounters relatable to his Swiss audiences. That link made his preaching relevant and applicable. Caspar Hedio, who heard Zwingli preach in 1519, lavished praise on his oratory skills, exclaiming, "I was greatly charmed by an address of yours, so elegant, learned, and weighty, fluent, discerning, and evangelical ... That address, I say, so inflamed me that I began at once to feel a deep affection for Zwingli, to respect and admire him."[37] Zwingli's preaching was colloquial and his prose transformative. This accessibility made him more trustworthy to his audiences with every sermon. The Zurich people slowly began to see and embrace him as their own.

IRE DIVERTED TOWARD ROME

The trust earned during those first few years proved valuable when Zwingli's patience with the papacy ran out. Though he never abandoned his political or nationalistic concerns, by 1522 the preacher's attention turned more exclusively toward religious matters. His immersion into Scripture uncovered a stark contrast between the Christianity presented in the New Testament and the one embodied by Catholicism. Guided by a desire to shepherd his flock toward truth, Zwingli could not remain silent about this delineation. Following a template set by Erasmus, Zwingli was quick to name those who were a danger to the Zurich people and a direct threat to the gospel.[38]

Drawing on the rising waves of anti-clericalism in the 1520s, which vehemently opposed the clergy's focus on temporal, self-serving interests to the detriment of eternal, Kingdom concerns, Zwingli's sermons became accusatory and incendiary in nature. Such anti-Catholic invective resonated especially with Reformation-minded partners. It also appealed to those Zurich political brokers keen on asserting independence from the intrusion of papal oversight. Zwingli's rural sensibilities also allowed him to tap into common virtues held by most Swiss, especially the laity.[39] Themes like truth, honesty, hard work, and service saturated his sermons. These virtues were contrasted against moral deficiencies that he increasingly cast as indicative of Catholicism: hypocrisy, idolatry, avarice, and self-gratitude. Those things characterized false religion, according to Zwingli. Given that he "emphasized righteous living as evidence that one has saving faith," his preaching ire was increasingly set against Catholic hypocrisy.[40]

Zwingli's concern with the Catholic clergy extended beyond moral deficiencies. His preaching also showed how the papacy was leading God's people toward false, idolatrous forms of worship. Promoting what he believed was an archetype of faithful ministry, the Reformer contended that godly shepherds must "learn to administer their office and commission from no other model than the only true Word of God."[41] God's voice, not that of the church's, was most important. The church's dependence on the Bible's normative instruction was even to shape the pastor's exegesis. He cautioned against any preacher "who comes to the Scriptures with his own opinion and interpretation and wrestles the Scriptures into conformity with it."[42] Both the Word and the faithful preacher were "a sweet smell or savor, but a savor of life to some and of death to others."[43] The preacher was to follow wherever the text led and proclaim whatever reforms it required. One of his early supporters, Simon Stumpf, said of the preacher, "Master Ulrich Zwingli repudiated and annihilated all the doctors, who did not form themselves in accord with the Gospel, but rested on human acts ... He also struck down petitions and prayers to Mary and the saints—who are in heaven—proved from many texts that one should pray to no creature other than God alone."[44] For Zwingli, the Bible made clear how the Zurich church was to anchor and orient itself. The Swiss preacher was keen to unleash those prescriptions with a passionate urgency.

The more Christ's words exposed the Zurich community to their sin and exhorted them to live gospel-transformed lives, the more evident a disconnect between their former faith and the one presented in Scripture became. Zwingli's use of vivid illustrations highlighted this incongruity and fostered a growing awareness among the Zurich community of their shortcomings. The role of memory played an important part in Zwingli's preaching at this point. From his childhood days at Weesen, learning his letters and Latin grammar meant hours of verbal repetition at a time when paper was scarce.[45] This fostered in him an aptitude for assimilating ideas, alongside a deft recall. Mind and mouth were forged as one. Once the classroom was supplanted by the church, these same tools proved useful whether he was shepherding his flock in biblical truth, speaking prophetically to contemporary political or social issues, or castigating Rome's errors. The biblical path toward life was clear. He gradually enticed many at Zurich to follow him down that road, even if it meant veering away from Catholic prescriptions more native to them.

THE FIRSTFRUITS OF PREACHING

Any boy who grows up in the Swiss countryside understands that planted seeds take time to germinate. The hope of a fruitful harvest requires patience and long-term commitment. Zwingli's preaching demanded a similar posture. For years he labored faithfully, laying the text of Scripture bare before his people. Week by week he sowed God's Word, hoping that his labors might one day yield discernable changes in his people. One of the firstfruits of Zwingli's preaching came in March 1522 when a group of men took his ideas about Christian freedom to heart. Emboldened by his words and incensed by what Rome had forbidden them, several men broke their Lenten fasts by eating sausages in the home of the Zurich printer Christoph Froschauer.[46] Zwingli did not consume meat, but he was present for this defiant act. Although this may appear trivial to certain Christians today, it was an egregious violation of Catholic canon law. Thus, this meal was an affront to the authorities and a blatant defiance of papal authority.

Rather than downplaying this rebellious meal and allowing it to retreat into obscurity, Zwingli preached about the scandalous act on March 23, 1522, in a sermon titled "Choice and Liberty Regarding Food."[47] The decision to support such defiance from the pulpit was strategic, albeit risky. The preacher leveraged the moment to build upon and expand his vision for reformation. If he could persuade the people to embrace the freedom found in the evangelical gospel, then he could reap a reformation harvest at Zurich.

Zwingli leveraged food as a thematic illustration in this sermon. Old Testament allusions to a promised land abounding in luscious fruits or the Apostle Paul's exhortation to move from milk to meat offered vivid word pictures embodying the rich spiritual sustenance available to God's people.[48] Zwingli employed these biblical examples toward his own ends by stressing the spiritually famished state of the Zurich people under Catholicism. He also highlighted how Rome had monetized religious dietary restrictions among the Swiss people to its own selfish ends. For the preacher, selling exceptions to eat native Swiss foods otherwise limited by the church "abused our [the Zurich people's] simplicity," instead of encouraging them to measure "sin according to God's law."[49] In contrast to Rome's oppressive overreach, the meat of Scripture, which he offered to the community through his sermons, provided a bountiful spiritual feast. The people only needed to taste of that which was their divine birthright. For a Swiss people familiar with savory meats supplied by their livestock, the spiritual renewal offered to them by their preacher was tangible and real. Biblical truth could almost be tasted.

This sermon, which was later preserved in print, helped solidify Zwingli as the leader of a forthcoming renewal movement at Zurich. By publicly supporting the offenders, the preacher could no longer be considered a passive observer of the rising tremors of reformation in the region. Nor were ethereal matters of theology guiding his polemical criticisms of Rome. He cast his lot with the lawbreakers and supported their example of what modifications to religious practices might look like. The Lenten meal became a visual form of reformation that went well beyond even the change in gospel language espoused by Zwingli for years.

Once the Word took root in the people, reformation ambitions were ignited. Zwingli agitated the Zurich community through his provocative preaching for years. Nevertheless, something else was alternatively positioned as the reason for reform. The Word, not his pastoral labors, provided this gospel harvest. Despite his growing notoriety as a preacher, Zwingli quickly deflected attention away from himself. He amplified this distinction by declaring, "This is the seed I have sown. Matthew, Luke, Paul, and Peter have watered it, and God has given it wonderful increase, but this I will not trumpet forth, lest I seem to be soliciting my own glory and not Christ's."[50] Gospel seeds sown produced Reformation fruit. But what he could not have known was that those same seeds were about to yield a harvest of unrest also for both Zwingli and Zurich.

CONTINUED LABORS AND SECURING SUPPORT

The Zurich Council offered an innocuous ruling in response to the sausage affair, attempting to carve out a political middle road on the matter. The Lenten offenders received fines for their participation. But the Council also encouraged the Bishop of Constance to consider the matter based on Scripture, to explore whether extrabiblical laws were burdening the people.[51] These responses, alongside the magistrates' refusal to discipline the fast breakers more strongly, suggested that reformation was within reach. The key questions moving forward related to how far and fast the preacher would push for his proposed changes. Perhaps more importantly, who would follow this ambitious preacher into uncharted reformation waters? Zwingli began to walk the perilous path that most pastors face at some point in their ministries. His spiritual ambitions for the flock were measured by the people's tolerance for change. Zwingli labored from the pulpit during the next few years in the hope of establishing more reformation gains. Yet his efforts were met with mixed results. His vision for reform persuaded some, while his proposals left traditionalists aghast. Others wanted to go far beyond his plan.

Zwingli emerged from the Lenten controversy relatively unscathed. He faced growing criticisms from the Bishop of Constance for his bold ideas. However, the Zurich Council continued supporting him. Seeing how the Bible fanned the flames of his reform efforts, Zwingli preached a sermon purposed to provide clarity amid a season rife with confusion. This sermon was well received, hence its later printing under the title "On the Clarity and Certainty of the Word of God."[52] The themes of Scriptural authority, gospel clarity, and God's revelatory work through His Spirit anchored the sermon's prose.

The *imago Dei* from Genesis 1:26 took center stage from the outset.[53] Highlighting veiled allusions to the Trinity, Zwingli stressed an innate human faculty for properly engaging with the Bible even post-fall. This anthropology spoke of a human agency that positioned humanity in a receptive posture toward God's authoritative Word. The power of Scripture, what was meant by the term "certainty," then took center stage. Zwingli declared, "The Word of God is so alive and strong and powerful that all things must obey it, and as often and at the time that God himself appoints."[54] The theme of the inner illumination of the Word by the Holy Spirit, framed through the term "clarity," built on the preceding premise. In this sense, clarity did not suggest unfettered, open accessibility to biblical truth. Instead, it focused on the Spirit's determinative power to illuminate the human mind with God's Word, thereby generating action via the human will. As Zwingli contended, "When the Word of God shines on the human understanding, it enlightens it in such a way that it understands and confesses the Word and knows the certainty of it."[55] Human response was a product of divine activity.

By highlighting the dual themes of clarity and certainty, Zwingli positioned the Bible as the normative authority for the church. Earlier understandings of tradition had previously sought to preserve an apostolic way of interpreting the biblical text. However, late medieval Catholicism expanded upon this early model beginning with the Fourth Lateran Council of 1215.[56] Since the thirteenth century, the church had affirmed a dual fount of authority, setting tradition alongside the Bible as a second, equal authority. Where the biblical text was silent or contested on certain matters, the church offered its own pronouncements, which were as binding as those of Holy Writ.[57] Zwingli's elevation of the Word and the Spirit's illuminating work undercut these assumed norms of authority.

Zwingli also affirmed *sola Scriptura* in the sermon. Questions about the nature of biblical authority famously surfaced in Luther's debate with Johann Eck at Leipzig in 1519. Like the Wittenberg Reformer, Zwingli stressed "that even Popes and councils have sometimes fallen into serious error."[58] Given humanity's natural inclination for deception, he reasoned,

"Only God Himself can teach us the truth with such certainty that all doubts are removed."[59] Accordingly, clerical elites were refused a monopoly on accessing God's Word. The laity had an equal share in the Spirit's illuminating work. They too could hear from God. Referencing the Spirit's anointing from 1 John 2, Zwingli stressed, "This anointing is the same as the enlightenment and gift of the Holy Ghost ... once God has taught us with this anointing, that is, His Spirit, we do not need any other teacher."[60] Such an idea enfranchised those previously taught that to hear from their Lord required clerical mediation. It also paired well with Zwingli's proclamation of the gospel that emphasized Christ as the sole Mediator.[61]

Zwingli believed Scriptural clarity removed the papacy's grip on theology. The Roman magisterium was not to exclusively oversee the interpretation of the Bible. People from all sectors of society received an invitation to take part in hearing from God and proclaiming his gospel truth. The laity's inclusion in this work attacked the clergy/laity divide that was already dissolving. At the close of his sermon, Zwingli pointed out that God spoke to and had an affinity for the lowly of society, the humble, and the least of these.[62] The elevation of the doctrine of the priesthood of all believers is unmistakably evident here. This view, when polemically framed against the Roman Curia's presumptuous oversight of theology, was an effective weapon for Zwingli in these early years. However, this position had unintended consequences that left the preacher vulnerable. As dissenting readings of the Bible within his own reform movement began emerging in 1523, opponents weaponized this principle against Zwingli. The attacking preacher soon found himself on the defensive, much like Luther had in the mid-1520s with Karlstadt and the German peasants. His assumed belief in the perspicuity of the Bible proved to be flawed and overstated.[63]

Ten days later, Zwingli shifted attention away from the Bible's authority toward its salvific message in a sermon to the nuns at Oetenbach. In this September 17, 1522, sermon, later titled "Sermon on the Eternal Purity of the Virgin Mary," Zwingli focused on the atoning work of Christ.[64] He contended, "Christ shed his blood for the sake of our salvation. Now one is a useless soldier who will not shed his blood for the sake of his Lord and Captain, but who runs away when the Lord has already suffered death for him and before him."[65] Even though Mary's perpetual virginity was maintained, Zwingli refocused attention on the saving work of Christ. This was an important contrasting distinction regarding Mary's place in redemptive history. The Holy Mother retained her elevated standing in the gospel narratives. However, Zwingli now positioned her as "an edificatory, not an intercessory figure."[66] For the nuns at Oetenbach who identified with Mary and drew inspiration for their work from the Holy Mother, this must have been an offensive domestication of her esteemed position. Yet Zwingli's introduction of the language of Christ as "Captain" demanded an allegiance to this truth by all Christians regardless of the cost. Confession of this biblical conviction came with a potential risk to those who followed Christ.[67]

The contrast of Zwingli's growth into a Reformation preacher with his early time as a Catholic priest was unmistakable. As a parish priest at Glarus, he once stirred people's support of Roman sacramentalism.[68] Now he deployed those same preaching tools to undercut historic Catholic norms like the veneration of the saints, the use of images, and clerical marriage. He offered these attacks while also elevating Scriptural authority to the detriment of the papacy, arguably the most scandalous of his ideas in the early 1520s. That both sermons were quickly edited and printed for public dissemination demonstrate that the ideas contained therein were portable to the community. Biblical truth was not simply for the clergy.

Shortly after Zwingli's return from Oetenbach, on October 10, 1522, the Zurich Council established a preaching office to fund Zwingli's work.[69] This was a noteworthy move on three fronts. First, relinquishing his benefice formally released Zwingli from his priestly duties, marking his personal break with Rome. Second, the decision implied the Council's authority in religious matters and set a trajectory for the civil magistrates' oversight of ecclesiastical issues at Zurich. Last, it denoted an important vote of confidence in Zwingli at what was a pivotal moment of the Swiss Reformation. The affirmation of his work must have been refreshing and life-giving. The Council's backing continued when the preacher faced heresy charges months later. That support allowed him to proceed forward, justified in his preaching. The hope of a greater gospel harvest lay in the coming season of ministry.

BEARING FACTITIOUS FRUIT

From the outset, Zwingli's sermons cut across demographic lines. His voice resonated with clergy and laity, the wealthy and the poor, and men and women alike.[70] However, little did he know, his work would soon be undermined by some of his followers. Certain co-laborers took his preaching to heart and got out in front of him, driven by their reformation ambitions. Men like Conrad Grebel, one of Zwingli's mentees, Wilhelm Reublin, and others began agitating Zurich's religious ethos. Some of these gospel partners either directly took part in or incited others to anti-clerical actions like disruptions of homilies, attacks on monasteries, and the destruction of paintings and icons.[71] Simon Stumpf, another of Zwingli's allies, stirred dissension in the rural communes around Zurich. Stumpf promoted independence for the rural churches mostly by questioning the tithe, which functioned like a tax and funneled money into the Zurich city center.[72]

Rebellious measures, like the violation of the Lenten fast, were useful means to Zwingli's reformation ends. These actions especially showed the disunity he believed stood between the Bible's commands and Catholic practices. However, similar destructive anti-clerical activities soon were turned inward and against the Swiss Reformer. In most cases there was a general accord between Zwingli and these radical factions on the nature of ecclesiastical problems. The divide now mostly related to the pace and extent of the correctives. On these two matters the sheep were beginning to stray from their shepherd. And where they were going, Zwingli was unwilling to follow.

Questions regarding the relationship between the civil and religious authorities further exacerbated the splintering of the reform camp at Zurich. The greater the fires of religious radicalism raged in the community, the more sternly state officials felt forced to respond with oppressive measures aimed at extinguishing the flames of discord. But who was more biblically justified in their actions: the agitating Radicals or the civil magistrates? The Swiss preacher quickly offered clarification to the devolving situation. To confront the rising wave of unrest during the summer months, Zwingli preached a sermon in June 1523 titled "Divine and Human

Righteousness."[73] This sermon, along with its publication in July 1523, promoted the evangelical gospel and aimed to quell dissent.

Zwingli centered his argument on two distinct yet interrelated ideas: divine and human righteousness. Divine righteousness, Zwingli argued, flows from God's character and bids humanity adhere to His holy standard, per Matthew 5:48.[74] Knowing humanity's inability to achieve this measure without divine intervention, Zwingli framed the gospel as mercifully connected with God's divine righteousness:

> Now since He who was innocent suffered death for us guilty sinners, He paid off for us the beautiful righteousness of God, which otherwise no human being can satisfy; thus, He earned for us the right to come to God by virtue of his free grace and gift. Whoever hears this and believes it without doubt shall be saved. That is the gospel.[75]

The simple, gospel clarity is staggering. Through Christ's atoning work, God Himself made the necessary payment for humanity's sin while also meeting the holy standard of living set before us all. Human righteousness was different, yet no less needed for the Christian community than its divine counterpart. Though God's Word offered a superseding voice, human standards of conduct were appropriate and required for ordering society. Zwingli's emphasis on the distinction between one's inner heart disposition and outer actions, which he drew from Erasmus, shines brightly here.[76] Since not all are elect, one should not expect reprobates to live according to God's divine righteousness. Therefore, temporal boundaries must be established. These ethical and moral guardrails are for the safety and good of society, though obedience to them does not grant one access to God's divine righteousness.[77]

Referencing Jesus's words from Matthew 22:21 about granting to Caesar what was rightfully his, Zwingli argued for God-ordained human authorities.[78] Similar to Augustine and Luther, he reminded his audience that temporal authorities were established for society's protection, not their oppression, and that these temporal powers are now to establish laws consistent with Scripture.[79] Citing Romans 13, Zwingli offered a stern warning: "Whoever sets oneself against the authorities opposes the divine order."[80] To disobey the Zurich Council was to defy the Lord. That was precisely what Grebel, Stumpf, and others had done. This sermon consolidated support for Zwingli's Reformation via the civil magistrates, who were keen to receive the preacher's empowerment. However, it further alienated his erstwhile gospel partners.

HERMENEUTICS AND HOMILETICS

The Protestant doctrine of *sola Scriptura* elevated the Bible as the normative authority for establishing doctrine and practice. This set a vision for the church in contrast to Rome's. One important qualifier to *sola Scriptura* surfaced almost immediately: the text needed to be interpreted. Accordingly, sermons allowed the Reformers to mediate God's Word to His people, but through each preacher's unique interpretative lens. In Zwingli's case, this enabled him to present a humanistic reading of the Bible through his sermons. It also allowed for his Reformed, covenantal commitments to be impressed upon the Zurich church, as those convictions increasingly surfaced in the Reformer's theology. The nature of the preacher's interposing work was often indiscernible to his audience. God's divine Word and the human preacher's voice are not easily disentangled. This allowed the Zurich preacher to guide the form and shape of forthcoming reforms amid a sea of other competing Reformation voices.

While appeals to the plain meaning of the text abounded during the era, such a reading proved problematic from the outset of the Reformation. As we will see exemplified later in Chapter 6, the notion of a plain or literal reading of the text did not account for the polyvalent nature of those hermeneutical designations applied by different parties. Given Zwingli's humanist commitments, an Erasmian distinction between the "letter" and "spirit" of Scripture framed his exegesis.[81] The letter of Scripture corresponded to the basic, surface meaning of the text. The spirit of Scripture contained the deeper, more important theological truths hidden under the letter. These deeper, veiled realities were the true words of life. Based on this hermeneutic, Zwingli began a multitiered approach to reading the

Bible drawn from the fourfold tradition of medieval exegesis and Origen's spirit/soul/body delineation.[82]

Zwingli's hermeneutic began with a search for the "literal sense" of Scripture. This pursuit corelated to the immediate historical context of the biblical text and served as the foundational axiom of interpretation. Word studies based on philology were a crucial step to discerning the text's literal meaning. This approach did not abandon allegorical interpretations, but it focused attention on the literal-grammatical-historical sense in the tradition of Erasmus. Zwingli relied on rhetorical devices like alloeosis, synecdoche, and metonymy to guide interpretation toward the most natural reading of the text given its unique context, always allowing Scripture to interpret Scripture. This approach avoided an overbearing literalism that he believed led to things like transubstantiation.

Subsequent calls to understand the deeper theological meaning of Scripture expanded from this literal interpretation, culminating in contemporary application. This is where Reformation sermons became about shaping more than ideas or beliefs. The interpretation of Scripture also came with calls for decisive action. Sermons transmitted more than content alone. They also invited audiences to cast aside passivity and become active participants in the reshaping of their communities. Reformation sermons were practical. They focused attention on personal application and spiritual renewal. This focus was especially true for preachers, like Zwingli, who were influenced by Renaissance humanism. A concern to craft argumentative forms that directed people toward *besserung* ("moral improvement") and spiritual renewal characterized the movement. As individuals drew closer to God through the preached Word, becoming active participants in society, a residual collective gain for the Christian community was realized.

The Zurich shepherd labored diligently in each of his sermons to connect the Bible's teachings with everyday realities. Zwingli's fascination with "finding parallels to the present times in the biblical text" allowed for the ethical prescriptions of Scripture to inform the Zurich community through the preached Word.[83] Exhortations to decisive action, most notably through an amended life, pervaded his preaching. Calls to repentance based on what was gleaned from the past were a characteristic of humanism's pedagogical tradition. As Zwingli turned his attention more acutely toward the Old Testament in 1525, this meant that Israel served as the model for the Zurich church.

The peeling back of Scripture was not just to find meaning and morality in the text. More importantly, it was about finding Messiah. Zwingli's reading of the Bible through multiple senses was saturated with a Christocentricity, likely derived from Erasmus, that stressed the imitation of Jesus.[84] This focus on Christ was important for two reasons. First, this amplification of Jesus put him out of step with many traditional Catholic preachers of his day. Zwingli was now free to preach Christ and His atoning work on the cross. Accordingly, the customary preaching themes that highlighted purgatory, the saints, Mary, or the apostles faded against the backdrop of the Son and His more dominant story. Following and imitating Christ became the means to the renewal of Zurich's society.

Second, this shift toward a Christocentric reading of the Bible became foundational to making sense of the relationship between the two Testaments of Scripture, situating Jesus as the anchor between the two. Prior to the mid-1520s, the preacher had already begun speaking in covenantal terms. However, from 1525 onward, he did so based on a strong connection between the Old and New Testaments, which also interweaved the old and new covenants. This link first surfaces in his late-1525 "Reply to [Balthasar] Hubmaier" amid the baptismal controversy. Subtle differences between the two testaments still existed for the Reformer, mostly relating to the inclusion of gentiles and the arrival of Messiah.[85] The sign of the covenant also shifted from circumcision to baptism. For Zwingli, "baptism is an external covenant symbol that all who are in the covenant receive without exception."[86] Still, covenant continuity was key. The ecclesial consequences of these convictions were profound. As Zwingli understood it, "to be in the covenant meant to be in the church, to be a part of the people of God," including children.[87] In the end, Zwingli maintained a strong commitment to "the basic unity of the Old and New Testaments, which is based in the unity of God and his word, which possesses in Christ its center, but also its guiding principle."[88] Consequently, Christ, and Jesus as the fulfillment of God's promise made to

Israel, saturated his sermons. From 1525 onward, it also meant that Zwingli increasingly framed the Zurich community as partakers of that promise, a contemporary representation of Israel.

This development in the Zurich Reformer's hermeneutic also coincided with the appearance of an exegetical principle called the Rule of Faith and Love. Initially surfacing in Zwingli around 1524, this rule established *charitas* ("love") as an axiomatic grid of interpretation that helped to embody the practice of neighbor love in a divisive era. Drawing especially from Erasmus on this point, this rule sought accommodation and allowance, especially when differing interpretations of contested texts threatened ecclesiastical unity.[89] Thus, while mired in the baptism controversy with his own students, the Reformer stressed, "We [Zwingli and the future Anabaptist Radicals] mutually obligated ourselves most conscientiously to discuss everything according to the norm of love."[90] Of course, this was how things looked from Zwingli's side of the debate. Things were much different for his counterparts, the Anabaptists. Based on magisterial persuasion, this exegetical premise was practically little more than a tool to keep dissenting groups silenced.[91]

This argument became useful to Zwingli when the Waldshut Reformer Balthasar Hubmaier arrived in Zurich under duress for his Anabaptist convictions in December 1525. According to a report from Joachim Vadian, a discussion with the Zurich preacher on December 19 led Hubmaier to recant his radical commitment to a believers' church.[92] When conveying the reason behind his shift in thinking, Hubmaier spoke specifically of Zwingli's exegetical Rule. Hubmaier's previous rejection of infant baptism was now amended based on the assertion that "love is to be the judge and referee in all Scriptures."[93] Zwingli's usage of the Rule of Love became such a valued weapon against Anabaptism that both Bullinger and the Reformed ministers at Bern leveraged the tool in their polemical responses to Anabaptism into the 1530s.[94] In all of these cases, 2 Corinthians 13:10 was used to highlight the Swiss Reformed ministers' pursuit of building up the body, as opposed to the destructive impulses of the Radicals. Thus, Zwingli's biblical interpretation extended his exegetical influence onto the Swiss Reformation well beyond Zurich.

PASTORAL REFLECTIONS

The religious controversies from summer 1523 lingered for several years. This persistent volatility undermined Zwingli's work and threatened the Reformation's viability. With a growing chorus of voices arguing for divergent visons of the church, confusion soon set in. Now into his forties, Zwingli had both a wealth of biblical knowledge and years of ministerial experience to draw on as he desperately tried to reorient his reformation efforts at Zurich. To help stabilize matters while also steering the Zurich church away from Rome, Zwingli crafted two important works that helped convey what he believed a true, biblical pastor should look like.

The first of these was a sermon preached in October 1523 at the Second Zurich Disputation. When later published in March 1524, the piece was titled "The Shepherd."[95] This choice created an intentional allusion to the second-century work *The Shepherd of Hermas* and insinuated that Zwingli's preaching was linked to apostolic tradition. In this sermon, the preacher contrasted true, faithful shepherds who abide in God's truth with godless, false ones who lead the flock astray. The use of contrast, a favorite literary tool of humanists like Zwingli, allowed him to highlight the Catholic clergy's failure to faithfully dispense their important charge.

The first half of the sermon positioned true shepherds as those who follow the Great Shepherd's model. Jesus is "the Shepherd who has led us out of the dark stall of ignorance and the bondage of human teaching into the light of the divine wisdom and the freedom of sons."[96] Zwingli cast faithful pastors as those focused on eternal matters and spiritual deliverance. The second half of the sermon warned of ministerial imposters, wolves dressed as sheep, who posed a grave danger to the community. Their sights were set on temporal, self-serving concerns. The task of a good shepherd was to preach the Word, with emphasis on repentance, a hallmark of Jesus's proclamation.[97] Ministers were no longer framed as mediating intercessors of God's grace, which was characteristic of late medieval Catholic theology. Instead, a prophetic obligation and task marked the calling of true preachers. These men exhorted the flock to believe and act rightly, befitting their standing as God's people. For Zwingli, this prophetic voice extended to all areas of Swiss life, including the social community. Thus, the preacher avoided the modern bifurcation between the sacred and secular. Concerns for things like the mercenary service, money lending, care for the poor, and business monopolies were all situated within the prophet's purview.[98]

Divorcing oneself from the pursuit of temporal, distracting concerns was paramount to the preaching task. Otherwise, pastors might become guilty of the hypocrisy Paul warned about in Romans and Titus.[99] This is where the Catholic Church not only permitted but promoted the allure of wealth, power, and pleasure. Like the ravenous wolves who regularly crept in among the herds of sheep who roamed the tranquil Swiss countryside, the papacy's self-indulgent behavior brought only danger and destruction. Was maintaining this high ministerial standard a monumental task? The tumult of the past two decades of ministry proved that it was. Yet Zwingli believed a divine support buttressed the minister's calling:

> It is apparent that nothing other than divine love can bring the shepherd to deny himself, to leave his father and mother, to go forth without purse, knapsack, and staff, to be dragged before the princes, beaten, falsely accused, and killed and that love may not exist without the fundamental of undoubting trust.[100]

The images of purse, knapsack, and staff signified the rejection of temporal, worldly trappings while also highlighting the sustaining power of God's divine hand for the work to which pastors were called.[101] Presently embroiled in religious controversy, Zwingli reminded the people to remember God's faithfulness. Just as the Lord brought the Israelites out of Egyptian bondage and into freedom, so too would He do the same for them through reformation.[102]

The rise of Anabaptism incited Zwingli to pen the second of his works from this period. His treatise *On the Preaching Office* was not a sermon but a detailed explanation of the pastoral office and the importance of preaching in the Zurich church.[103] In fact, the Reformer used the terms "prophet" and "pastor" synonymously in this text. This esteemed office was so foundational for Zwingli that he subsumed the other biblical offices (along with their work and commission) from Ephesians 4 into a single prophetic, preaching one.[104]

For Zwingli, the pastor's calling, commission, and work were important themes validating one's ministerial standing. Proper, state-sanctioned authorization was something that the Anabaptists did not have since they detached themselves from the Zurich churches. The Anabaptists' lack of ministerial qualification was subsequently linked to their dangerous preaching and unbiblical practice of adult baptism. According to Zwingli, "The former act [preaching without authorization] serves to confound the truth, while the latter [rebaptism] leads to disorder ... both these are wholly against Christ."[105] Zwingli believed that Anabaptist pastors were overseeing false churches.

Like in the Old Testament, true prophets labored to prevent or to root out idolatry.[106] Yet they did this without sowing discord and confusion among the community. This is what the seditious Anabaptists had done. According to Zwingli, gospel order was exactly what Paul promoted in 1 Corinthians 14. While all might speak about Scripture, only pastors were to offer the normative interpretation of the text for the church. This shift away from Zwingli's earlier emphasis on the doctrine of the priesthood of all believers coincided with his elevation of the importance of proficiency in the biblical languages for proper biblical interpretation and his establishment of the Zurich *Prophezei*.[107] His exegesis of 1 Corinthians 14 went directly against the Anabaptists' reading of that text and their demand for a broader community of biblical interpreters, which culminated in their law of sitting.[108] It is easy to see the balance that Zwingli was trying to strike between avoiding what he perceived to be the Catholics' idolatrous failings while not devolving into the Anabaptists' radicalism, which he believed would unravel the Zurich society. A crucial part of the pastor's calling was to carve a *via media* on such matters.

GOSPEL HARVEST

In the mid-1520s, Zwingli portrayed true shepherds as those who stressed the importance of faithful biblical instruction. Only in the sacred Scriptures could the people of Zurich meet Jesus Christ. And the Reformer believed that Christ's voice alone would lead the people toward not only faithful patterns of worship in the present but also salvation for all eternity.

The Zurich preacher labored to model such a shepherd, sowing the truths of Scripture through his sermons. While doing this, the boy from rural Wildhaus knew that reaping and sowing went together. If this was true of the rhythms of agriculture, how much more would a gospel harvest be realized given the authority of Scripture. Zwingli reasoned, "The Word of God will always want to be manifested. For just as snow and rain fall from heaven and moisten the ground to make it green, so also does the Word of God work. It does not remain ineffective."[109] As he anticipated, the Word did not return void.

Countless Zurichers embraced the evangelical gospel through Zwingli's pulpit ministry. And as we will see in Chapter 2, by the mid-1520s, many eagerly embraced new patterns of worship they believed were prescribed by the Scriptures. To avoid idolatry, the Zurich churches removed images from their buildings, silenced organs, and whitewashed walls previously adorned with religious renderings. The motivation behind such moves was simple:

> We should be taught solely by the Word of God. Instead, the idle priests, who should have taught us without ceasing, have painted the teachings [of the Lord] on the walls for us. And we poor simple people have therefore been deprived of the teaching and have fallen to images, and have honored them. We have begun to seek from creatures what we should have sought only from God.[110]

The cost of blindly following Roman traditionalism and not listening to God's voice in the Scriptures was too high. Idolatry was a grievous offense. Zwingli believed that "Christians have a rule that we ought to endure death rather than depart from or keep silent the truth we know."[111] At great risk to himself, the Zurich preacher laid the text of Scripture bare before the people. He believed too much in the transforming power of God's Word to do otherwise.

A key premise guided Zwingli's preaching: "The pure Word of God is to be proclaimed without ceasing, for in it one learns what God demands of us and with what grace He comes to our aid."[112] By spring 1525, Zwingli had proclaimed the risen Christ for years. He now believed that the Zurich church was ripe for a Reformation harvest. As will be outlined in Chapter 2, this meant abolishing the Roman Mass and installing a new Reformed liturgy. Zwingli believed the Spirit had tilled the soil of the people's hearts through Scripture. He, along with a host of other faithful preachers, sowed the seeds of the gospel for years. The transforming power of the Word watered those seeds over time, and the Lord would produce the beautiful, abundant gospel harvest that surely lay before him in a Reformed liturgy.

CONCLUSION

In summer 1524, Zwingli exhorted his beloved Swiss people to make certain "the Word of God is faithfully preached among you ... and when you see how this alone brings God glory and holds out salvation to souls, then further it, regardless of what others may say."[113] He modeled this commitment from the outset of his preaching ministry in 1519, always sowing the seeds of the gospel in his sermons. Zwingli also knew opposition would come. Faithful gospel proclamation always brings detractors in tow. Disapproval first came from papal apologists who lamented Zwingli's departure from the Pope's authority and Catholic practices. Radicals from within his own camp also brought resistance. These opponents believed their former mentor was not practicing what he preached.

Yet the words of others were not important to Zwingli. Only the voice of the Lord, which he believed Holy Writ preserved, did matter. Amid the ever-present battle between fear of God and fear of humanity, Zwingli chose surrender to the Lord. He pleaded with his audiences to assume a similar posture of submission: "That word [the Scriptures] makes you pious, God-fearing people ... For where there is the fear of God, there is the help of God. Where it [the fear] is not present, there is hell and everything is miserable and wrong. Therefore, let loose the Word of God because that alone will make you right again."[114] Only as the Swiss people surrendered themselves to God's voice could the pathway toward salvation be realized. The sheep needed to hear from their Shepherd.

The Haeberlin rendering of Zwingli preaching at Stein am Rhein artistically captures Zwingli doing what was at the heart of his ministry, proclaiming the Word of God. Though the Swiss preacher is the focal point of the painting, the surrounding assembly tells an important part of his narrative. Seated in the choir portion of the building is a cluster of clerics easily identified by their black robes. Several of these are tilted with inquisitive postures. One rests his head on his hand in confusion. Another figure, adorned with a tall bishop's miter and holding a golden mace, appears aghast. He recoils in a posture of rejection and shock. Each of the clerical figures symbolizes Rome's suspicion and ultimate rejection of Zwingli's preaching. However, the laity in the foreground tell a different story. Men on both sides frame the portrait, each leaning inward, captivated by Zwingli's preaching. One even cranes his head sideways to find an unobstructed view of the Reformer. Two women kneel while clutching their hands, an allusion to their submission to God's Word. Though some, like the Catholics, rejected Zwingli's preaching, countless others did not. Meeting Christ in the Scriptures, these experienced a transformation that forever changed the Swiss church.

During the proceedings of the First Zurich Disputation, Zwingli declared, "God does not require of us what popes, bishops, and councils have established, nor what is a laudable old custom, but how His divine will, His Word, and His commands are to be followed."[115] The only way to know what God desires, to find true religion as Zwingli framed it, was to hear God's voice that had been preserved in Scripture. The church had only confused and obfuscated true religion, ultimately leading the people into what the Reformer perceived were idolatrous practices. Zwingli's Reformation focused on liberating the Scriptures so the people of God might hear from their Maker and commune with Christ their Savior.

Chapter 2

The Reformation of Worship

"Also, the Church of Christ has its model for posterity to observe and imitate, and how can these endure to posterity unless there be someone to commend them to the coming ages?"[1]

EACH DAY, SCORES OF PEOPLE visit the picturesque Grossmunster Church in the Zurich city center. Per the request of attending ushers, the large medieval building remains mostly silent. This quiet sensitizes visitors to the reverential nature of a building where God has been the focus of Christian worship for centuries. The shuffling of feet, the whispers of tourists, and the occasional cough are lone sounds in an otherwise awe-inspiring silent venue. The stillness of the setting today stands in stark contrast to what was once regularly found in the sanctuary. Five hundred years ago, the Swiss Reformer Huldrych Zwingli regularly thundered eloquent sermons to masses of Zurich citizens throughout the week in this space. His bold gospel proclamation inspired and encouraged some of those in attendance. Others were aghast and angered. All of those present witnessed the reshaping of the Swiss church's ecclesiastical landscape through Reformation preaching.

During Zwingli's tenure at Zurich, the Reformer oversaw several reforms aimed at reorienting the community's worship toward what he believed was a more biblical pattern. The greatest of these changes was the dramatic elevation of the sermon in the Swiss church's liturgy. For hundreds of years, the Eucharist dominated worship in the Catholic Church. Every part of the Roman Mass pushed toward the climactic moment when Jesus appeared before His people in the bread and wine. The preached word was an important part of the Mass, alongside things like Scripture readings and singing. However, preaching was more tangential to the wondrous rite where God, in Christ Jesus, met with His people through the miracle of the Eucharist. Zwingli knew that communion with God was a crucial part of the Christian experience. However, he believed Roman abuses to the Eucharist, including over-emphasis, missteps in practical application, and theological error, veiled that important interaction with God.

Zwingli's Reformation vision sought to reorient the place of preaching in the Zurich liturgy by making it central. His work as a humanist taught him that the Word needed to be elevated as the primary means of realizing the human-divine dialogue in Zurich. Upon arrival at Zurich, Zwingli labored to bring preaching to the fore of Christian worship. Yet this was not the only required change. Other substantive reforms, like the removal of images and icons from the Zurich churches, were also needed, along with a more active role for the laity in their corporate gatherings for worship. Reformation would be realized only after these corrections were made.

These revisions did not come overnight. Nor did they come easily. But for Zwingli, they were essential. By 1525, the Reformation sermon was established as the primary means by which the people communed with God. This elevation of the preached Word replaced the rite of the Eucharist, which had dominated the church's liturgy for hundreds of years. That same year, Zwingli also oversaw a new Reformed form of the Lord's Supper at Zurich. For Zwingli, the liturgical trappings of the Roman Mass would no longer mute or misconstrue God. He could now be heard by the Swiss people clearly and in a transformative way.

A DRAMATIC ECCLESIAL SHIFT

The elevation of the Holy Scriptures was one of the defining characteristics of the Reformations that swept across Europe in the sixteenth century. During the medieval era, the Eucharist served as the centerpiece of Christian worship. The Eucharist, with all its mystery and ceremony, was more than just a familiar rite and central activity of the Christian community. It was the climactic moment of the Mass, when one could taste God's divine grace. It was a unique, albeit fleeting, event when one encountered God in an intimate and salvific way. Clerical priests played a crucial part in this occasion. They were mediators of this divine encounter by virtue of their ordination. Without them, this brush with heaven could not be realized.

That all changed with the Protestant Reformation. From the outset, most of the Reformers had concerns about what they perceived to be Rome's mistaken overemphasis on the Eucharist as the central place where God's people met with their Lord. According to these same Reformers, the interface between God and humanity found through the elements was stifled and obfuscated by egregious errors in both Catholic theology and practice. It was difficult to see the living Christ through the repeated sacrifice of their Savior they believed regularly played out before them in the Roman Mass. The communicants' inability to understand the Latin Mass or partake of the cup only added to their distance from God.

The unfurling of the Reformation ushered in substantive changes to the Eucharist. But reforms did not end with this rite alone. Ecclesiastical revisions extended to the entire liturgy. Abuses relating to the Mass became one of the Reformers' primary concerns demanding redress. Formally abolishing the Mass was so highly valued that it now serves as the defining historical marker establishing when Reformation was realized. However, the Reformers were divided over what changes were required. Martin Luther declared he had "no intention to abolish the liturgical services of God completely, but rather to purify the one that is now in use from the wretched accretions which corrupt it and to point out an evangelical use."[2] Though Luther had several liturgical reforms in view, one dominated his concerns: the Roman Mass was mistakenly being understood as a sacrifice. In fact, Luther called the canon prayer "that abominable concoction drawn from everyone's sewer and cesspool," since this prayer conveyed the idea of Christ's re-sacrifice.[3] For the Wittenberg Reformer, this could not remain. Luther believed substantive changes to the Mass were required, though much remained the same in the German liturgy.

Many of the Swiss Reformers, like Zwingli, shared Luther's concerns. However, they also believed the Mass needed a larger overhaul. They contended that Catholicism's understanding and administration of the sacraments were stunting the human-divine encounter that was at the heart of Christian worship. Medieval innovations related to the Roman Mass veiled the gospel instead of proclaiming it. The Mass unintentionally distanced people from their Lord rather than drawing them near Him. As reliance on medieval forms of the sacraments waned during the early days of the Swiss Reformation, something had to fill the vacuum left behind in their worship. Something needed to supplant the Eucharist as the primary ecclesial location where one communed with God. For Zwingli, the sacred Scriptures became that replacement. In the text of Holy Writ, one heard the voice of the divine. One could taste salvation.

EMBRACING THE WORD

By the early 1520s, several different vernacular Bibles were available. At roughly the same time, the revolutionary Protestant doctrine of the priesthood of all believers surfaced.[4] Christians were not only gaining access to Scripture but were also afforded theological justification to engage with it. Given the confluence of these revelations, the Scriptures became the common property of all Christians. True communion with God was no longer primarily found in the bread and cup. It could be realized through a divinely inspired text, the Word of God breathed out for humanity. The Bible, Zwingli argued, was a "touchstone" of truth.[5] Any doctrine could be set against that benchmark to see if the words of humanity "reflected the same color or rather that the doctrine could bear the brilliance of the stone."[6] This belief in the Bible's authority became a guiding compass for Zwingli and many of the other Reformers. The Scriptures would navigate the church through the era's tumultuous waters.

This access to the text came much later than many today might imagine. Most of the Reformers' vernacular Bible translations did not surface until the mid-1520s. Even then, illiteracy proved a formidable obstacle that left much of society without access to the text. In some places as little as five percent of society could read.[7] With such abysmal literacy rates, how could the people commune with the Lord via the Scriptures? In the absence of widespread literacy, the sermon became an important tool making God's Word accessible to His people. Priests no longer mediated God's grace in a sacerdotal system that divided the clergy from the laity. Rather, pastors now stood alongside their people with a shared priesthood, but also with a unique appointment to proclaim God's Word. Given this reality, it is not surprising that Reformation preachers like Zwingli, Luther, and others quickly saw themselves as contemporary prophets. They believed God tasked them to mediate the Lord's voice to the people.

The displacement of the Eucharist by the preached Word was a dramatic departure from the medieval tradition. God was still speaking to His people. However, that exchange had changed in at least three ways. The first related to language. For hundreds of years, the Mass was offered in Latin. There was something elegant and reverential about Latin, especially when contrasted with the harshness of certain brogues, like German. However, this left God's voice distant from the people, unintelligible to most. The Reformers' vernacular preaching presented a stark contrast to this heritage. Zwingli argued that the liturgy should be enacted "not in the Latin tongue, but in the vernacular, so that all shall understand what is going on."[8] Communication was crucial to communion. God's voice was no longer to remain muted by the Latinate tradition. According to Zwingli, the people needed to hear from the Lord in their native Swiss German tongue.

Second, God's voice also shifted in medium. The Reformers communicated in a variety of forms to persuade the people of their visions for the church. These included mass publications of pamphlet literature and personal letters alongside participation in public disputations. Yet none of those mediums were as powerful as the Reformation sermon. Only there did the words of Scripture coalesce with Zwingli's to create one powerful voice that spoke to the Zurich people. Such a union, when combined with the visual authority symbolized by an elevated pulpit, generated an avenue of influence unparalleled by other media. Given that Zwingli's sermons were embodied expressions, they offered him an opportunity to convey biblical truth with human emotion and a personal appeal unmatched by print. The preached Word created incarnational moments. God not only spoke to the Zurich community but was also with His people, guiding them forward in their faith through His appointed servant.

Third, the message itself was also different from the one offered by Catholicism. This change was central to what the Reformers saw as their recovery of the true gospel. The Catholic Church's preaching and sacramental theology focused attention on what the people needed to do to rightly relate to God. The Reformers' message was different. Zwingli and others focused attention on the need to embrace by faith what Christ had already accomplished to secure salvation. Zwingli contended, "Since, therefore, we have learned by the teaching of the Holy Spirit that there is but one offering and that was made by the Son of God," the Zurich liturgy became "a simple and Christian form of celebration."[9] Roman Catholicism's encouragement to participate in the sacraments as a means of infusing salvific grace was viewed as an abomination. Zwingli and most of the Reformers directed their verbal proclamation of the Word toward an already accomplished historical reality, Jesus's work at Calvary and God's divine election. This emphasis reshaped the nature of the human-divine relationship and directed attention toward God's activity in redemption.

LOOSING GOD'S VOICE

From the outset of his Zurich ministry, Zwingli recognized the sacred trust placed in him by the community. To mediate the Lord's voice through the pulpit was a weighty task. He also understood the nature of the sermon and how crucial it was for his ministry's success. If the Reformation he envisioned was to be realized, then Zwingli needed to leverage that persuasive form. Success and failure would be measured by two things: contrast and recovery. Reformation required that he eloquently contrast the Word of God with what he believed were Catholicism's unbiblical practices, such as the Mass being portrayed as a sacrifice, the use of images in worship, and the invocation of the Saints. The changes he envisioned also demanded that he persuasively move the Zurich people toward recovering biblical patterns of worship he believed were prescribed by Scripture. Years of study, especially his work as a humanist, provided him oratorical eloquence for this task. His time serving at Glarus and Einsiedeln seasoned and equipped him for the ministry that lay before him. Nevertheless, questions about his work remained. Would his new parishioners listen to him? Might Rome intervene and crush his prophetic voice? Could he help guide Zurich toward the heavenly city promised in the Bible? These questions began to find answers as the preacher arrived at Zurich.

On January 1, 1519, Zwingli stood behind a pulpit ready to address his new congregation for the very first time. This sermon may have been offered from an elevated, ornate, hand-carved wooden pulpit affixed to a stone column supporting the roof in front of the choir portion of the building. Or it might have been preached from a portable stool, which had become commonplace in parts of the Swiss Confederation.[10] Either way, the Reformer preached in the nave portion of the building. This positioning set Zwingli perpendicularly adjacent to and well in front of the High Altar, which was elevated atop a steep flight of stairs, though veiled from the laity's view by a wooden rood screen. This arrangement also likely situated him to the side of the main sanctuary, architecturally embodying the prevailing theological belief that the Eucharist, not the sermon, was the focal point of worship. It was at that High Altar where priests presided for centuries over the miracle of the Mass, the transformation of the bread and wine into Christ's body and blood.

The Grossmunster sanctuary was replete with colorful stained-glass windows and a dazzling array of iconography commonplace for the era. Glass and plaster depictions of Christ, the Virgin Mary, and canonized saints filled the cavernous building with visually stimulating sights from the Bible. For centuries, these renderings served as the laity's Scripture in a medieval world where Bibles, due to cost, were as scarce as the literacy required to read them. They also connected parishioners in a familial way, not only with Jesus but also with a historical Christian tradition. These artistic representations kept watch over the day's proceedings, as they had for centuries. There was no shortage of eyes and ears attending to the new preacher, ready to oversee his every word.

While Zwingli stepped into the pulpit in a common manner, his words were anything but typical. He was preaching on the eighth day of

Christmastide, a feast day in the church's calendar devoted to the solemnity of Mary. However, his preaching was about not Mary, the Mother of God, but the Lord's voice as recorded in the sacred Scriptures. Why such a shift? As he later reasoned, he came "to have trust in nothing and in no words except those which proceeded out of the Lord's mouth."[11] The Latin term for "words" employed here is *sermone*, thereby connecting God's word with pulpit proclamation. This was a voice he believed the people of Zurich needed. Based on that conviction, Zwingli made a commitment to the people.[12] He would offer all his future sermons *lectio continua*, that is, based on an expositional preaching form that jettisoned the church's historical pericope.[13] This decision was a stunning revelation to those present and was the first formal liturgical change ushered in by Protestantism.[14]

For centuries, the lectionary ordered the church's liturgy on Sundays and feast days.[15] Each week a group of prescribed readings walked the people through the Scriptures. This reading plan allowed for select biblical texts to strategically complement various seasons and festivals in the ecclesiastical calendar. According to Zwingli, this practice had shortcomings. For instance, he feared that lectionary readings moved the reader around the canon in a disjointed manner, with little to no consideration for the immediate, historical, and canonical contexts he believed were required to understand the text. This disjoined and ahistorical approach was particularly problematic given his commitments to Renaissance humanism. Moreover, he believed that the traditional lectionary allowed the church to impress ecclesiastical themes into its corporate worship by dictating the weekly readings of Scripture, rather than allowing the Bible to shape the church's worship directly. For Zwingli, this approach subjugated the voice of God to the church's ecclesial concerns.

Zwingli planned to reform worship so the weekly liturgy focused attention more purposefully on the text of Scripture. He would strategically select a book of the Bible and subsequently work verse by verse through the text. Similar preaching forms may be familiar to many contemporary audiences, but their appearance in the sixteenth century was a revolutionary departure from the typical lectionary orderings for worship.[16] This pedagogical decision was guided by the preacher's growing affinity for the biblical text, which had been nurtured by his studies as a Renaissance humanist. Sequential exposition and interpretation of the biblical text elevated the Scriptures as an authoritative priority to the church's traditions.[17] Zwingli believed that the whole counsel of God's Word, offered in its canonically given form, was the proper diet for the Zurich community. For Zwingli, it was the Catholic Church's ecclesiastical innovations, such as the lectionary, that left the people unable to fully feast on the Word as God intended.

There are no surviving sources capturing the audience's immediate response to Zwingli's promise. However, one can easily imagine that those present would have been astounded by his plan. This preaching plan would have been scandalous to those who esteemed Roman traditionalism and papal authority. To them, this idea must have seemed an outrageous proposition offered by a distrusted outsider to the community. But for some of those who had already caught wind of early Reformation musings emanating from Germany and elsewhere, or those with an affinity for humanism, Zwingli's promise likely would have been intriguing, perhaps even hopeful. The people of God would hear the Word of God as the prophets and apostles intended, loosed from the scholastic glosses and the binding shackles of Catholic tradition. They would be fed a steady diet of Scripture, which must have been appealing to those hungry for spiritual renewal. All present, regardless of their posture toward Zwingli's promise, would have to wait and see how this drama might unfold in the coming days.

SOWING SEEDS OF SCHISM

Zwingli honored his preaching promise. By the following year, the civil magistrates showed signs of being won to their new pastor's convictions, as evidenced by a new mandate. Ever since 1520, the Council had forbidden the Zurich ministers "to preach anything which they had not drawn from the fountain head of the two Testaments of Holy Writ."[18] This ill-defined preaching declaration afforded Zwingli and the other Reformation-minded preachers at Zurich a unique opportunity. From their pulpits they legally contrasted the doctrinal and ethical teachings of Scripture with those offered by Rome. The Council permitted such preaching freedoms so long as the preachers did not evoke Luther's name, given the controversy stirred by the German monk's famous 1520 polemical treatises.[19] This legislation helped facilitate a gospel harvest on one level, but it also placed the Zurich church in an untenable situation.

The paradox of gospel preaching alongside traditional Catholic practices left worship disjointed and confusing. In short, preached words did not correspond to liturgical movements. Zwingli employed Christocentric language focused on Christian freedom, but without an accompanying liturgy that embodied and connected with that same gospel proclamation. He regularly preached thundering sermons highlighting Christ's completed redemptive work through His sacrifice on the cross and victory over death through resurrection. Yet these gospel-saturated sermons conveyed a discordant message when paired with observance of the Roman Mass and preached in settings where iconic statues watched over worship. For Zwingli, this disconnect between doctrine and practice was disingenuous at best, idolatrous at worst.

Believing Zurich was on the precipice of reformation, Zwingli began to address with greater intensity aspects of Catholicism he believed undermined the gospel and were without biblical prescription. Repeated attacks questioning the perpetuity of monastic vows, clerical celibacy, and the use of images in worship dominated his sermons from 1521 and 1522. He also railed against the community's observance of the Eucharist, perhaps the greatest offense against Scripture. Each of his proposed correctives related to Catholic norms and, much like the breaking of the Lenten fast in 1522, were tangible expressions of reformation.[20] Changes to these religious forms meant that reformation was felt and experienced. A break from Rome loomed on the horizon. However, these calls for change also meant a fissure within his own reform camp was soon to surface.

The next several months proved to be some of the most challenging of Zwingli's pastorate. A myriad of voices and circumstances forced him to serve as mediator between advocates and opponents of long-established ecclesiastical norms. Traditionalists like Conrad Hofmann, an older canon at the Grossmunster who was one of many voices of opposition, seemingly always challenging the Reformer's ideas. Others, like the young humanists

Conrad Grebel and Felix Manz, chided Zwingli to move further and faster than he believed prudent. Rumblings of unrest in the rural communes over financial matters relating to the tithe during this time only exacerbated the situation. Zwingli's Reformation found itself "torn as it was between the conservatism of those who wished to change nothing and the spirit of the innovators to whom the slightest survival from the past became suspect."[21] His proceeding steps would be as momentous as they would be tenuous.

In summer 1523, Zwingli tried to blaze a conciliatory path, one that he hoped most would find agreeable. He helped introduce small innovations like the use of German vernacular in mid-week baptismal ceremonies through Leo Jud's translation of the *Baptismal Office*.[22] Nevertheless, the need for more substantive changes to the liturgy persisted. On August 29, 1523, Zwingli published *An Attempt Regarding the Canon of the Mass*, a pamphlet written in Latin formally outlining his proposed changes.[23] This work raised questions about the historic origins of the Roman Mass and recorded Zwingli's ire especially turned toward the re-sacrificing of Christ in the Roman Eucharist. In it he also portrayed the Supper as a memorial, which will be discussed at length in Chapter 6. But those reforms not proposed constitute the most fascinating part of this pamphlet. Things like the use of clerical vestments, singing in Latin, and liturgical prayers all remained.[24] The retention of such practices was not arbitrary. After all, Zwingli later removed these same things from the Swiss liturgy. Instead, this conservatism stood as a pastoral concession for the weak, those still clinging to Catholicism. Defending his proposals less than two months later, he spoke of a "dutiful restraint" in relation to "the weak" on such matters.[25] Regarding vestments, the Reformer stated, "But if any peril threatens them, then let the weak first be taken in hand and clearly taught what vestments have to do with the case and the consequences if they are not abolished."[26] Such conciliation was a hallmark of his ministry at Zurich, even though he proved unrelenting and uncompromising on other issues. Similar concessions were also something soon challenged by those closest to him.

Zwingli was not alone in his aspirations. During 1523, others pushed for a variety of changes that swelled into a chorus of concerns. In fall 1523,

Zwingli's close friend Leo Jud demanded the removal of statues, paintings, and other iconic depictions from the Zurich church during an impassioned sermon on September 19. Five days later, Ludwig Haetzer published a work, *On the Abolition of Images*, in which he expressed similar concerns, drawing many of his ideas from the Wittenberg iconoclast Andreas Karlstadt.[27] Zwingli agreed with Jud and Haetzer about removing images. But he was not as keen to do so swiftly for fear of social discord. Among gospel partners, agreement on the nature of reforms and their pace of implementation eluded even close friends.

Shortly thereafter, some took Zwingli's exhortations and those of his fellow Reformers to heart, and a season of iconoclasm swept through the community. From the close of September until November 1523, iconoclastic incidents sprang up with alarming frequency. For instance, critics of the church destroyed an altar, while others defaced a series of decorative panels at St. Peter's Church, the site of Jud's sermon one week earlier. Lampstands were also upended and holy water tossed about the sanctuary in the Fraumunster Church.[28] Another offense occurred when a wooden crucifix just outside the city walls was taken down. To justify his actions, the offending party cited a desire to follow the Bible's prohibition against images and his subsequent hope to use the wood from the cross to help the poor.[29] The dual themes of image removal and care for Zurich's downtrodden connected this iconoclastic action with Zwingli's preaching. While these iconoclasts shared many of Zwingli's convictions, they were also more cavalier in their violent reformation actions.

AFFINITY FOR IMAGES

The use of images in Christian worship has a long and storied history stretching as far back as the late patristic era. For centuries, religious icons and artistic renderings served as books for the illiterate. Images were often cast as necessary accommodations based on the educational limitations of commoners. Visual representations became a unique conduit or didactic aid that connected people with biblical stories and theological truths through a human sense different from that engaged by traditional education. As the eighth-century Syrian monk John of Damascus noted, "For just as words edify the ear, so also the image stimulates the eye. What the book is to the literate, the image is to the illiterate. Just as words speak to the ear, so the image speaks to the sight; it brings understanding."[30] Images were not considered a barrier of separation, nor a visual lens obfuscating the divine. Rather, images were an important medium many believed helped provide crucial access to religious knowledge for large sectors of society.

However, during the medieval period, images offered their audiences more than just static propositional knowledge. They also helped bridge the physical and metaphysical worlds by offering a relational experience between God and faithful followers of Jesus through a remembrance of past works. This important point about medieval iconography is frequently lost on modern audiences. Iconic depictions and artistic renderings did not directly relate in an ontological sense to the thing being represented, nor did they offer a one-for-one representation. These are modern misperceptions. Rather, icons connected people with God and the saints through metaphor. A crucifix, for instance, did not directly cohere to Jesus's death on the cross. But the rendering could work mnemonically, eliciting a remembrance of Jesus's work. The observer's eyes and imagination worked together symbiotically, providing a powerful encounter with Jesus at His passion.

Connections with a person or event from the past were not merely for receiving propositional knowledge or truth. That was only part of the experience. Perhaps more importantly, encounters with icons and images helped shape the whole person. These experiences directed affections and promoted a distinct way of living based on memory. Thomas Aquinas spoke of religious images as arousing more than just the human intellect. Images spoke especially to the affections. Images were able to affect mood and engender the disposition of one's heart in a way distinct from print or auricular mediums.[31] Images connected one's eyes and heart, extending their value to the educated sectors of society and to uneducated, illiterate ones.

REJECTING IDOLATRY

At the dawn of the Reformation, buildings throughout Europe were awash with religious images and icons. Statues, stained glass depictions, murals, carved furniture, and other visual forms framed worship settings and were as much a part of the liturgical rhythms of the Catholic Church as the sermon. Though these objects were ubiquitous in Swiss worship, Zwingli increasingly feared their presence on at least three fronts. First, the use of icons signified a departure from the Bible's clear prohibition in Exodus about crafting graven images. To allow these renderings to remain in the Zurich churches was to disobey the Lord. Second, God forbade the making of images specifically because they obscure and veil God from the people while also enticing them to worship the creation, not the Creator. Images, for Zwingli, were a steppingstone to image worship, a gateway to idolatry.[32] The distinction between the icon and that which was imaged was not easily distinguished in his mind. Last, images betrayed an improper love not only for God but also for neighbor. This was especially true of the poor. Money spent on what he pejoratively called the "cult of visible worship" should have been leveraged for the destitute and poverty-stricken people of Zurich.[33] Images were a misappropriation of funds to the detriment of the whole of society, most notably the poor.

Zwingli's stance on images did not make him an opponent of Christian art. But he was keen to make certain that images remained outside the confines of the church's walls, far removed from its theater of worship. Though the Reformer was not always consistent in his use of language, he did make a theological distinction between the German terms *Bilder* ("image" or "picture") and *Götzen* ("idol").[34] For Zwingli, the former of these, the image, was an artistic depiction that could be visually stunning or beautiful yet did not engender worship or elicit devotion. The latter, the idol, was a representation of Jesus, Mary, or the saints, for instance, that erroneously offered the people hope, peace, and comfort, perhaps even salvation itself. The people often mistakenly worshiped icons, and this was why he believed they must be removed from houses of worship. Here, Zwingli's pastoral concerns strategically overlapped with his reformation ambitions. These artistic renderings embodied the Catholic faith from which he was increasingly trying to separate the Zurich church through his reformation. To remove icons from communal worship offered a dual effect: it further established the independent nature of the Swiss church from Rome while also drawing the Zurich people closer to their Lord through a purer form of worship.

Icons represented more than just idolatry and Catholicism. They also signaled a failure to care for fellow humanity. In the mid-1520s, Zwingli began contrasting the "images of God," a phrase he used metaphorically of humanity, with the "image of man," which he used polemically to reference icons. Attending to the latter at the expense of the former was unthinkable. Regrettably, that had been the church's practice for centuries. Decrying this misalignment of priorities in a letter to Valentin Compar, Zwingli stressed, "What we, however, should give to the needy images of God, to the poor man, we hang on the image of man; for the idols are images of man, but man is an image of God."[35] The Reformer assigned much of the blame for this travesty to those who funded the crafting of icons. Zwingli judged that "all patrons of idols will have to give account to God, that they have let his own images go hungry, freeze, etc. and have so expensively adorned their own idols."[36] He knew that pastoring his people meant caring for the whole of the person, not simply the soul.

Although Zwingli was keen to remove icons from Swiss worship, he balanced that desire with an equal concern to care for his people during the transition away from their usage. The Reformer believed a biblical shepherd persuasively walks alongside his sheep, gently leading the flock, not dragging them behind. Therefore, before these abhorrent representations could be removed, he believed the people's dependence on them must first be cast aside. This is where the preacher's pastoral inclinations helped guide and steady his reformation. He later clarified during a sermon at Bern in 1528, "One should first remove the idols from one's heart, and then cast them away from one's eyes."[37] People's reliance on external things must first be purged personally and internally, well in advance of any broad, corporate changes to worship. To proceed in reverse was to risk rebellion and civil disruption. The preacher only needed look to the unrest caused by the iconoclast Andreas Karlstadt during Luther's isolation at the Wartburg for an example of such danger.[38] Like Luther, Zwingli desired an ordered Reformation, one free from social unrest and religious radicalism. That his own words, along with those of his co-laborers like Leo Jud, played any part inciting iconoclasm around Zurich must have been particularly painful for him.

The incidents of iconoclasm and other forms of radicalism eventually forced the Council's hand. These magistrates convened a debate on reforms as much to quell religious dissent as to secure biblical truth.[39] The Second Zurich Disputation met October 26–28, 1523.[40] On images, Zwingli swayed the Council's judgment. They concluded that images did not meet the biblical standard for usage in Christian worship. Zwingli argued during the debate, "Images should not be made, should not be worshipped, should not even be honored ... for the Word is clearer than day" on the matter.[41] Where Zwingli laid the blame for the appearance of images was just as evident: "Had the useless priests and bishops earnestly preached the Word of God as they ran after useless things, it would never have come to this that the poor layman who is ignorant of Scripture has to learn about Christ from the walls and from pictures."[42] Regardless of blame, images existed. But how were they to be removed?

The following month, Zwingli penned *A Short Christian Instruction*. This work focused on a host of Reformation themes, including the practical removal of icons. It remains a fascinating piece, given that it was written by Zwingli at the behest of the Zurich Council. However, once published, it was designated as sent from the Council, not from the Reformer, to the ministers and preachers of the State.[43] In essence, the Council was ratifying and validating Zwingli's words, as the two entities spoke in one accord on several issues, including on images. This cooperation serves as a reminder of how interwoven Zwingli's reforms were with the magistrate's authority, a relationship that soon helped birth the Swiss Anabaptists at Zurich.

Zwingli and the Council's shared commitment to remove images was to be carried out in an orderly manner. Once again, Zwingli's pastoral consideration resurfaced for those whose hearts and minds were still committed to Catholic worship patterns. The preacher stressed, "It is reasonable for everyone to teach, as has been found, that images are forbidden by God so that, after they have been instructed and strengthened, the unlearned and weak ones may soon accept what should be done with the images."[44] Images must go. They were leading the people astray and providing instruction that only the Bible should offer. Yet the Zurich community needed to come to grips with this truth themselves. The people needed to be persuaded, not coerced. His subsequent attempts at reform were slow, deliberate, and purposeful. According to Zwingli, "one is to proceed carefully so that evil is not the result."[45] The evil Zwingli had in mind was the disorderly, violent outbursts of iconoclasm that had sporadically been perpetrated only weeks earlier.

What remains fascinating about Zwingli's departure from images was how important memory was for him as a Renaissance humanist. The idea of remembrance, as we shall later outline, dominated the Reformer's understanding of the sacraments, especially the Lord's Supper.[46] In that act, the bread and the cup evoked a visceral remembrance of and reflection upon Jesus's work at Calvary. Tangible, material items, the bread and the wine, connected communicants with a past act. Could images not function and serve to edify and strengthen believers in a like manner?

Zwingli did not think so, arguing that such belief was as foolish as it was dangerous. Not only did the instruction offered by images supplant the authority of Scripture, but the presence of such things was leading the people astray from true worship.[47] The blurring of the lines between the Creator and the creation was a real danger. As he warned, "We have begun to seek from creatures what we should have sought only from God."[48] Zwingli framed image worship as idolatry.[49] Even the images of saints, which some contended might inspire observers toward similar forms of pious action, offered only faulty instruction. These renderings promoted a humanity-focused faith, not a divinely oriented one. As Zwingli reasoned, images of saints "cannot make the heart faithful."[50] That was a work of God alone.

THE SOUND OF SILENCE

Zwingli did not believe that images were the only liturgical form leading the Swiss away from true worship. Beginning in the early 1520s, he also addressed the issue of music, first criticizing both the priestly and choral singing that were common in the church's liturgy. Much of Zwingli's concern stemmed from his Erasmian distinction between the spirit and flesh, the form of worship and its content. For instance, people could sing a beautiful, melodious song, even one based on Scripture, yet still "not understand a single verse of the Psalms which they drone out."[51] External expression did not always mean internal comprehension. Moreover, because of humanity's finitude and frailty, liturgical acts like singing could easily be derailed from their desired purpose. Much like with prayer, Zwingli stressed, "Heart and mind are usually not connected for long, much less heart and song."[52] The human mind and heart are prone to wander. This was especially true for worship. Zwingli's understanding of humanity's psychological constitution meant singing naturally devolved into an assumed act of piety, often without a corresponding internal heart disposition of praise. External worship did not necessarily indicate a virtuous inner disposition, nor an understanding of the divine.

For Zwingli, the public form of worship was cause for concern and reform. All worship mediums risked devolving into "hypocrisy" when employed in public venues. Corporate singing, much like pilgrimage or the veneration of images, provided an opportunity for a public display of worship that could turn self-serving. As he reasoned, "Devotion does not parade itself before people, as a foolish paramour."[53] The human heart knows how to craft a façade of religion to its own selfish ends. Zwingli knew humans often carry themselves differently in public than in private. That there was a monetary benefit to this practice only exacerbated the problematic nature of such singing. Once again, as with images, money that could have benefited the poor was being funneled into what he believed was a godless practice.[54] Singing at Zurich violated both biblical commands to love God and love neighbor.

There was one exception to the Reformer's concern for the impious nature of public worship: the teaching of the Scriptures. He clarified, "Devotion diminishes in large crowds, unless, of course, one was to instruct the multitudes in God's Word."[55] While he believed some acts were hindered by a public form, biblical proclamation thrived in a corporate context. For Zwingli, understanding the Bible was always a communal endeavor. Once again, the reorientation of the Zurich church's liturgy around the Word of God drove Zwingli's reform agenda. As liturgical practices like public singing faded away, the elevation of God's Holy Word as the primary and foundational act whereby the Zurich community interacted with the divine took center stage.

It was not merely professional singing that Zwingli sought to remove from the Zurich church's worship. Beginning in 1525, the Reformer silenced the pipe organ and abandoned all forms of public singing. These remained absent from the Zurich church's worship until just before the seventeenth century.[56] For a gifted musician like Zwingli, this may seem odd. But a closer look at his desire for these unique musical reforms helps explain the Reformer's aversion to images. The Bible always informed his decisions on what was to be retained and jettisoned in the liturgy. Yet music was a part of worship in Scripture, especially for Israel. Throughout the Hebrew Bible, the Israelites used musical instruments and song to celebrate their God. Many of the Psalms, of course, not only were written to be sung but spoke of praising the Lord through the lyre, harp, or trumpet. Guided by his Reformed, covenantal theology, Zwingli did desire to recreate a contemporary form of Israel through his Zurich community. However, not all things were translatable from one community to the other. How was one to distinguish what was to be retained from what was to be avoided?

Scripture provided him the answer. For Zwingli, only God's clear commands would suffice when determining liturgical norms. Citing rhetorical objections to his stance on the removal of singing, Zwingli defiantly declared, "Now, if the mumbling of the Psalms is good, it must come from God. But show me where God ordered such droning, stammering, and mumbling."[57] As the Reformer pointed out, the prophet Amos specifically commanded setting aside vocal and instrumental forms of music.[58] Zwingli's usage of an early form of the regulative principle of worship, which states that only those things found in the Bible are utilized in worship, guided him. This hermeneutical approach paired well with his humanistic focus on the human heart. The Apostle Paul never exhorted the church to worship God by external means of song and voice primarily, "but rather with the heart."[59] The Zurich church was to follow such a commitment.

Zwingli believed music, much like images, was a distraction to true Christian worship. Such external forms muted the Word of the Lord, which he refused to tolerate. Citing 1 Corinthians 14, he stated, "Paul prefers to speak five words of understanding for the edification of others than to speak ten thousand words in tongues."[60] Whether lips or lyre, neither offered true instruction to the people of Zurich like God's Word. Therefore, Zwingli's beliefs about music in Christian worship may best be summarized as follows: "Music, choral or instrumental, no matter how religiously inspired, artistically beautiful, or superlatively performed, must be prohibited from the worship because Scripture has made its existence there impossible."[61] Zwingli desired an unfettered form of pure worship that not only elevated God's voice via Scripture but also accounted for humanity's innate proclivity to morph worship into idolatry.

PURIFYING THE CHURCH

The iconoclasm that first erupted in the Zurich city center eventually spilled over into the rural communes and persisted until summer 1524. Images began to vanish or were found ruined by iconoclasts. Church windows were shattered, altars destroyed, and furniture broken. In one famous incident, iconoclasts tossed into Lake Zurich an image of Jesus seated on a wooden donkey used annually during Holy Week.[62] Although individual dissenters and small roving groups of iconoclasts committed these destructive acts in a diffuse and unorganized manner, the unrest eventually forced a coordinated, magisterial response.

To allay concerns about a return to Catholic idolatry while also dissuading radicalism, Zwingli worked with the Council to remove the images and icons scattered throughout the Zurich State. The Council oversaw this purge, instituting a programmatic form of iconoclasm that sought the removal of images "with love, without anger, or divisiveness."[63] This meant that artisans who crafted images, or those who commissioned them, were free to remove items peaceably, while each local congregation removed images at its own unique pace.[64] By July, the Council went a step further. The magistrates forced the removal of all images and icons from the Zurich churches, mostly through a purge hidden from the public. Some of the items were carefully returned to those who fashioned them. Others were destroyed. Anything made of valuable material was used to fund benevolent ministries for the poor.

The same images that once watched over his first sermon at Zurich no longer stood in judgment over Zwingli's Reformation. He was also able to dissuade the community from observing religious relics or traveling to Catholic pilgrimage sites, like the one he formerly attended to at Einsiedeln. Similarly, church walls were whitewashed. The buildings that once offered visually stimulating settings now lay sanitized and barren.

The Council's legislative acts maintained the delicate balance Zwingli sought between honoring biblical commands, considering weaker brethren, caring for the poor, and retaining societal integrity. The look and feel of worship transformed in just a few short years. There was cause for celebration. Nevertheless, for all these successes, one great gospel harvest still eluded the Reformer. The Roman Mass remained in place, with the Eucharist still dominating the focus of the Zurich liturgy.

A BOUNTIFUL HARVEST

In March 1525, Zwingli decried this state of affairs: "For I fear that if there is anywhere pernicious error in the adoration and worship of the one true God, it is in the abuse of the Eucharist. If this had retained its proper use, according to the institution of Christ there would not have crept in such atrocious sins against God's people, the church."[65] Despite his desire to rid the church of this abomination, Zwingli only endured the Roman Mass as a "concession," patiently sowing gospel seeds, "not wishing to put forth things at a time when no one would receive them."[66] By spring 1525, he believed the time was right to abolish the Roman Mass. The Zurich shepherd desired an evangelical Supper for his sheep, a feast that was as much biblical as it was spiritually nourishing.

Reformation in this context meant not liturgical innovation but the reinstitution of past prescriptions. Returning to January 1519, Zwingli's preaching set the practical agenda for reforms designed to help the Zurich church more faithfully follow the pattern of worship set forth in Scripture. The same held true for correcting the Mass. Still, the preacher believed that any ecclesiastical reforms had to be initiated by the Zurich Council. To abolish the Mass would require that his persuasive preaching be supplemented with strategic political maneuvering behind the scenes.[67] He proved masterful at both. As he later revealed, it also helped that he believed the Lord divinely provided his argumentation. In his 1525 *Subsidiary Tract on the Eucharist*, Zwingli shared how God revealed to him in a dream the night before he met with the Council that the Lord's Supper was a continuation of the Passover for the Zurich church.[68] While this vision later served as polemical fodder for Catholic and Lutheran critics, the magistrates found it compelling.[69] Two days after making a formal request to install an evangelical liturgy at Zurich, on April 13, 1525, the Council formally abolished the Roman Mass.

What did this step mean practically? Fortunately, we are not left to wonder. Detailed orders of worship at Zurich remain preserved in Zwingli's 1525 work *Acts or Custom of the Supper* and his treatise *An Exposition of the Christian Faith*.[70] Reforming worship patterns for Zurich meant more than offering both the bread and cup to the people. Nor would refusing to elevate or consecrate the host provide enough of a departure from Rome. Liturgical reform meant an entire reorientation of the ways God's people encountered their Lord in worship.

The preached Word played a crucial role in Zwingli's new liturgy, just as it had sparked Reformation six years earlier. The most striking point of contrast with medieval patterns of worship came with the reduction in the Supper's observance to a mere four times a year, though this went well beyond the once-a-year requirement demanded since the Fourth Lateran Council.[71] This change deliberately set the Zurich church's practices apart from the more frequent observance of the Roman Eucharist. It was important for Zwingli that specific times were set aside so the entire community could take part in the rite.[72] Such administration made both practical and theological sense. It also allowed for the preached gospel to be prioritized over the visual depiction of the gospel represented in the two sacraments of baptism and the Lord's Supper.

Verbal proclamation of the gospel was not the only way in which the community interacted with the divine. Using specific language and purposeful movements, gospel preaching was connected with the observance of the elements through a new liturgical drama. This deliberate link avoided what Zwingli believed was the disjointed nature of the Roman liturgy. Catholics focused too heavily upon the Eucharist to the neglect of the preached Word. Zwingli's changes made preaching central to the new form of worship, but not the exclusive means of communing with God. This liturgical change demanded two new requirements. The observance of the Lord's Supper needed a new liturgy during those four special services of remembrance. The regular weekly services also needed to be overhauled. Abolishing the Mass required replacement and corrective.

WEEKLY GATHERING AROUND THE WORD

The relegation of the Supper's observance to four occasions (Easter, Pentecost, All Saints' Day, and Christmas) required modifications to the regular weekly corporate gatherings at Zurich. Although some modern worship services only observe the Supper quarterly, their weekly expressions of worship deviate widely from what Zwingli installed in 1525. In fact, the pattern of weekly worship at Zurich would seem foreign to many Christians today.

To set the order of worship for these non-Eucharist services, Zwingli built upon his preaching emphasis going back to 1519. Drawing inspiration from Ulrich Surgant, under whom Zwingli studied during a stint at Basel, Zurich's new liturgy reached back to a late medieval pattern known as the *Pronaus*.[73] This order of worship, familiar to many at the time, offered a brief vernacular preaching service that was employed in conjunction with the Roman Mass or, alternatively, just prior to or after the rite.[74] Before the Mass was abolished at Zurich in 1525, this meant evangelical, gospel preaching in a vernacular service offered alongside the regular observance of the Roman Eucharist in Latin. However, from April 1525 onward, this preaching service comprised the entirety of the service itself.[75]

The proclamation of the Word was the focal point of worship in these preaching services. Scriptural centrality is easily discerned given that the pulpit was the only piece of furniture not removed from the church buildings during the iconoclastic purge. Though the look of the building changed, the order of worship remained familiar, as the liturgy retained traditional catechetical elements from late medieval worship. The order of worship for the weekly services at Zurich included the following: opening prayers and intercessions, communal recitations, Scripture reading, the sermon, announcement and remembrance of those recently deceased, more communal recitations, and closing prayers of confession and forgiveness. A cursory glance at this ordering reveals a strong dependence on familiar liturgical norms. But these were offered with their own Zwinglian flavor, as he reimagined the community's encounter with God.

The pastor's opening prayer acknowledged the people's dependence upon the Lord to reveal His will in the Bible. Once God spoke through the Scriptures, only then could Zurichers "live according to His divine will."[76] The dual themes of God's sovereignty and the Christian's obligation to live rightly, ideas prevalent in Zwingli's theology, were key to communal worship. Subsequent intercessory prayers for both the civil magistrates and those "intimidated and oppressed for the sake of his Word" followed.[77] These intercessory prayers highlight Zwingli's commitment to a territorial church. They also offer a contextual reminder that some in this sacral society were still being oppressed for the gospel despite Reformation advancement. One must remember that not everyone embraced the important ecclesial changes the Swiss church realized in 1525. The people at Zurich were still confessionally divided during this tenuous moment. Zwingli's new liturgy reflected that reality.

A communal recitation of the Lord's Prayer followed in advance of Scripture readings and the sermon. Once the sermon concluded, deaths from the past week were announced, much as they had been in Surgant's *Pronaus*. Praying for the dead was not intended as posthumous intercession affecting the deceased's eternal standing. Instead, these announcements reminded the community about their own mortality. They also encouraged the community to see God's providential hand in the deaths of those whom "God has called out of this time."[78] Referencing Jesus's own words from Matthew 24 and Mark 13, Zwingli wanted the community to "always be prepared and [to] be on the watch at all times," for "nothing admonishes man more about himself than death."[79] The preacher knew the truth of this statement all too well given his near-death encounter with plague in early 1519.[80] The weekly liturgy forced congregants to face their own mortality as a means of rightly orienting their lives.

After the sermon ended, the weekly services concluded with the pastor confessing sin on behalf of the community and praying God might forgive them all on account of Jesus. This finale was crucial to the liturgy. As Zwingli had recently noted about confession of sin in his *Commentary*, "It is God alone who remits sins and puts the heart at rest."[81] By ending the weekly services this way, the people left their corporate gathering confident not only in their status before God but also in Christ's salvific work.

Despite all these changes, to view Zwingli as a liturgical innovator misstates the matter. The bifurcation of the liturgy into a weekly service and a quarterly Eucharist service was a revolutionary shift. However, the Zurich liturgy retained many earlier worship patterns, though these were framed in a way that allowed Zwingli to emphasize themes and ideas he felt were crucial to recovering true religion. For Zwingli, the Zurich liturgy did not convey a new theology. Rather, it recovered an older biblically ordered one.

A NEW MEAL

On Wednesday of Holy Week 1525, the Mass was conspicuously absent. One day later, the drama of Zwingli's new Eucharistic liturgy played out before the Zurich people on Maundy Thursday. Shortly after 7:00 a.m., Zwingli stepped behind the wooden pulpit just as he had done for the first time in January 1519. Though the scene was vaguely reminiscent of his initial sermon, much had changed. The images that watched over him that cold January day were now gone. The clerical vestments donned during his first sermon were also missing, replaced instead by "only the usual garb."[82] More importantly, instead of making a promise about an innovative preaching plan, Zwingli did something else. He presented God's salvific promise of Jesus Christ. Before the Lord's Supper was observed, the Reformer reminded the people of "the goodness of God which He has shown us through the Son."[83] After the sermon, a Eucharist service unfolded that was designed to be "a simple and Christian form of celebration."[84] The Zurich liturgy was intended to be as much purposeful as it was biblical. It was to mediate a divine encounter with God in a way that the Roman Mass could not. The service that Zwingli presided over that day served as the model for the Zurich liturgy from 1525 on.

The sermon offered in advance of the Supper was a key movement in this drama. The preached Word not only pointed to but also represented Jesus. The Word, the *logos*, was God's gracious gift sent from above to deliver His people from their sin. This proclamation of the Scriptures coming from the pulpit's elevated position in the sanctuary provided a twofold illustration. The spatial nature of the preached Word offered an image of God's voice situated authoritatively over the people. But God would not remain distant from His children. The preached word projecting from the raised pulpit imaged God's Word as descending to the community, an accommodation to their need as fallen humanity. God not only spoke to His people as their Creator, but He was also with them as their covenant-keeping Savior. The preacher, Zwingli, served in that moment as God's vessel in this unfolding drama of redemption and communion. He acted as a contemporary prophet, divinely appointed as God's representative spokesperson to the people. This prophet mediated God's truth about the Messiah, Jesus Christ, and called the people to repentance. Biblical allusions to the Old Testament prophets and the New Testament apostles were striking and clear.

The preached Word also came with a call to action. As any humanist preacher might desire, truthful instruction was supposed to elicit a response, as Zwingli exhorted his listeners to amend their lives. This call to action was not based on future actions alone but was set in motion immediately. The preacher then invited the people to repent prior to their consumption. This move invited the communicants to take an active part in the Eucharist in a way that was foreign to the Roman Mass. In this sense proclamation was instigation. A liturgical lethargy would no longer characterize the assembled congregants. The community was encouraged to move from passive lay observers to active priestly participants.[85] Zwingli invited his community to take part as a royal priesthood in the sacred rituals that God set in place for His people, including the Lord's Supper.

The Word subsequently invited those assembled to join Christ at the table, to eat of the Bread of Life and drink of Christ's saving blood. However, the people did not come to the High Altar to receive the elements, as was typical in the Catholic Church. When the time came to partake of the elements, once again the preacher played a crucial role in this administration. He carried the bread and the wine from the altar down a steep flight of stairs, eventually standing among the people to distribute God's gracious accommodation to them.[86] As Zwingli had argued months earlier, "The bread of God is that which comes down out of heaven," not attending to bodily sustenance but to offer spiritual life that is "abundant and efficacious."[87] As one historian has astutely noted, "Propinquity, for Zwingli was an essential element of Christian worship."[88] Zwingli's service purposefully removed the elements from the altar, which was in the elevated choir portion of the building. Instead, the bread and cup were now distributed from the nave. This move signified God coming to His people, meeting them at their place of need. It also purposefully connected the Eucharistic depiction of the gospel with the verbal preaching of the Word of God.[89]

Entering the presence of the Almighty demanded a certain human posture. Before receiving the elements, the Reformer offered a corporate preparatory prayer. The congregants knelt, denoting a posture of submission, while an overseer offered the following prayer:

> O Almighty, eternal God, whom all creatures rightly honor, worship, and praise as their Maker, Creator, and Father; grant to us poor sinners that we may observe with true fidelity and faith Your praise and thanksgiving, which Your only begotten Son, our Lord and Savior Jesus Christ, has commanded us believers to do as a remembrance of His death, through the same, our Lord Jesus Christ, Your Son, who lives with You and reigns in the unity of the Holy Spirit, God forever and ever. Amen.[90]

A desire for true worship framed Zurich's Eucharistic liturgy. And yet, as the prayer denoted, not just any worship would suffice. Only that which Christ commanded, worship undertaken as "a remembrance," would honor

Him. And God had to facilitate this form of worship, for He directed the Zurich worshipers' praises just as He dictated their place as His people. Following the opening prayer, the people inwardly considered their sinful shortcomings. The Apostle Paul demanded this contemplation, according to 1 Corinthians 11:27–32. Personal introspective reflection came before observing the Supper, Zwingli's preferred term for the Eucharist. The liturgy subsequently paired the internal meditations of the mind and heart with an outward confession or dual pledge of the communicant's commitment to both the local body and Christ. This moment was an important part of Zwingli's liturgy. The rite acknowledged that "we are indeed miserable sinners," just as it confessed "we are brethren" to one another.[91] A foundational aspect of Zwingli's Supper, and a key component of his Eucharistic theology, was the vertical and horizontal nature of the Supper's observance.[92]

The *Gloria* followed next. The Roman Mass had always included this hymn of thanksgiving. Though Zwingli retained its presence in the liturgy, in keeping with his work to remove music from Zurich's worship, the *Gloria* was not sung. Instead, it morphed into an antiphonal reader response in which the men and the women of the community recited alternating verses from the famous hymn.[93] The inclusion of female participation in this act was just as innovative as the removal of clerical choral singing.[94] Equally important, lay people now took an active role in expressing thanks to God, freed from a human mediator. Just as the people collectively acknowledged their shortcomings as a sinful people, so too did they declare their praises for God's provision in the Son through this hymn.

The next movement of the service included the reading of Jesus's words from John 6:47–63. The selection of this passage insinuated that the Zurich church was a contemporary manifestation of Israel. As Christ spoke of the temporary provision of the manna, the Supper's bread—which memorialized His body—brought eternal life to those who partook of Him. Zwingli's choice to conclude the reading with verse 63 was purposeful, a final qualifying reminder that this eating was spiritual, "done in commemoration, praise, and thanksgiving."[95] The Zurich community would not corporeally consume Christ.

At the close of this Bible reading, the preacher kissed the text, a sign of appreciation for God's Holy Word. The people then recited the Apostles' Creed and the Lord's Prayer. In each of these acts the subtle echoes of the Roman liturgy undoubtedly stirred a comforting familiarity to an otherwise unusual experience. However, dramatic and unmistakable changes to the observance of the elements subsequently broke this historic mirroring.

For years, the elevation of the host and the words of consecration in the Roman Mass had been "the single most important gesture of the priest, theologically and devotionally."[96] In that moment, the people not only caught a glimpse of Christ's body and blood but also witnessed the miracle of transubstantiation. If Zwingli was going to abolish the Mass, by "both desertion and defection," then a new institution was required.[97] To begin the new Zurich Supper, rather than allowing the priest to remain distant, with his back turned to the people in the choir portion of the building, the presiding minister stood among and faced the people in the nave. He also abandoned the traditional silver and gold utensils used in previous Eucharistic observances. Wooden chalices and plates replaced these opulent items. These were subtle but important changes. Zwingli contended, "We deemed it best for our people to prescribe as few ceremonies and as little churchly pomp as we could" to aid in the recovery of biblical patterns of worship.[98] The decision also offered a historical reenactment of the scene from the upper room.[99] The recitation of 1 Corinthians 11 preceded the actual eating and drinking. The Apostle Paul's language of memorial was crucial for Zwingli. To imply any notion of a real sacrifice was to make Jesus "much like the sacrifices in the Old Testament," which were "imperfect."[100] Here, he wanted to avoid any confusion. There was no magic in the institution, only memorial of the once-sacrificed Christ.

Clerical assistants then took the bread and the cup to those assembled for worship. This action continued the spatial idea of Christ coming to the people. It also allowed the congregants to take hold of the elements themselves, an important reminder of both their active participation in this rite of remembrance and their place as a royal priesthood. Zwingli even provided a pastoral accommodation for those who feared to reach out and grab the sacred elements with their own hands.[101] In such instances, assistants distributing the elements offered them instead. Zwingli knew the long shadow that the Roman Eucharist cast in the minds and hearts of his people.

After the Supper's observance, the people read Psalm 113. The minister opened the passage and the men and women in the assembly alternated its verses thereafter. What better response was there to the remembrance of Christ's sacrifice than a Psalm of praise? To close the Eucharist service, the presiding minister offered a final exhortation:

> Be mindful, dearly beloved brethren, of what we have now done together by Christ's command. We have borne witness by this giving of thanks, which we have done in faith, that we are indeed miserable sinners, but [we] have been purified by the body and blood of Christ which He delivered up and poured out for us, and [we] have been redeemed from everlasting death. We have borne witness that we are brethren. Let us, therefore, confirm this by love, faith, and mutual service.[102]

The people departed reminded of their former standing as sinners once condemned by God but also now rejoicing in the cleansing that Jesus's shed blood and broken body had brought them. They were formerly sinners. Now they were God's people, a community set apart for Him. The people returned to their daily lives with a twofold exhortation: the community was to remember their corporate confession of Christ, and they were to walk in a manner worthy of their standing as God's people.

In all these reforms, "the popish Mass was abolished, and the Lord's Supper instituted."[103] The imagery of the once-distant Word now present among the people was clear and powerful. From start to finish, the Zurich liturgy was incarnational. It was initiated by Christ and focused on Him. It also invited those present to commune with Jesus in a real and tangible way. This occurred not through consumption of his actual flesh and blood but through a faithful remembrance. For Zwingli, it was not physical food but a spiritual faith that "allays all hunger and thirst."[104] Humanity craved reconciliation with God more than anything. Zwingli believed the completed work of Jesus, not the sacramental grace of Rome, was "the only thing that can give such food and drink to the heart that it shall want nothing further."[105] The contrast with the Roman Mass was not lost on those present. This was not a religious act in which the Lord seemed distant from them. It was an intimate and relational moment. The new liturgy provided an encounter with the Divine, in which the people of God communed in a powerful way with their Heavenly Father because of the eternal Son's sacrifice. As has been rightly expressed, "Liturgy for the Swiss Reformers was not some mere external act of piety, but the temporal and spatial expression of the divine drama manifested in the local community."[106] Worship was an encounter with God, a relational reflection on what had been accomplished for the Zurichers that also set them forward as a redeemed people.

CONCLUSION

In April 1525, Zwingli presided over the first evangelical Reformed Supper. In contrast to what he believed was a passive, stale Roman Mass, "the Zurich liturgy was a brilliant piece of humanist rhetoric in which mind and body were moved, passions aroused, the faithful persuaded and ultimately charged to live according to the truth they had heard."[107] In terms of the narrative arc of Protestant history, this was a pivotal moment that helped launch a religious movement. It also established unique patterns of worship, many of which continue to this day in certain confessional heritages.

For Zwingli, this liturgy marked a personal milestone. Watching his parishioners receive the bread and cup proved that his labors were worth the struggle and that he kept his promise to faithfully preach God's Word. There were opposition and detractors to his vision for a renewal of the Zurich church along the way. Nevertheless, as Zwingli expressed in the months after implementing his evangelical Mass in 1525, "the number of those who looked back to the garlic pots of Egypt was far less than expected."[108] This was the gospel harvest that he once hoped for and why he came to Zurich.

Following years of observing the Roman liturgy, which left Swiss worship "long in error and darkness," Zwingli believed the light of the true gospel was finally shining forth through an evangelical Mass.[109] As the Reformer understood, only now had true religion been realized at Zurich through a meal reminiscent of Christ's celebration of the Passover. Liturgical life had been renewed, and consequently, the worship at Zurich in the coming years was as God had intended. Scores of people even from outside the Zurich community came to witness and marvel at this accomplishment that evidenced Reformation success. The busyness and brilliance of this worship was tangible, an experience all but forgotten by and lost on most visitors to the Grossmunster today.

Chapter 3

Unveiling the Gospel

"Now since He who was innocent suffered death for us guilty sinners, He paid off for us the beautiful righteousness of God, which otherwise no human being is able to satisfy; thus, He earned for us the right to come to God by virtue of His free grace and gift. Whoever hears this and believes it without doubt shall be saved. That is the gospel."[1]

THERE ARE MANY PICTURESQUE PLACES to explore in Zurich today. Though often known for its financial sector, public green areas, and upscale shopping boutiques, the city center also boasts a wonderful assortment of Christian sites. A series of church spires lining the Limmat River reminds visitors of the spiritual axis of a city with Christian roots extending back a millennium. Each of these destinations offers visitors a chance to connect with the contemporary, though dwindling, religious life of Zurichers today. These locales also link visitors to the distant world of the Reformation, a place far removed from the bustling life of wealth and innovation now characterized by Zurich.

Tourists who come to experience Zurich's rich Christian offerings often visit the most famous of the city's religious destinations, the Fraumunster Church. This building houses the famed Chagall windows, a series of colorful stained-glass windows created in the late twentieth century by the expressionist artist Marc Chagall. A unique depiction of Jesus on the cross anchors the five windows. The Messiah is presented through Chagall's typical cubist style in vibrant green hues complemented by a smattering of red to illustrate Christ's shed blood. A short walk north is St. Peter's Church, a parish once pastored by the Zurich Reformer Leo Jud. Today it attracts visitors hoping to see Europe's largest clockface housed in its towering lone spire. A jaunt eastward over the Limmat River provides access to the Wasser and Grossmunster Churches. The former of these, as outlined in the Introduction, is a wonderful diminutive chapel offering shadow to a Zwingli statue. The latter is a colossal structure dominating Lake Zurich's north shore and was the epicenter of Zwingli's reformation efforts.

Each of these places offers vestiges of the past and echoes of the Reformation in a context otherwise dominated by modern secularism. Yet perhaps the greatest contemporary connection to the Reformation at Zurich is not found in memorials or cathedrals but hiding in plain view in the variety of free-standing sausage vendors and traditional Swiss restaurants that line the Limmat. Wursts of all varieties are things commonly associated with the Swiss. Zurich boasts many restaurants and local food stands that carry on the tradition of serving up this famous Swiss fare. In an odd turn of events, sausages also helped to incite and embody Reformation at Zurich in the early 1520s.

In spring 1522, a small group of men consumed the familiar food. It was not their menu but the timing of their eating that proved controversial. The men ate forbidden fare during Lent. To those in modernity, such an act may appear benign. However, this was an outrageous move deviating from religious and cultural norms intended to harmonize late medieval society. During Zwingli's day, "feast and fast defined the church. Fasting and the Eucharist were what everyone had in common."[2] To jettison this custom was to disconnect from the community in a defiant act of individualism and a blatant rejection of Catholic authority. Given the context, the breaking of the Lenten fast was not merely a religious scandal. It also threatened the integration of Zurich's society.

One culinary decision soon embroiled Zwingli's parish in controversy. As any pastor might, Zwingli leveraged the moment for instruction. He believed partaking of a common Swiss cuisine helpfully illustrated the most uncommon of all realities, Jesus's work on the cross. It was an important reminder that one is not made holy based upon religious rite and human action but only through Jesus's atoning work at Calvary, which is appropriated by faith. Christ's redemption had ushered in a new era of liberty, which the Catholic Church had forgotten.

As it was for much of his ministry, controversy surrounded Zwingli's work at Zurich. Unrest was the norm, not an outlier. But the preacher welcomed this violation, for this inflammatory, rebellious meal clearly exhibited gospel truths. Moreover, the event bolstered in Zwingli a conviction that had been growing for years: the gospel, which had been veiled by the Catholic Church, needed to be uncovered and proclaimed. The good news of Jesus could turn the heart of stone into one of flesh, eager to obey the will of God. Thus, the inner transformation of a person via the gospel brought external realities, not vice versa. Accordingly, recovering the gospel became a driving force behind the Swiss preacher's ministry at Zurich.

The Reformer believed salvation through Christ alone was the hope of humanity. He also thought the gospel was key to establishing the Christian society he longed for Zurich to become. So he labored to unveil the gospel in all its splendor to a people he believed were eager to taste of good news. Along the way, this recovery caused quarreling and division, as the preacher warred against adversaries on two fronts. Zwingli found himself at odds with the Catholic Church that he sought to reform and that increasingly saw him as an apostate. The Swiss preacher also faced a rending of his own reform party, as figures within his own circle sought to detour his gospel recovery down a radical path. Amid the controversy, the Reformer held tightly to his convictions regarding the evangelical gospel. The reconciliation Jesus brought via His atoning work on the cross was an anchor of truth for Zwingli's ministry and the focus of his preaching. It also served as a guiding premise demarcating true and false religion for the Zurich community he loved so dearly.

A NEW MEDIATOR

When it came to the awakening of the gospel in Zwingli's life, according to the Reformer, it was tied to the reordering of his understanding of clerical mediation. As a Catholic priest, Zwingli was steeped in a tradition that emphasized the importance of clerical priests acting as mediating agents of God's grace. During the medieval era, the Latin term for priest, *sacerdos*, connoted the idea of a person who offers a sacred, holy, or consecrated thing on behalf of the community of faith.[3] The sacerdotalism of the medieval era elevated the clergy to a unique position. They welcomed individuals into the church via baptism, uttered prayers on behalf of the people, and offered absolution for sin via the sacrament of penance. Most importantly, ordained priests oversaw the miracle of the Mass, the Eucharist. Their consecration and administration of the elements situated clerics as those presiding over the dispensing of God's grace via Christ's body and blood. From start to finish, the priest was a figure standing between God and humanity, mediating salvation.

Zwingli's break from this understanding of priestly mediation occurred during his time at Einsiedeln. Ironically, this break happened after reading a contemporary who never departed from the papacy's ecclesiastical authority. Pleading his case before the people at the First Zurich Disputation in 1523, Zwingli explained his new position:

> I do not wish to keep from you, most beloved brothers in Christ Jesus, how I have reached the opinion and firm belief that we do not need a mediator other than Christ. Some eight or nine years ago I read a comforting poem by the great scholar Erasmus of Rotterdam which was addressed to the Lord Jesus in which Jesus in many beautiful words bemoans the fact that not everything good is sought with Him, though He is a fount of all goodness, a Savior, the comfort and treasure of the soul.[4]

The Dutch humanist Erasmus helped open Zwingli's eyes to a basic gospel truth: "Christ is the sole mediator between God and us [humanity]."[5] Jesus accomplished what humanity could not.

Zwingli believed a mediator was a type of "referee," who secures "a peaceful solution for two who are fighting or at odds, thereby making friendship" between two previously opposed parties.[6] Adam's sin created a gulf of separation between a holy God and a fallen, sinful humanity. But this severed relationship was not neutral in nature. After Genesis 3, humans inevitably and eventually become children of wrath warring against their Creator.

Attempts to find salvation outside of Jesus's intercessory work plagued the Swiss Church in Zwingli's mind. He rhetorically opined to such people, "Do you not hear that Christ does everything [for your salvation]? You are lacking in that you still do not recognize Him, for you do not trust yourself to Him as a father and yet you call Him Father."[7] The Reformer wanted others to understand how prideful and foolish it was to presume that meritorious works could restore a broken relationship with God. Stressing this point, Zwingli argued, "You cannot come to God other than through Christ. With him alone, you must find grace and mercy. To ascribe that to your own good works is to deceive yourself."[8] The Reformer believed humanity was impotent regarding the work of redemption. This was true of his flock at Einsiedeln just as it was for those at Zurich. The geographic location of ministry had not altered the human plight of his parishioners.

It was equally delusional to believe anyone other than Christ—even the Church—or any act beyond Jesus's atoning sacrifice could reconcile humanity's broken relationship with God. This was a belief championed at the close of his tenure at Einsiedeln. Within months of the posting of Luther's *95 Theses*, Zwingli became concerned with and an outspoken critic of the church's use of indulgences. Bernhardin Sanson, pejoratively called "the Tetzel of Switzerland," who peddled the forgiveness of sin for money in the region, incited in Zwingli a disdain for indulgences.[9] Incensed by Sanson's indulgence sales, Zwingli attacked the practice in summer 1518:

> Jesus Christ, the Son of God, has said, "Come unto Me all you that labor and are heavy laden, and I will give you rest." Is it not then audacious folly and insensate rashness to say, on the contrary, "Buy letters of indulgence! Run to Rome! Give to the monks! Sacrifice to the priests! And if you do these things, I absolve you from your sins?" Jesus Christ is the only offering, the only sacrifice, the only way![10]

The false sense of salvific security indulgences engendered in his parishioners mortified Zwingli, as it had Luther. He wanted his flock to feel the lightness of the Great Shepherd's yoke, to be loosed from the shackles of their presumed meritorious works.

Zwingli reaffirmed his disdain for the indulgence industry years later at Zurich. In 1523, he asserted about external human acts, "If you point to popish indulgences, masses, vigils, chanting, vestments, the holiness of the fathers [for reconciliation], I say to you 'No, it cannot be done that way; everything must come through Christ.' "[11] The reason for his resolve was clear: "Whoever robs Him [God] of his honor and ascribes it to creatures, is an idolater."[12] Such statements demonstrate Zwingli's belief in salvation *solus Christus*, by Christ alone, as a guiding aspect of his shepherding at Zurich.[13] To credit human works with any reconciling power was to supplant Christ.

Indulgences were leading the people astray in two specific ways. First, Rome's salvific prescriptions were making people idolaters. Zwingli often situated idolatry as the antithesis to the true gospel, in contrast to Luther's departure from human works in relation to justification, for example.[14] Second, the papacy was minimizing Jesus's unique place in redemptive history. Using rich Christological language reminiscent of Anselm's *Why God Became Man*, Zwingli contended that Jesus, as the God-man, was uniquely able to both act on humanity's behalf and accomplish what was befitting only the divine.[15] Christ did what no Catholic priest could do.

Zwingli regularly offered stern warnings to those who viewed human works as a means of reconciliation with God. However, he provided a distinction between intolerable ecclesiastical acts and those that might be endured for a time. Such accommodation was especially needed during this transitional period for the Swiss church, as the Reformation was being unfurled in the early 1520s. For instance, the preacher silently suffered practices like intercessory prayers to the saints. This temporary tolerance was not ideal. However, his patience had a redemptive end in mind. Zwingli spoke of a pastoral tolerance for the "simple minded": "Thus I nurtured them [those dependent upon non-Scriptural traditions] with milk so that several of them who once were dead set against me, now cling the firmer to God alone."[16] A season of compromise eventually bore deeper commitment once the Bible found fertile soil in the people's hearts. Tolerance had its bounds though. When it came to such things like using the honorary title, "Our Father ... [being] addressed to anyone other than the one God," such was strictly forbidden.[17] There were always limitations to what Zwingli would suffer, even for a season.

SCRIPTURE AND SALVATION

A shift in Zwingli's understanding of authority was a crucial conviction that helped him usher in Zurich's recovery of the gospel. His earlier commitments to Catholic sacerdotalism receded over time as the Reformer embraced *sola Scriptura*. This doctrine reestablished the Bible as the normative authority when considering doctrine and ecclesiastical practice. Scriptural primacy was so foundational to Zwingli's recovery of the gospel that it was the first argument in his *Exposition of the Sixty-Seven Articles*. There he contended, "Everyone who says that the gospel is nothing without the sanction of the church, errs and blasphemes."[18] Some people argued not only that the gospel was dependent upon the papacy but that "should the gospel not exist at all, the church could establish laws by which one might be saved."[19] In the hypothetical absence of Scripture, some thought the church could offer definitive pronouncements regarding salvation. Zwingli was aghast at such a presumptuous and blasphemous notion.

The Reformer began contrasting what he believed was true, biblical Christianity with the papists' idolatry. As he did, much like Luther, the Reformer recognized an emerging fault line that existed between two irreconcilable ways of understanding how one identifies theological truth. The Reformer soon faced heresy charges in 1523 after pressing the church on the question of its authority. While defending himself, Zwingli blamed the papacy for mistakenly following the rule of earthly kingdoms by presuming to determine doctrine and practice for the church.[20] Zwingli believed such a task belonged exclusively to Christ, who shared His divine will via the Bible.[21] Jesus was the final arbiter of truth through the Scriptures, just as He was the only true mediator between God and humanity. Drawing from his military background, the preacher frequently spoke of Jesus as a captain to illustrate this point.[22] Referencing Hebrews 12, Zwingli encouraged the Swiss, "Let everyone look to his captain, Christ Jesus, who will not lead us astray."[23] Christ was a trustworthy guide, not Rome.

This captain metaphor was an asset to Zwingli on two fronts. First, it established Jesus's voice as normative. As the "guide and captain" of salvation, "his deeds, teaching and life must, as a result, be above any human counsel."[24] This was precisely why Scripture was so important to Zwingli's pastoral ministry. In the Bible the people could see and experience Jesus with gospel clarity, rather than having the beauty of the good news veiled by the papacy's extrabiblical prescriptions. Christ, not the papacy, was to lead the Swiss church. Second, according to Zwingli, this Captain was the Son who "suffered inhumane opposition and now sits at the right hand of God."[25] By following Christ through faith, a new life marked by repentance was realized. Paradoxically, this faithful following included a call to death. Such faith required the ongoing mortification of the flesh through moral improvement and, should it be required, a martyr's death. There was a steely allegiance to Christ required of His people.[26] Still, this Captain could be confidently followed, for He already secured the victory over sin and the grave.

The elevation of Scripture as the normative authority for Zwingli's Swiss congregants did not mean the rejection of other sources of authority outside the Bible. One scholar astutely reminds us, "*Sola Scriptura* was not *nuda Scriptura*" ("Scripture as norm" versus "Scripture in isolation") for Zwingli, any more than it was for Luther.[27] Zwingli believed valuable authorities, like the church fathers, could aid the Zurich church in its recovery and maintenance of the gospel. But these human voices were always subservient to God's voice preserved in the Bible. Writing to Luther in 1527, Zwingli leveraged church fathers like Augustine, Chrysostom, and Cyril to defend his views on the Lord's Supper.[28] He even cleverly cited a contemporary authority, Luther's own beloved protégé, Philipp Melanchthon, as a way of personally skewering the German friar.[29] Extrabiblical authorities were a great aid to Zwingli. These same authorities also helped him better understand the gospel. As he argues in the same 1527 letter, "I call God to witness that I learned the highest embodiment of the gospel from reading the treatises of John [the Apostle] and Augustine and from the diligent study of Paul's epistles in the Greek."[30] Both human reflections and biblical revelation were pathways to the Swiss preacher's discovery of the gospel. He believed the same could be true for his Zurich flock. Yet these two unique avenues were not of equal authority. The Bible was always supreme.

Sources outside the Bible could be valuable and leveraged as helpful guides. Nevertheless, for Zwingli, all sources, regardless of their vintage, must be validated by Scripture. The papists often cited the church fathers to defend their ecclesiastical practices and doctrinal convictions. However, Zwingli demanded that even the most revered of the church fathers "prove by the word of God" what they contended.[31] Their human authority was always derived from, subservient to, and dependent upon the biblical text. Even the greatest of the church fathers "were still potentially harmful to the gospel if held in a similar esteem as the Word of God."[32] This truth was why the Bible had to remain the final, authoritative arbiter. In this sense, the preacher's understanding of church tradition related to acceptable, apostolic interpretations of the Bible, not to a papal authority outside of the text.[33] And the more intently Zwingli looked at the Scriptures, freed from the papacy's authority, the more clearly he saw the pure evangelical gospel. This gospel clarity was precisely what he wanted his Zurich flock to see, experience, and embrace.

Zwingli began his ministry at Zurich by preaching *lectio continua* precisely because of the Bible's authority. He believed that only in the text of sacred Scripture could the Zurich community find Jesus in a real and meaningful way. This was also why the Reformer was adamant Jesus could not be corporeally present in the elements of the Lord's Supper. Arguing against both the Catholic and Lutheran Eucharists based on John 6, Zwingli stressed, "Christ has held out to us no other food to secure our happiness than the gospel, that is, He suffered death freely for us."[34] Zwingli's understanding of the gospel anticipated his later articulation of the Supper, while not confining the appropriation of the gospel to the sacraments.

The Reformer believed Zurichers needed to meet Jesus and hear the gospel in the text of Scripture, which was an idea likely learned from Erasmus. In the close of his 1516 critical edition to the Greek New

Testament, Erasmus says of Scripture, "But these writings [the New Testament] bring you the living image of His holy mind and the speaking, healing, dying, rising Christ Himself, and thus they render Him so fully present that you would see less if you gazed upon Him with your very eyes."[35] Zwingli located Christ physically in heaven but believed His voice could be clearly heard in the text of Scripture. Christ mediated the gospel to the Zurich community through the Bible, not the ceremonies of Rome. And His Word was to be the requisite diet leading to salvation and the banquet feast of the Lamb.

LOOSED FROM LENT

Zwingli's gospel proclamation in the early 1520s was drawn directly from Scripture. Through New Testament texts like Matthew and the Acts of the Apostles, the preacher's sermons stressed the need for Zurichers to find freedom from Rome's extrabiblical prescriptions. This was an appealing message to some in the community who grew eager to put their preacher's declarations into practice. On March 9, 1522, during the evening meal of the Old Carnival festival, a group of men broke their Lenten fast by eating sausages in the home of the printer, Christoph Froschauer.

More than a dozen men were present at the meal, including Zwingli and his fellow Reformer Leo Jud. One by one, these men paraded into the Froschauer home that night. They came for a Carnival meal. Few, if any, knew they would be involved in what was later considered a pivotal moment, even the start, of the Swiss Reformation. Servants later recounted how the men shared a fried dough dish commonly associated with the Carnival.[36] The kitchen staff also provided the diners two succulent smoked sausages. These wursts were equally divided and distributed among the guests. Based on the size of the gathering and their means of sharing, some have argued this dinner was deliberately modeled after Jesus's institution of the Last Supper. This biblical allusion, however relevant, may be a later addition aimed to enhance the moment's lore.[37]

This meal was a private, intimate affair that eventually became public. When it did, Froschauer tried justifying the meal to the Zurich Council by citing a demanding work schedule that required substantive nourishment.

The accused also suggested that the excessive price of fish had forced his wife's hand at the market.[38] Therefore, economic and practical concerns possibly provided some motivation for this sausage affair. However, Zwingli's presence at the meal, despite his refusal to partake of meat, suggests a different impetus behind the eating. In fact, as one historian has noted, it is more than likely this meal was "a well-staged provocation."[39] Furthermore, this meal was not an isolated breach of the Lenten restrictions, as one may easily assume. A host of other violations in the community surfaced as the Council made further inquiry into the scandal.[40] Zwingli's gospel preaching had made a tangible impact on many in the community who were eager to taste of the freedoms proclaimed from his pulpit. These violations also suggest some Zurichers were not as committed to Catholic traditions as otherwise assumed.

Perhaps what is most important about these events is not the meal itself but Zwingli's subsequent defense of the Lenten breach in a sermon two weeks later. Published by Froschauer under the title "Concerning Choice and Liberty Respecting Food," this sermon enabled the preacher to illustrate the outworking of the gospel through a relatable medium. By focusing on the people's choice to eat meat during Lent, Zwingli highlighted the liberty found in the gospel. The preacher positioned Jesus's work as having ushered in a new era of freedom for the Swiss, who were no longer bound by institutional rites.

Despite the accessibility of this freedom, Zwingli knew that many at Zurich still pined for the bondage of Rome. In the sermon he said of these, "As when the children of Israel were led out of Egypt, at first impatiently and unaccustomed to the hard journey, they sometimes in vexation wished themselves back in Egypt, with the food left there."[41] Blind obedience to Catholic traditions like the Lenten fast was akin to the Israelites clamoring for a return to the shackles of Egypt despite the freedom they had through God's intervening exodus.[42]

Drawing on an Erasmian distinction between the inner and outer aspects of religion, Zwingli pointed to Jesus's teachings. The Lord reminded the Pharisees, "No food can defile a man"; rather, "those things which come out from him, those are they that defile a man."[43] To underscore this important point, Zwingli crassly asserted, "A man may eat shit if he would like."[44] Food consumption had no impact upon the spiritual condition of the eater. A person's heart posture, not the timing or nature of any food consumed, determined true or false religion. The contrast between the freedom offered by Christ and Rome's oppressive mandates was striking.

The Froschauer meal accused the Catholic Church of holding to a counterfeit faith. This mistaken overstep was why the Froschauer group partook of the fruits of their freedom in Christ. Zwingli explained their motivation:

> In time they [the fast breakers] have become so controlled by and accustomed to the salt and good fruit of the gospel, which they find in abundance, that they not only avoid the former darkness, labor, food, and yoke of Egypt, but are also vexed with all brothers, that is, Christians, wherever they do not freely apply Christian liberty.[45]

Some Zurichers refused to covet their former lives. A small taste of the freedom Jesus's atoning work provided them would not allow it.

As he often did, Zwingli leveraged the theme of memory to elicit action. Like Israel with the Passover meal, the Zurich community was to reflect on their former bondage while they took hold of their newfound freedoms through Christ. The Froschauer meal, much like the Supper, provided opportunity for such reflections. This focus on *memoria* ("memory") provided "a visceral, emotive recollection of God's salvific promises and actions in history that fired faith and restored person and community."[46] Some from the community were acting based on the remembrance of God's perfect provision in Jesus Christ. Many had simply forgotten that important biblical truth. Others had not heard, which made Zwingli's ongoing preaching of the gospel even more paramount.

The fines imposed on the offenders by the Zurich Council spoke to the scandalous nature of the group's actions. This public violation of the law was a brazen act that the magistrates felt obliged to address. Yet in that tense moment, Zwingli leveraged the controversial event to highlight the gospel. A rudimentary form of resistance theory that soon made its way into the Reformed tradition possibly shaped his thinking on this matter.[47] As he later contended in 1524, a godly pastor must stand for truth despite opposition from the civil authorities. If magistrates failed to promote biblical principles, "the shepherd has to risk his skin and hope for no other help nor liberation than that from God."[48] The Swiss preacher was compelled to prophetically speak to the moment, expressing the truth of the gospel as he understood it. Zwingli spoke up despite leaving himself vulnerable. It was a risky but calculated move that soon paid gospel dividends.

THE HEART OF THE GOSPEL

Being freed to eat foods without fear of ecclesiastical retribution was a welcomed consequence of the gospel. However, it was not the greatest for Zwingli. Reconciliation with a heavenly Father was far superior and spoke to the essence of the evangelical gospel. In his compendium of doctrine from 1525, Zwingli wrote, "This is the gospel, that sins are remitted in the name of Christ."[49] Through Christ's work, the sinner's debt had been paid. The relationship between humanity and God, once severed by sin and further marred by humanity's subsequent failings, had been restored again. One only needed to embrace Christ's sacrifice by faith, which was "the key that opens to the heart the chest of the forgiveness of sins."[50] Given the alternative of death and eternal separation from God, this new relational alternative was not just good news but the best of all news. It was news all Zurichers needed.

Highlighting a demarcation between true and false religion, Zwingli labored to make certain his people did not follow the prevailing soteriological convictions of the day. He challenged those he labeled "self-righteous" for pursuing their own right standing before God.[51] The popular late medieval adage *facere quod in se est* ("do what is in him"), which posited that God would not withhold His grace from those who acted rightly based on the good found within them, dominated much of the intellectual landscape of the day.[52] This idea was an anathema to Zwingli and reeked of Catholic sacramentalism. Citing Romans 7, Zwingli believed the "disease" or "defect" of sin, which all contracted from Adam, left humanity woefully deficient.[53] The optimistic appraisal of humanity and human freedom championed by Erasmus was altogether absent in Zwingli. Instead, the preacher reminded his Zurich flock that God was the One who brought life from death by His sovereign hand. This was a truth drawn from Scripture and wrought in his own experience battling plague early in his ministry at Zurich.[54]

Against the backdrop of late medieval Catholicism, Zwingli could not have been more adamant about the gospel. Humanity's broken relationship with the Lord was restored at God's initiative and based solely on Christ's sacrificial atoning work. Humanity did nothing. God's holiness set a standard that humanity could not accomplish after the fall. No act of piety or participation in the church's sacraments could assuage the guilt of humanity's violation of the law. The divide between the Creator and fallen humanity was only bridged from one side. As he stressed in his 1523 sermon "Divine and Human Righteousness," "Thus God commands what is appropriate to His righteousness; but we are incapable of keeping His commandments. Yet no one can aid us in this our impotence except God alone. He has done it through His Son, Christ Jesus."[55] Human weakness required divine intervention. This deficiency made the gospel that much sweeter for Zwingli. Considering humanity's impotent state, God, in Christ, accomplished what we could not.

Zwingli contrasted Jesus's atoning work with the meritorious works promoted through Rome's sacramental system. This gaze toward Golgotha was purposeful and driven partially by his context. Zurich witnessed a steady increase in the community's participation in pilgrimages, icon construction, and religious processions during the years leading up to the Reformation.[56] To shine a light on Christ was to shepherd his flock away from familiar community norms Zwingli deemed idolatrous. Highlighting Christ's redemptive work, he clarified, "Now since He who was innocent suffered death for us guilty sinners, He paid off for us the beautiful righteousness of God, which otherwise no human being is able to satisfy; thus, He earned for us the right to come to God by virtue of His free grace and gift. Whoever hears this and believes it without doubt shall be saved. That is the gospel."[57] The people's need to hear the gospel drove Zwingli's preaching from the outset of his ministry at Zurich.

But what precisely did Christ accomplish? Zwingli's humanist studies guided his answer, leaving him dependent on the work of earlier Christians for his language. Some have noted in Zwingli an Anselmian gloss, highlighted by a dependence on the medieval thinker's satisfaction theory of the atonement.[58] The Swiss Reformer frequently tempered the two taproots of God's justice and love when framing redemption. In his *Commentary* Zwingli contended, "Since His [God's] justice, being inviolably sacred, had to remain as intact and unshaken as His mercy, and since man was indeed in need of mercy but wholly amenable to God's justice, divine goodness found a way to satisfy justice and yet to be allowed to open wide the arms of mercy without detriment to justice."[59] With echoes of Athanasius and Anselm, Zwingli concluded that the God-man, Jesus Christ, was the mediating pathway chosen by God to accomplish salvation. He reasoned, "For as God created humanity through His Son, so He determined through Him to restore humanity when they had fallen into death, that the Son might be at once their creator and restorer."[60] Jesus's work allowed God to punish sin, while not eternally leaving Him separated from the crown of His creation. The Son became "forever a gate and a valid offering for the sins of everyone."[61] All who came to God must enter through that door, which only swung open from God's direction.

GOD'S HEAVENLY PLEDGE

Zwingli worked to make certain his parishioners saw Christ as the only pathway to God. The Son was also the fulfillment of a promise God made to His people back in the book of Genesis. This was why the Reformer frequently spoke of Jesus by using the Latin and German terms for pledge or promise. This "pledge language" is littered throughout his *Commentary*. There he opined, "When once there is faith in Him [Jesus], then salvation is found; for He is the infallible pledge of God's mercy."[62] Later, he stressed that Jesus was the "infallible pledge of hope," the one promised long ago.[63] The preacher believed one finds hope in God's mercy, which was manifest in the person of Jesus Christ. Just as Abraham lovingly encouraged his son, Isaac, to trust the Lord to provide an animal for the burnt offering on Mt. Moriah, Zwingli wanted Zurich to know that God's promise to secure an unblemished Lamb for their salvation stood as well. Jesus's substitutionary sacrifice, which satisfied the justice of God's wrath, culminated in Christ becoming "the indubitable pledge of salvation."[64] Jesus was an oath regarding the promise of atonement, God's pledge of redemption. The Lord never fails to fulfill His promises. His commitment to the covenant was guaranteed by the Son. In this sense, Jesus, as the sacrificial Lamb of God, served as both the promise of atonement hoped for and the provision of the sacrifice required.

Writing to King Francis I in 1531, Zwingli contended that when God wanted to give the greatest of all gifts to humanity, namely salvation, He did so by giving Himself. "The Son of God has, therefore, been given to us as a confirmation of His [the Father's] mercy, as a pledge or pardon, as the price of righteousness, and as a rule of life, to make us sure of the grace of God."[65] The promise of a fulfilled commitment to His covenant meant the giving of Jesus. That the Eternal Son took on the fullness of humanity was an important point for Zwingli relating to this divine promise. After carefully outlining the fully human nature of Christ, Zwingli reiterated to the French monarch the importance of God's pledge through a rhetorical question: "Who shall take from me what God Himself has bestowed, giving His Son as a pledge and surety?"[66] Christ's humanity serves as an assurance of God's gift of salvation. Whereas Luther found solace and relational proximity to God in the nearness of divinity through Christ's corporeal presence in communion, Zwingli looked elsewhere. His eyes were set on the promise of God via a covenant made with Abraham, which the incarnate Jesus fulfilled. That Christ was physically seated at the right hand of the Father, interceding on our behalf, further proved that God honored His pledge and that the work of atonement was complete.

In God's giving the Eternal Son as a pledge of His kindness toward humanity, Zwingli stressed the deeply relational nature of Christ's work. Salvation went far beyond God addressing an assault on His honor. The cross was not merely some cosmic correction by an offended God. The work of redemption was about God reconciling Himself with a people. It was the fulfillment of a promise that He would be their God and they, the Zurich community, would be His people. As Zwingli stressed while commenting on the Ten Commandments, "What goodness was lent to us in Christ, for He is the pledge of divine goodness, mercy, and grace."[67] The very heart of God, which beat with a desire to commune with humanity, led the Lord to send the dearest of all things, the Son, to fulfill the law and accomplish the payment required for reconciliation. Zwingli wanted Zurich to know that this work was not required of God. Rather, it came out of the overflow of His grace and mercy. God lavished His affections upon the Zurich community, not on account of their worth or pious actions but because of the Father's love for His Son.

Building on the notion of covenant, the Zurich people had their part to play as well. Though Jesus was the pledge of God's promise, the people's salvific hope was conditional and connected with a new way of life. Christ satisfied God's justice on the cross. But, as Zwingli stressed, that work was applied to the Zurich people "on condition that we become new creatures and that we walk having put on Christ."[68] A Zwinglian ethic connected God's salvific work with the people's new lives in Christ. The inner reality of God's salvific work wrought by His Spirit inevitably ushered in an external manifestation characterized by *besserung* ("moral improvement"). Otherwise, if such works were not present, faith was not real and was more akin to the papists' false religion.

Zwingli stressed that only those "who believe that Jesus Christ is our 'pledge' and recompense, should approach the table [the Lord's Supper]."[69] Acknowledging God's promise to humanity in the Son was part of what it meant to participate in the community of faith. The very nature of a covenant demanded commitment and actions from two parties. This was why, as we saw in Chapter 2, the Lord's Supper served as humanity's reciprocal act of pledging to God and to each other in the covenant community. God promised to redeem for Himself a people by means of His Son. In response, the Swiss pledged themselves both vertically toward God and horizontally toward each other. That act of pledging was an ongoing commitment offering a tangible reminder of the communicants' standing as God's people. Zwingli believed salvation was deeply communal, never intending to focus exclusively on the individual's personal relationship with God. Such is a modern notion that would have been foreign to Zwingli's soteriological and ecclesiological convictions. Zwingli also highlighted the papists' false religion through this pledge language. Rather than Christ being offered up to God through the Roman Eucharist's elevation of the host, Zwingli shifted the imagery. The reformer now positioned, God as having sent the Divine Son down to humanity as the pledge of the covenant through the Incarnation. In response to God's work, the people subsequently pledged themselves to God by lifting their hearts toward Him and by committing themselves to each other. This Eucharistic reversal was practical in relation to the laity's active involvement in the Supper. The reversal was profoundly theological in nature as well, assailing a core aspect of Catholicism's sacerdotal focus on the work of the ordained priest in the Eucharist.

THE ZURICH CHURCH AND ISRAEL

Zwingli's covenantal theology, coupled with his commitment to the *corpus Christianum*, had profound consequences for his understanding of the gospel. These two convictions informed the way he understood how the gospel shaped, related to, and was promoted within the Zurich community. For Zwingli, the gospel was never merely appropriated by individuals internally but always shown forth externally into and through society. He wanted to make clear to his Zurich flock that the gospel renewed both person and people. The notion of Reformation in this context went far beyond an individual finding freedom from the bondage of sin. It also extended to the renewal of Christian society, hence his desire for a Christian renaissance at Zurich. Returning to the illustration from the Froschauer home, this meant that the Christian never ate alone. Christian freedoms were always connected to and manifested in the community.

Zwingli defined the gospel as follows: "The summary of the gospel is that our Lord Christ, true Son of God, has made known to us the will of His Heavenly Father and has redeemed us from death and reconciled us with God by His guiltlessness."[70] The repeated use of the first-person plural pronoun was purposeful in this definition. Zwingli believed Zurich was a contemporary representation of Israel. Much like the Hebrews in the Old Testament, God tasked Zurichers with a special purpose, namely, to live as a holy people called out by God to a distinctly Christian life of obedience. Instead of merely gazing eschatologically toward the coming of Christ's eternal Kingdom, Zwingli's eyes were also set on Christ's present temporal rule over Zurich. The awakening of the gospel meant Zwingli's Reformation sought to make new again a Christian society, the *corpus Christianum*. And though this ostensibly Christian society existed before the dawn of the Reformation, he believed the sins of individuals and the corruption of the Catholic Church derailed the Swiss church from reaching that goal.

For both church and state, Zwingli's gospel proposal did not mean the official inauguration of God's eschatological Kingdom. Rather, it meant establishing a contemporary, shadowy representation of Christ's rule as a vibrant preview of that promised Kingdom to come. Based on these convictions, the preacher argued that God had tasked the Zurich Council to create legislation promoting things befitting a Christian society. Therefore, the laws established by divinely instituted civil magistrates should "be in conformity to the will of God, not exactly like it, but in some measure in the form of the divine law and will."[71] Drawing from a neo-Platonic foundation that viewed God as the *summum bonum*, or supreme good, Zwingli encouraged the magistrates to establish Zurich's moral standards, as best they could, based upon God's character and nature.[72]

Much like the civil authorities, the church was to mirror God's coming Kingdom in a real, though admittedly imperfect, form. This is where it is helpful to understand Zwingli's delineation between various forms or senses of "the church." Early in his time at Zurich, the preacher spoke about the church via two categories: (1) the elect, "all those who are founded and built upon the one faith in the Lord Jesus Christ," and (2) individual churches or "special gatherings which we call parishes or ecclesiastical communities."[73] This worked well when dealing exclusively with the papists. However, after the rise of Anabaptism in the mid-1520s, a shift took place and a tripartite definition surfaced.[74] In his 1530 *An Account of the Faith*, a third more generic definition of church was added. Zwingli said the church must also be "taken in a general sense," which included those "who acknowledge Christ publicly by confession or participation in the sacraments, and yet at heart shrink back from Him or are ignorant of Him."[75]

There was both the universal church and the individual local parishes, but there was also the more generic Zurich church. That church was analogous to Israel and, therefore, was admittedly a mixed body. Thus, an already/not yet tension characterized the current standing of the Zurich church. This church stood in contrast to the regenerate, free church embraced by the Swiss Anabaptists in January 1525.

To clarify this point, Zwingli contrasted the visible and invisible forms of the church, a distinction later employed by John Calvin.[76] For Zwingli, the universal church was "called invisible, not as if they that believe were invisible, but because it is not evident to human eyes who do believe."[77] The Zurich church, much like Israel, was a temporal, visible expression of God's people. Nonbelievers were admittedly contained within that visible expression. Not all descendants of Israel were of Israel, as Paul reminded his readers in Romans 9. This reality guided the Reformer in his understanding of the magistrate's role: "Therefore, since this church which is visible contains many rebellious and traitorous members who having no faith care nothing if they be a hundred times cast out of the church, there is need of a government, whether princes or nobles, to restrain such shameless sinners."[78] Israel served as the model for Zurich. The Jews were a people set apart by God, imaging the Lord to others. The Israelites were guided by holy standards designed by God to promote their flourishing, while also governed by laws and rulers who reigned in unfaithful community members living among them.

Zwingli's belief that Zurich was a contemporary representation of Israel had profound consequences for his understanding of the gospel. Writing on May 4, 1528, to the Constance Reformer Ambrosius Blaurer, Zwingli stressed that though the gospel transforms an individual internally, "Christ's Kingdom is also external."[79] The gospel's dual transformative focus meant that "Zwingli's Kingdom was not primarily an eschatological conception … [but] rather, a legitimate goal in the earthly life of the Christian person and the Christian community."[80] The two soteriological realities for person and community, though distinct, were inseparable. Unlike the Swiss Anabaptists, Zwingli did not see society as inherently evil and something to be eschewed. He believed the gospel could positively impact Zurich. The inner transformation of the person naturally renewed the external community in which the redeemed resided. One was the consequence of the other. Both salvific realities were symbiotically and inextricably connected.

The Zurich church was also to act in a manner befitting a covenant community. To do otherwise was to veil God's glory and diminish their legitimacy as a Christian people. This meant that Zwingli's Reformation "was primarily moral in character, affecting attitudes and actions, rather than ensuring correct beliefs. Zwingli was concerned with the moral and spiritual regeneration of Zurich along New Testament lines, rather than with any doctrine of justification."[81] His articulation of the gospel focused on the community's reconciled relationship with God and a subsequent obedience to His commands, as opposed to Luther's emphasis on an individual's justification.[82] Focus on the transformed person was subsumed into and a part of Zwingli's concern for the transformation of the whole of Zurich society.

The civil authorities and Zurich pastors played a shared role in the promotion of the gospel among the community. For the magistrates, the good news of Jesus was not a competing authority. Instead, the gospel "strengthens the magistrates [and] teaches them what is right."[83] For Zwingli, God granted the Zurich Council authority as a part of His "divine order" for the promotion of a gospel order.[84] The magistrates helped lead the people toward righteous living in a gospel-saturated community. Ministers and magistrates alike promoted the gospel. God ordained both offices, yet each was limited in its authority. For instance, Zwingli argued that when a civil authority "obstructs the free course of the heavenly word, the best people turn away from the government and behold everything that can preserve the heavenly teaching."[85] Nor would he stand for pastors "who do not resist the kings and people who sin, but allow them constantly to go on sinning unashamedly, to the vexation of all the godly folk."[86] The gospel was too sacred a trust to allow for either God-ordained authority to detour the Zurich community from its divine calling. Both church and state were to promote godliness, or the people should resist them so that the truth of God's salvation might be made manifest in the community.

KNOWING THYSELF AND FINDING CHRIST

Despite strong beliefs regarding salvation for the covenant community, Zwingli still wanted his flock to understand the importance of an individual response to the gospel. Here, the preacher stressed the notion of mental assent as a key catalyst to one's participation in the promises of God via repentance. Zwingli contended in 1525, "In order, then, that one may repent of their errors, it is necessary that one knows that their errors are errors."[87] He had offered a similar sentiment two years earlier: "For those who recognize their sin which descends from Adam, and their own inner deceit which every person knows resides within them, [these] see their own misery and impotence to attain salvation."[88] Knowing one has violated God's holy standard was also to despair of believing the Lord's measures are obtainable by humans. Knowledge of one's shortcomings became a crucial pathway toward embracing the gospel by faith.

Zwingli viewed the preached word as a catalyst to this requisite despair. Through Spirit-empowered gospel preaching, "humanity knows oneself and is disgusted with oneself known."[89] Zwingli's humanist bent, with its emphasis on intellectual assent, made this an important part of how he understood and preached the gospel. Yet this belief did not deviate from his convictions regarding God's sovereignty. He even situated this human self-deprecation as an act ushered in by God, for "it is a result wrought by the divine Spirit alone that humanity knows oneself."[90] To know one's moral deficiencies was equally crushing as much as it was a grace from God. Both were gifts from the Lord. With his emphasis on knowing oneself as a crucial component of gospel-awareness, Zwingli offered a foretaste of the bifurcation that was the methodological frame for Calvin's later work, *The Institutes*, namely, that all true knowledge is founded upon knowing God and knowing self.[91]

Awareness of one's moral impotence was only part of the pathway toward a renewed life for Zwingli. Recognizing and embracing Jesus's perfect and all-sufficient work of redemption was the other. Building on this notion of self-repudiation, he stressed that those who "see the grace and salvation of Jesus Christ and trust in them have been born of God."[92]

Deliverance came through Jesus alone. One only needed to believe in His perfect atoning work to taste salvation. Christ accomplished what humanity could not. The Reformer maintained, "He who was perfect in every way and without blemish was able to take away all our blemishes. Whoever firmly believes in this activity and trusts in the precious fruitfulness of the suffering of Christ has already believed the gospel and will be saved."[93] Jesus's salvific work was unique and not to be conflated with the work of humanity.

Self-awareness was not merely a pathway to embracing Christ's atoning work. It was also requisite to freeing the conscience burdened by sin. Given Zwingli's humanist pedagogy, introspection had an experiential component to it. In his *Commentary*, Zwingli says of the regenerate, "The minister of the word, therefore, evangelizes you; and when you have been evangelized, that is, when you have received Christ, you are absolved and delivered from the burden of sin, and this relief you feel in your heart, even if no pontiff pronounces the words of any formula over you."[94] The external working of the Bible wrought an internal, felt awareness of the gospel. This emphasis on the Word's ministry to the burdened conscience coincided with Zwingli's move in the mid-1520s away from the Eucharist's salving properties.[95] The redemption birthed through the preached Word freed the elect from the mental and emotional burden of their culpability before a holy God. This deliverance happened without the human aid of a priest. The faithful preacher simply ministered the Word of God, which the Holy Spirit used to initiate faith.

THE FRUITS OF FAITH

While Zwingli stood alongside other Reformers in affirming *sola fide*, or faith alone, he never envisioned true faith to remain alone. Zwingli frequently spoke of two parts or aspects of the gospel. The first, as we have outlined, was based on God's work to make alive that which was once dead. The second part emphasized both the need and capacity to obey God's commands and to walk in accordance with one's confession of faith.[96] Even after Christ paid the sinner's debt, Zwingli declared, "That which God demands still remains, namely, to live as pure, clean, unspotted and right as God wants it."[97] Zwingli did not bifurcate the external work of God via divine declarations (justification) from the ongoing growth of the believer in Christlikeness (sanctification). He saw these two salvific components working together symbiotically in one gospel reality. The outworking implications of the gospel were bound up in the reality of one's new life in Christ. Therefore, Jesus's righteousness was "the initial and continuing source of a life like Christ's."[98] This meant Christ's righteousness was both imputed and imparted. To belong to Christ in a salvific sense was to be like Christ in moral terms. Zwingli always wanted his people to know that how they lived mattered. Though human works did not secure one's salvation, the transforming reality of the gospel was to be evident in the godly lives of the Zurich people.

Stressing this point in 1523, Zwingli argued that although the gospel "means everything which God has made known to us through his Son; indeed, it is the gospel, too, when He says, 'You shall not be angry with one another.' "[99] Confession and action were inextricably linked. Reasserting this premise, the preacher clarified, "I call everything 'gospel' which God opens to human beings and demands of them. ... For whenever God shows his will to people, it delights those who love God and thus it is to them certain and good news."[100] God declared the elect to be righteous positionally in relation to God, while He also made his children to live righteously in relation to their neighbors. A similar sentiment was conveyed in a 1524 letter to the Strasbourg Reformers: "Unless faith is present, you will sing the song of the law in vain, as is clear because only the ones who are his sheep hear the voice of the shepherd."[101] Those who hear the Great Shepherd's voice act accordingly. They love the Lord's laws and His precepts. As he stated in *A Short Christian Instruction*, "If they are now the sons of God, then they will act like sons."[102] Action mattered equally to confession, "for piety is a matter of fact and experience, not speech or knowledge."[103] Accordingly, Zwingli's soteriology may perhaps be best framed in terms of a gospel/law symmetry, as opposed to Luther's famous law/gospel dichotomy. The gospel frees the believer to a life of obedience. The one previously enslaved to sin now became a slave to righteousness because of Christ's redemption.

This important connection between the fruits of one's faith and divine election shaped the way Zwingli shepherded his Zurich flock. His territorial mixed-church ecclesiology, which he derived from Augustine, demanded as much. Admittedly, there were non-regenerate people in the Zurich church. In a 1524 letter to Jerome Emser, he concedes, "But among the Christians there are always evil and unfaithful ones, although we do not always recognize these unless they betray themselves by their fruits."[104] The Reformer believed spiritual fruit inspection was important. Yet it was also a task fraught with limitations. This was why God demanded the church permit each type of crop, "both grain and tares," to "grow [together] until the day of harvest."[105] In Zwingli's mind, to demand that all church members act in accordance with their confession was presumptuous and impossible in a pre-glorified era. While the person with genuine faith may "know that they themselves are members of this first [universal] church," they also "are ignorant about members other than themselves."[106] For anyone to make definitive pronouncements about another's eternal standing was foolish. Such was a determination best left to the divine.

Accordingly, when it came to employing church discipline, rather than stringently applying Matthew 18 to all his parishioners' transgressions, Zwingli opted for a different tactic. He suggested patience and longsuffering for a people living this side of glory. The Reformer addressed only those pressing issues deemed corrosive to the fabric of society or heretical to the Christian faith. Reasoning to Emser, he emphasized, "Here we learn that the whole population of Christians who consider themselves faithful are called one faithful people, one church, and yet it is not an undefiled church; for it has many blemishes, some of which it is not foreign for Christ to overlook [literally, "wink at"]."[107] As Zwingli reiterated in 1527, "For when He [Jesus] says to Peter that one is to be forgiven seventy-seven times, and in another place orders the tares to be permitted to grow until the harvest, He shows that there are some things at which fraternal love may wink."[108] This winking imagery, which Zwingli frequently employed, was not tacit tolerance.[109] It was a gospel accommodation allowing sinners to remain connected with the faith community that proclaimed the very gospel that they needed to hear and receive.

Such a pastoral concession became more acutely necessary and explicitly affirmed with the rise of Anabaptism in the mid-1520s. Volatile discussion over the biblical veracity of infant baptism led some of his former students to establish what he described as an entirely "new church," one that they presumptuously gathered "without sin."[110] The Anabaptists' free-church ecclesiology promoted a regenerate church that was maintained via a stringent discipline. The Swiss Radicals' separation of the wheat and the tares made no sense to Zwingli. Given his ecclesiological convictions, he viewed the Anabaptists' attempt to gather a regenerate church as presumptuous, loveless, and societally corrosive. When addressing sin in the body, he suggested a tempered alternative: "Moderation therefore in this matter with the greatest diligence (which is to be sought from the Lord) is to be observed here."[111] Given his convictions regarding the anonymous nature of the temporal, visible church, it was foolish to believe anyone was able to police that which they were unable to perceive.[112] In a territorial church context, his prescribed "winking at sin" was practically necessary and always framed as a loving act. This is why he demanded the Swiss ministers "preach the law and faith at the same time on account of the variety of believers."[113] The regenerate and reprobate both needed repeated reminders about God's saving grace and His holy standards.

Zwingli believed that to expel sinners from the Zurich church was to mistakenly distance people from the proclamation of the true gospel. The shepherd was unwilling to separate the unregenerate part of his community from the healing salve of Scripture. Just as important, the Anabaptists' ideas threatened to rend society in two. In his polemical treatise decrying the Radicals, Zwingli argues, "There will ever be those who will oppose the gospel, even among those who boast in the name of Christ."[114] Thus, the schismatic Anabaptists could not be tolerated, even as Christ's gospel was to be proclaimed.

CONCLUSION

The Anabaptists' embrace of believers' baptism soon bore the fruit of martyrdom.[115] Not all held credobaptism to be an obedient act experienced only after one's confession of Christ and as an outward sign of the inward awakening of the gospel. Zwingli, as a Reformed theologian, certainly did not. Questions regarding the timing and recipient of baptism did not initiate the painful divide that ensued between Zwingli and his former students. Controversy was already stirred through issues like the tithe, the use of images, and the abolishment of the Mass, not to mention who had the authority to initiate such changes. However, baptism became the ecclesial act marking the Swiss Radicals' formal break from the Zurich church. The rite itself embodied reformation, while also offering a profound theological instruction.

This phenomenon was not unique to the Anabaptists. Across Europe, unique and contextual catalysts ignited different forms and tangible expressions of reformation. Reformation impulses often found their genesis during the most unlikely of events and from seemingly mundane things. In England, Henry VIII's personal ambitions and his desire for Anne Boleyn instigated the Anglican Church's separation from Rome. Most famously, the selling of indulgences sparked the German Reformation. For one German friar, the sale of God's grace was presumptuous and worthless, embodying all that was wrong with the papacy.

At Zurich, the breaking of the Lenten fast in 1522 marked change, the eating of sausages an appreciable expression of Christian freedom and renewal. Gospel proclamation by Zwingli and others was certainly more responsible for the spread of the good news about Jesus throughout Zurich. And the Mass's abolishment in 1525 marked the formal break from Rome and ushered in a new Reformed tradition. Yet perhaps no moment symbolized Rome's mistaken theology or the correctives that came via the Zurich Reformation than one forbidden meal.

So those present at Froschauer's house ate. They consumed what they believed the Lord had given them, an ever-present reminder of God's constant provision. They did this despite the church telling them they could not. No matter how seemingly innocuous the act of eating meat during Lent might appear to some, that meal left an indelible mark on Zurich. The act symbolized deliverance from the shackles of Catholic oppression. But more than reminding the partakers of what was to be refrained from, every bite of succulent meat spoke of Christ, a promised bounty sent from

Heaven. Jesus was the One who brought the Froschauer diners new life by means of His own death. He was both the promise of and the provision for their redemption.

This truth became the resounding theme of weekly sermons at Zurich and the focus of the quarterly observance of the Lord's Supper. Christ was the great Mediator between God and humanity. Rather than having a priest stand between them and God, the Zurich people had One who took their place on the cross and brought them reconciliation. Ironically, Jesus's mediating work invited all Christians to be a part of a holy priesthood in the covenant community, which was to reflect the glory of God and His gospel. Clerical elites no longer laid exclusive claim to that title. The Messiah's atoning work provided for the people a spiritual freedom that no religious act or ecclesial rite could. No longer dependent upon the Pope's musings, the Zurich people now had Jesus as their Captain, guiding them toward true worship by means of His Holy Word. The proclamation of this gospel became as prevalent at Zurich as were Swiss sausages.

Chapter 4

The Sovereign Lord of Zurich

"Even if death should take me in the middle of my days, let it be so! Do as You will, nothing shall be too much for me. I am Your vessel, to make whole or to break."[1]

FEW COULD HAVE ANTICIPATED the circumstances surrounding the start of 2020. News of the SARS CoV-2 outbreak dominated the headlines as people around the world became gripped with fear and uncertainty surrounding a novel virus. By late winter, what would be later classified as the COVID-19 pandemic made its way to Europe, including the serene lands of Switzerland. Despite the country's famous stance regarding political neutrality, no amount of distance from the world's affairs could spare the Swiss. Viruses do not respect national boundaries any more than they do persons. As the reality of the COVID-19 pandemic set in across the globe, many began bantering about the statement, "We are living in unprecedented times." For people captive to the moment and devoid of historical sensibilities, such appeared the case. However, this statement did not accurately reflect the historical record. This was certainly the case for the Swiss, who were all too familiar with pandemics going back hundreds of years. At one time in Swiss history—during the sixteenth century—seasonal waves of pestilence became as common and familiar as did calls for reform. In the case of Huldrych Zwingli, his ministry at Zurich helped lead to his own personal crisis related to plague both metaphorically and literally.

The Swiss Reformer encountered disease early in his ministry at Zurich. He frequently watched those in his parish suffer and die from the Black Death. He also endured the trauma of burying family members because of plague. Eventually the preacher himself became afflicted because of the pastoral care he provided for his flock. Though he faced many battles during his pastorate, nothing prepared him for the war with death that he was forced to wage. Yet what could have derailed his ministry at Zurich soon became a defining part of it. Through both his suffering and his healing, the Reformer saw the Lord's divine hand at work. He could not forget this foundational truth and the comfort it provided. But this was a hard-won belief, one that distanced the Zwingli at Zurich from earlier iterations of his younger self.

Prior to his arrival at Zurich, the young Zwingli had expressed late medieval convictions that affirmed a primary divine causality for the human experience that was subsequently informed by secondary influences embodied in human freedom. These two independent wills, one divine and one human, were affirmed and believed to work symbiotically in human history. These convictions allowed God to remain sovereign without unduly damaging human liberty and volitional choice, which were seen as essential to the *imago Dei*. This view helped a young Zwingli make sense of things like Swiss successes and failings in war during the early sixteenth century. It also initially aligned him with the Catholic Church's synergistic view of salvation that dominated the late medieval ecclesiastical landscape.

However, the preacher that emerged during his Zurich pastorate was a different man. He now maintained stronger beliefs about sovereignty and a monergistic soteriology that permeated his preaching and theology. The Reformer's renewed reading of the Bible, especially those sections related to Israel's history, instilled in him biblical convictions about God's oversight of humanity that he believed were undeniable. Personal experiences like his battle with the Black Death and the stark realities of ministry at Zurich also proved to Zwingli that humanity did not direct life's journey as he once thought. Only God did that. In the end, we will see how a confluence of Zwingli's immersion into the sacred Scriptures and a lived theology forged in the fires of life experiences reshaped his understanding of divine providence.

The Zurich preacher mediated to his people a divine Lord who not only oversaw the major and minuscule aspects of their lives but did so from the loving perspective of a good Father. Such an understanding of God's sovereignty spoke directly to the issue of election at a time when the topic was increasingly contested. Perhaps more importantly, this belief about God's providence helped make sense out of the seemingly random and often painful experiences of life in the early modern world. It also cultivated a disposition of trust toward the Giver and Sustainer of life. When humanity faced unforeseen battles or during hours of greatest need, the Lord was present and in control. And like any good Father, He could be trusted.

EARLY REFLECTIONS

The Zwingli we will meet at Zurich maintained different sensibilities regarding sovereignty from those of his earlier self. This reality does not mean the youthful Zwingli believed himself totally free from God's divine oversight. Although a particular reading of the Bible largely shaped his later views on sovereignty, the notion of God's divine care was implanted in the young Ulrich through different means during his youth. Before encountering the sovereign Lord of Scripture as a clerical priest and Reformer, Zwingli became acquainted with this God through the common experiences of a Swiss boy coming of age.

Living in a rural farming community offered unique instruction about cause and effect, seasons of provision and of want, and the cycle of life and death. As a young boy, Zwingli was familiar with the cyclical reality of nature and its seasons. At the close of each year, harsh conditions brought death to his native land. Flowers withered and foliage decayed as the chilling cold of winter descended upon his Toggenburg community. Despite darkness and death, spring would eventually return, and with it, patterns of restoration, the renewal of life. Seeds planted soon sprouted sprigs, which later matured into a life-giving harvest. Livestock multiplied according to season and kind, with each animal providing certain products that sustained his rural Swiss village. Given the deeply religious context of Wildhaus, people assumed God's providential involvement in their world.

In spring 1524, while drawing on remembrances from his upbringing at Toggenburg, Zwingli implied how these assumed rhythms from his own agrarian society shaped his thoughts regarding God's care for the Swiss people. As he reasoned, though "this land does not give us cinnamon, ginger, sweet white wine, cloves, oranges, [and] silk," the absence of such luxuries was not something to lament.[2] God's failure to provide these commodities to the Swiss countryside was not random. God chose not to provide such opulent things. Instead, the land produced what the Lord willed, not necessarily what the people wanted. For the Swiss, this meant daily staples like "butter, medicinal herbs, milk, horses, sheep, cattle, linen, wine, and corn in abundance."[3] The Lord provided all the people required for daily sustenance.

Even the gracious overflow of the land's resources, all framed as a gift from God, allowed the Swiss to subsidize the remainder of their needs. As Zwingli explained, "What we have others want; and our goods can easily be sold or exchanged for what we need."[4] God provided for the Swiss people's daily sustenance. This provision occurred directly through a unique variety of crops and animals native to the region. However, God also sustained the Swiss indirectly through an economic system that allowed for resource sharing. Provision from the Lord came in different forms, some more explicit than others. Yet there was still work to be done. Farming taught him that God manifested His provision for the Swiss through the farmer's hand and toil.

GOD AND WAR

The lush Swiss countryside regularly produced a harvest of crops that sustained the people. Yet other economic assets also shaped Zwingli's understanding of the human-divine relationship in his early years. The country's chief export of Swiss soldiers taught him similar lessons. Though the Reformer deplored the mercenary trade and was an outspoken opponent of the practice, he was not a pacifist. In fact, Zwingli argued that God's sovereign provision could be seen amid the cruelty of war.

Witnessing harrowing successes and heartbreaking defeats while on military campaigns alongside his countrymen guided Zwingli's thinking. In *A Godly Exhortation to the Swiss Confederates*, Zwingli spoke of God's care for the Swiss and the people's reciprocal reliance on the Lord in battle. He reasoned, "Our forefathers conquered their enemies and won their freedom exclusively through God's strength, and they were always ready, with great gratitude and love, to give God credit for His aid."[5] God's oversight of war, and the soldiers who waged it, were not to be forgotten.

Swiss victories were compared to Israel's exodus from Egypt. God oversaw the people's deliverance, but the people still had a part to play that informed the Lord's will in a substantive way. To illustrate this conviction, Zwingli highlighted how Swiss armies achieved victory when fighting for the noble cause of securing their independence.[6] However, he was quick to offer one key qualifier. Even for these Swiss triumphs, "there can be no doubt that such [military victory] was not due to human strength but [was] only possible by means of divine aid and grace."[7] For Zwingli, there was a moral cause and effect at play in war. God was in control of all things. But He also worked His will out through the people's decisions, especially through Swiss allegiances.

Despite Zwingli's beliefs about God's sovereignty, he warned his people not to assume or take for granted the Lord's hand of protection. Swiss failures during military campaigns in Italy had taught him that painful lesson. In Zwingli's mind, those defeats had nothing to do with a lack of tactful military strategy or might. The Swiss people's pride and dependence upon their own military prowess had caused their past failures. Referencing Isaiah 28, Zwingli reasoned that just as Judah had cut a covenant with death and made a pact with Sheol by relying on the foreign armies of Egypt and Babylon, so too had the Swiss people mistakenly followed Satan by making allegiances with foreign entities.[8] Political dependence on others betrayed a lack of reliance on God's protection and resulted in Swiss military collapse.

Even though Zwingli was nearly a decade removed from a series of horrific experiences on foreign battlefields, the Swiss people's obstinate reliance on the mercenary trade continued to vex him. Was this a profitable enterprise for the country? It had proven economically lucrative for centuries. However, Zwingli believed there was an unintended cost to this commerce. He warned that relying on the monetary support of foreign nations was an affront to God and a tacit rejection of the Lord's sovereignty. Idolatry was inherent in the accords made with foreign nations. In Zwingli's mind, the allure of foreign coin had seduced the Swiss people. An assumed national security came at the expense of God's perfect provision.

Drawing a parallel to Pilate's mixing of the Galileans' blood with their sacrifices (Luke 13:1), Zwingli pleaded with the Swiss to follow Jesus's exhortation to repent of their transgression by extracting themselves from foreign concerns.[9] His country needed to jettison its sinful dependence on the mercenary service. Preemptively addressing the loss of revenue they would incur, Zwingli once again reminded his audience of God's sustaining, providential hand: "If God is for us, who is against us?"[10] As the Lord's prophet once reminded Israel in Hosea 1:7, God's deliverance was not contingent upon military might and superior weaponry.[11] For a Swiss people with a proud heritage of pikemen known for their deft military prowess, this must have been a challenging appeal.[12] Yet Zwingli contended that the Lord could be trusted. The Father had already gone to great lengths by sending His Son to save humanity from sin. Consequently, as the Apostle Paul reminded the Romans, would not God's provision be found for the Swiss people regarding their temporal needs?

In his early years at Zurich, the Reformer seamlessly intertwined political concerns with biblical themes. He cast support for the mercenary industry in terms of idolatry, a dominant theme in Zwingli's theology. He also framed a shift away from the mercenary commerce in the theological language of repentance. This is where the humanist in him shone. He employed typology and parallel imagery to place his audience in the Scriptures. Once there, he guided his flock toward a practical response in their own context. As Moses reminded the people in Leviticus 26, obedience to the Lord yielded the rain that produced a bountiful harvest and military victory that ushered in peace and security to their promised land.[13] For Zwingli, this was a truth that was relatable, one that must not be forgotten. The cause of obedience to the effect of God's sovereign provision was as clear as it was pressing for the Zurichers. Just like Israel in the Old Testament, the Swiss people had all that they needed, in terms of both their land and their Lord.

HUMANITY'S HELPING HAND

It should not be surprising that Zwingli believed the Swiss had a tangible role to play in their military outcomes. Certain influences had directed him toward that position prior to his arrival at Zurich. Medieval convictions shaped his early thinking on divine sovereignty, leaving him with an optimistic view of humanity. As a Roman Catholic priest, Zwingli held to a scholastic understanding of providence, which saw God as the first catalyst or mover of all things, and this guided his theological commitments. The Lord's sovereign hand was seen in Genesis 1 when the Lord spoke creation into being but also extended to the new creation of humanity through Jesus's sacrifice. Aquinas's teachings on divine foreknowledge initially shaped Zwingli's early beliefs, especially when it came to God's sovereignty and the matter of predestination. Election began with "God, seeing all things before they take place" ahead of the Lord establishing a final decision based on "what humanity was going to be like."[14] A volitional will and choice were key here. The cognitive ability to choose highlighted humanity's reason and was foundational to what being made in the *imago Dei* meant. To make decisions was to be human. This conviction retained humanity's genuine freedom, yet this freedom remained situated under or subservient to God's primary causality. God ordered all things by His will according to foreknowledge.

Even as late as 1519 and 1520, after Zwingli's break with scholasticism, this synergistic understanding of the human-divine interchange lingered in his thought. Following a largely Erasmian program of spiritual renewal, which sought to appropriate the wisdom of Christ, Zwingli believed humanity played a crucial role in moving the church toward Christian rebirth.[15] God would renew His church, but something was required from the people as well. Immersion into ancient sources, especially the Bible, afforded people a pathway to the wisdom of Christ. This unique access to

Jesus facilitated an inner spiritual renewal that many longed for during the period. The principal catalyst to this transformation was God's external grace, but the Lord's renewing activity worked in a symbiotic way alongside humanity's intellectual pursuits. As we saw in Chapter 3, Zwingli believed that once internal rebirth was realized on a personal level, that change would flesh itself out in an external, transformed life mediated to the public square.[16] Each person had an important and active role to play in the transformation of Swiss society.

AN UNEXPECTED ADVERSARY

The early months of ministry at Zurich were chaotic and exhausting for Zwingli. As with any new pastoral appointment, establishing life rhythms was a necessary priority. The pulpit ministry to which the canons called him directed Zwingli's attention. Other ecclesiastical tasks ancillary to his office consumed the remainder of his time. However, just as he was settling into his new ministry, an unforeseen challenge abruptly confronted Zwingli. Throughout his life, Zwingli endured many opponents who threatened his work as a priest and Reformer. Yet the adversary facing him before the close of 1519 was like no other. This was an enemy that took him to the brink of death itself.

In August 1519, plague struck the city. Early modern communities were no strangers to pestilence. For centuries, plague washed over communities, leaving a wake of death and destruction behind. Most estimates suggest that more than one-third of the European population lost their lives once this plague descended. The deadly nature of the disease was exacerbated by the rise of cities in the early modern world. Poor sanitation, negligent burial practices that contaminated water supplies, and the intermingling of people with livestock on crowded cobblestone streets were just a few of the things making cities like Zurich vulnerable to infection. The Black Death, as it was commonly called, was no respecter of persons. All sectors of society were within reach of plague's cold, deadly hand. No amount of money, privilege, or power could provide immunity to it. Though it was all too familiar for the people, there was always something unnatural and unsettling for communities when plague visited.

Zwingli was away on holiday enjoying the refreshing springs at Pfäfers near his Wildhaus home when plague came to Zurich. Upon hearing the news, he rushed home to minister to the afflicted and dying. The flock needed its shepherd. The once lively city overlooking Lake Zurich that he returned to was different from the one he had left behind. The bustling enterprises of food and festival the citizens typically enjoyed during the summer months were now muted. Instead, the common fare of the day was fear. Those with financial means had already taken leave, hastily retreating to unaffected regions. Other citizens undertook spiritual routines of absolution, hoping to be spared impending infirmity and the looming specter of death.

Zwingli shifted his ministry focus. While he continued preaching, he was also pressed into service at the local hospitals. Zurich boasted three hospitals at the time, though they would hardly be identified as such today.[18] Rudimentary practices left little in the way of useful medical care. Illness was most often framed as spiritual affliction rather than biological infection, with sickness and death understood as divine judgments. In 1527, Martin Luther said of death caused by plague, "It is God's punishment, which he sends upon us for our sins, we must submit to God and with a true and firm faith patiently await our punishment."[19] Accordingly, the attention patients received for their illnesses was mostly spiritual in nature. The common prescription for the peoples' maladies was intercessory prayer offered by clerics at the bedsides of those teetering between life and death.

The contagious nature of plague, coupled with the primary care given by clerics, meant ministers were particularly at risk. Thus, it was hardly surprising when Zwingli took ill in September 1519. His service to the needy came at great cost to him personally. The priest had now become the patient. The morbidity rate for those afflicted with plague was nearly one hundred percent. As one historian notes, "In time of plague pastoral care was a death sentence."[20] All indications suggested Zwingli's ministry at Zurich was ending just as it was starting to begin.

ZWINGLI'S "PLAGUE SONG"

There is no historical evidence charting the medical struggle that ensued. However, we know the Reformer survived this bout with plague. Sometime after cheating death, Zwingli drafted a song offering a window into his dramatic brush with the grave. His choice to employ a musical medium to capture the drama is not surprising and was appropriate. Zwingli's musical proclivities are well documented. From his childhood days, the young Ulrich showed an interest in music that matched his talents on a variety of musical instruments. As a boy, he was as familiar with instruments like the flute, violin, and horn as he was his Latin letters. Zwingli's musical talents remained with him into adulthood, and he accessed these as needs like this arose. Humanists often leveraged music in their work, as songs connected past events with emotions in a medium that was deeply visceral and personally transformative. For Zwingli, a poetic hymn must have seemed a suitable way to catalogue all the experiences from that fateful time.

Zwingli's "Plague Song" invited his audience to suffer alongside him. It also encouraged others to encounter the providential God who comforted and sustained the Reformer during his torment. The song was divided into three separate parts chronicling his journey: the onset of symptoms, the apex of his sickness, and later reflections following his miraculous recovery. The opening of his song immediately charted a path outside the usual religious currents of the period. Zwingli cried out: "Help, Lord God, help in this trouble! I think death is at the door. Stand before me, Christ; for You have overcome him!"[21] What is fascinating is not the intensity of his opening cries. That should be assumed, given the grave nature of the moment. Rather, it was the Reformer's appeal to Christ and the confidence in Jesus's past work. When confronted by his own mortality, Zwingli quickly pled for Christ's intervention. This appeal evoked images of intercession, of the Great Mediator we met in Chapter 3 offering spiritual assurance in Zwingli's hour of greatest need. Jesus's work at Calvary and His subsequent resurrection buttressed the Reformer's hope. The empty tomb at Jerusalem was proof that his reliance on Jesus was not in vain. Christ could be trusted in this instance, for the Son had already overcome the grave.

Zwingli continued the first section by establishing a dominant theme of the song: the patient's submission to the sovereign hand of God. What remains striking was the solace the Reformer found in God's care precisely because of the Lord's divine will. As he prayerfully declared, "If it is Your will, take out the dart that wounds me ... [but] even if death should take me in the middle of my days, let it be so."[22] God could remove the illness that afflicted the patient. Or the Lord could let the disease remain and run its natural course until death. Zwingli considered either within the Lord's purview. Paradoxically, the patient experienced spiritual rest in that moment, while he was simultaneously laboring physically to remain alive.

Zwingli also spoke of the torment of disease. Not surprisingly, physical suffering produced spiritual pain as well: "The illness increases, pain and fear seize my soul and body."[23] This was not merely a battle of flesh and blood. This was a war waged by and for the whole of his being. As a confluence of symptoms ravaged his body, even an "hour's rest and repose" seemed out of reach to him at the height of the illness.[24] Though he assumed "the Devil's wiles and treacherous hand" instigated his calamity, Zwingli's eyes were fixed on God and God alone, in whom he believed rested the power of life and death.[25] God's grace was the only hope for him at this point. He yielded himself to the One who would take up this fight for him.

Zwingli's acquiescence to life or death was not merely the resignation of a man to the human condition, nor was it born of exhaustion battling a superior foe. This was the willing surrender of a person to the Giver and Sustainer of life. This was submission to a heavenly Father Whom he believed could be trusted and Who always had the interest of His children in mind. These months of sickness taught the Reformer that true freedom was found by abandoning oneself to God. This was a life-altering lesson that intellectual assent alone could not teach. Only human experience could provide such instruction through the coalescing of mind, body, and soul. There would be many challenges as Zwingli labored to reform the Zurich church in the coming years. Rarely would any of those threats be so deadly as the one faced in the waning months of 1519. And just as he believed God had been sovereign over every moment of his fight against the plague, so too would Zwingli look to the Lord as the overseer of whatever he would face in the future.

LESSONS LEARNED

Plague came quickly and without warning to Zurich. But the illness did eventually relinquish its grasp on the besieged city. As Zwingli's body recovered, the physical symptoms of illness faded away into memories. But he could not forget his spiritual struggles. Sickness forced Zwingli to lay prostrate before God, and he believed himself better for it. Plague was unable to leave the preacher visually scarred. However, this experience changed him as a person, ultimately reshaping his theology. The subsequent publication of his "Plague Song" signaled the Reformer's desire to share this pivotal teaching moment from his life with others. The lessons learned during his sickness were too important not to share with the community. Two motifs from the hymn became guiding principles for Zwingli's reforming work and themes dominating his theology: sole dependence upon Christ and God's divine providence.

The "Plague Song" was out of character for its time in relation to a prescribed dependence upon Jesus. There were no signs of the typical contours of late medieval Catholicism one might expect to find. Zwingli's cries offered no references to the saints or the Virgin Mary. He also made no mention of the sacraments, which were typically cast as the infusion of divine grace one especially needed while passing from this life to the next. Appeals to the Pope or even the Catholic Church, outside of which there was no salvation, were also absent. Instead, there was only resolute trust in Jesus Christ and a steadfast confidence in His salvific work.

The song was thematically anchored by certitude in God's providence. From the surfacing of the first symptoms, through the celebration of restored health, the "Plague Song" recounted a man who committed his care to the Lord. Zwingli later revealed how the Bible established in him deep convictions related to God's providence. The Reformer witnessed the sovereign Lord of Scripture caring for Israel amid its sufferings in the Old Testament, just as God later miraculously raised up Lazarus through Jesus in the New Testament. Page after page of Scripture sowed in him an important belief: nothing was outside the Lord's control; all occurred according to His divine will. These ideas became real to him in his sufferings. They were now grounded in the drama of his own life. He was the one who experienced firsthand the providential care of a Creator who could be trusted. Such a truth had to be shared with his Zurich flock.

For a Reformer who faced many trials and tribulations during his future efforts to return the Zurich church to a proper posture before God, this bout with illness was an important milestone. As one biographer reasoned, it was a baptism that thrust Zwingli down to the depths of death only to see God mercifully raise him back up again by His sovereign hand.[26] The preacher's health was restored. His reforming efforts would continue. But now a belief that God was still not finished with him as a preacher guided his work.

A SURRENDER TO GOD'S SOVEREIGNTY

It is difficult to discern when Zwingli shifted from humanist to Reformer, though we can say with some confidence that it took place in the early 1520s.[27] The difference between these two phases of life was subtle yet led to substantive changes on matters like his view of God's sovereignty. Synergistic sensibilities marked Zwingli's early theology. However, these early years of ministry at Zurich changed his thinking. The Zwingli that emerged in the mid-1520s was one wholly committed to God's sovereignty. Humanity's free choice, which he once believed a secondary causation to God's primary one, was now removed and replaced. All things now resided in God's providential hand. Consequently, a passive, even impotent anthropology surfaced in the Reformer. This loss of human agency might at first glance appear a loss of freedom. However, as Zwingli came to believe, total dependence upon the Lord's sovereign hand was one of the greatest liberties anyone could experience. One simply needed to acknowledge this truth and surrender to it.

Signs of this transformation began to materialize in 1520 and were evident in a July 24, 1520, letter penned to a dear friend and fellow Reformer, Oswald Myconius. The Reformation's viability was being tested at the time. Pope Leo X had threatened Luther with excommunication just one month earlier. For his part, Zwingli was embroiled in a battle with papal supporters at Zurich, mostly those from the city's monastic orders. Despite the opposition, the Swiss Reformer spoke of a need to remain committed to the evangelical gospel. Such resolve was required, even at the expense of his own well-being. Anticipating hostility against his convictions and tacit support of Luther, Zwingli wrote, "I beseech Christ for this one thing only, that He will enable me to endure all things courageously, and that He break me as a potter's vessel or make me strong, as it pleases Him."[28] It did not matter to Zwingli whether his life was threatened by disease or displeased authorities. He believed God was in control.

In Zwingli's mind, the Lord's divine will, not humanity's efforts, would determine gospel advances. Men like Myconius and Zwingli were to surrender themselves as instruments to the hands of their Maker. Even the strength to endure opposition to their gospel proclamation and the fortitude required to face the flood of impending adversity were not seen as found within oneself. These qualities were considered gifts from the Lord. To make this point, Zwingli employed metaphorical language from his "Plague Song." The image of the potter shaping clay evoked a posture of surrender, a submissive trust in the Lord. Once again, we find literary allusions to God's sovereignty, as Zwingli connected the divine potter from Isaiah 64 and Jeremiah 18 with the Lord. In God's hands, humanity could find comfort and rest as the potter's vessel.[29] Humanity, as the clay, was malleable and ultimately to be fashioned according to God's good purposes. As was the case during Zwingli's battle with disease, the Reformer positioned the Reformation's long-term prospects for success in the Lord's hands. God was to be trusted when facing the life and death prospects of plague. Why would the same not be true for the work of reform before him?

This commitment to God's providence became valuable when Zwingli faced charges of heresy at the First Zurich Disputation. This was a tenuous moment for the embattled preacher, as the stability of his Reformation remained precarious. The nature of the gospel dominated the January 1523 debate. Zwingli used this theme to highlight humanity's inability to facilitate salvation. Once again, he cast humanity as vessels in the Lord's hands. Using the blacksmith as an analogy, Zwingli contended, "God effects all things in us. We are nothing but vessels in His hand through which he works. ... A blacksmith will not credit the hammer, but himself, for having made the plowshares; for he made the hammer, too, and both hammer and plowshares are the blacksmith's handiwork."[30] The word picture was purposeful and clear. Humans were instruments in the hands of their providential Maker. And God purposefully crafted His ends in and through them.

Like we saw in Chapter 3, Christ's exclusive standing as the Mediator framed this important instruction. The people were warned not to believe that humanity cooperated in the work of salvation through supposed righteous acts such as purchasing papal indulgences or giving alms to the poor. According to Zwingli, considering such efforts meritorious not only made "the suffering of Christ itself not sufficient to pay all debt," but also effectively served as a "cutting off of Christ's hands and mouth."[31] Zwingli determined that for humanity to play any part in the beautiful drama of redemption, which Rome believed, was an arrogant assumption. It was mistaken and dangerous for the people to believe they cooperated in God's salvific work. Zwingli cautioned, "Whoever robs Him of His honor and ascribes it to creatures, is an idolater."[32] Such pursuits blurred the lines between creation and Creator. The preacher was adamant his people must not walk down that idolatrous path.

Zwingli continued promoting God's determinative oversight by attacking scholastic interpretations of Matthew 10:40–42.[33] Some believed giving a cup of water to the thirsty or welcoming a foreign stranger spoke to human participation in God's divine work. Zwingli rebutted such notions. An exegetical principle frequently employed by humanists, which stressed canonical context, refused such interpretation. Jesus's previous words in Matthew established God's authority over the human body and soul as a preceding premise. Therefore, this pericope affirmed God's providence in all matters, including the acts of mercy in question in verses 40–42. The Reformer concluded, "We cannot but admit that not even the least thing takes place unless it is ordered by God," which included knowing the exact number of hairs on any person's head (Matthew 10:30).[34] The

Reformer reasoned that since the Lord was omniscient and omnipotent, "how much more then are all our works ordered by divine decrees? Since this is so, we cannot ascribe any credit to ourselves."[35] Was the gospel visible in and embodied by the kindness of filling a cup or welcoming a stranger to one's home? As we saw in Chapter 3, it certainly was. However, for Zwingli, human works did not offer anything either to the inner transformation of the gospel in a person's heart or to the outworking of spiritual renewal in the public sphere. Both were of divine genesis, established by means of His Spirit.

Zwingli believed that God's providence extended beyond salvation and included the ordering of mundane and seemingly obscure matters of life. In a letter to Joachim Vadian written the following year, Zwingli acknowledged that something as trivial as his own forgetfulness amid the busyness of life was to be attributed to God's providence.[36] The Bible taught such things regarding God's sovereignty. This belief also undoubtedly comforted Zwingli in that stressful moment, as his standing with the church, his work at Zurich, and his life hung in the balance.

UNDERSTANDING THE SHIFT

The change in Zwingli's anthropology from his arrival at Zurich to the mid-1520s was dramatic and extensive. In addition to his increasingly viewing the biblical text through a covenantal lens, several life experiences helped to alter his beliefs regarding humanity's relationship with God and provide important historical context for this shift. A lived, experiential theology modified much of the Reformer's thinking.[37] As stated earlier, his battle with plague provided an important lesson about his own reliance on God that no theology textbook could teach. The death of his brother Andrew on November 18, 1520, further entrenched this conviction in him.[38] While corresponding with Myconius just one week later, Zwingli declared, "God is grace."[39] Even while Zwingli decried the loss of his brother, whom he believed of "the best young character and greatest of hope," the Father's will provided him solace amid his suffering.[40] The affirmation of this theological truth amid the devastating loss of his brother spoke volumes. It appears that his acknowledgment of the Lord's will was the only way he could make sense of the ostensible randomness of his own return to health in contrast to Andrew's sudden death. To believe otherwise was to reject the clear teachings of Scripture about the nature of God. It might also plunge his mind into a pit of despair, where random chance overshadowed divine intention. That seems to have been too much for him to bear.

A second catalyst to Zwingli's theological modification surfaced shortly after his experiences with the plague. In a letter to Myconius on January 31, 1519, he expressed great optimism about his reforming program, even anticipating the people's move from spiritual milk to solid food.[41] However, six months later, he lamented that hopeful exuberance. His humanist agenda, with its emphasis on ancient sources, was not eliciting the change he desired. As Zwingli came to believe, only God could change people. One historian has astutely noted that Zwingli came to understand that Reformation victories were to be won by God's divine hand, not his own theological brilliance or eloquence.[42] Only God could accomplish what human efforts could only hope for, especially the renewal of humanity and the Zurich community.

By mid-1520, the preacher had become increasingly disillusioned by the lack of Reformation successes based on his humanist agenda. He had also become frustrated by institutional pushback from Rome. Education and exposure to the truths of God in the sacred Scriptures were supposed to have fanned the flames of change throughout Christendom. Instead, Luther and Zwingli were facing the literal fires of hell and damnation through Rome's threats of excommunication and execution. The papacy's understanding of the gospel, especially in relation to papal indulgences, compelled Luther to raise substantive and legitimate concerns about the church. Similarly, Zwingli hoped the church would see its shortcomings and institute reforms to rectify any problems, based on his work at Zurich.[43] However, Rome was unmoved. The June 1520 publication of *Exsurge Domine*, the papal bull threatening Luther with excommunication, and charges of heresy against Zwingli amplified this obstinance. Zwingli began seeing himself, like the Old Testament prophets, opposed for calling the church back to biblical standards. He slowly came to realize that the renewal he longed for was not going to come from books or religious institutions. It was to be found by the Lord's sovereign hand and only on account of His grace.

In August 1522, while defending his teachings to Hugo the Bishop of Constance, the Reformer deflected blame away from himself for inciting change among the Zurich people.[44] Any present controversy had its roots in the transforming power of the gospel, not in his work as a Reformer. Zwingli likened that gospel to a seed, one that the Holy Scriptures nurtured in the people and that God Himself brought to a rich harvest. The reason for the Reformation impulses at Zurich was God, not humanity. And He was to be glorified because of it. Zwingli described himself as a sower of the seed, a vessel the Lord used to transform the community. The Reformer knew he was not responsible for the spiritual harvest at Zurich any more than a farmer could create the crops vital to the trade. It was all the Lord's doing.

MAKING SENSE OF EVIL

The strong determinism undergirding Zwingli's view of providence extended to the matter of theodicy and helped provide him biblical responses to questions related to the problem of evil. As is often reasoned, if God is providential and His governance extends over all creation, then how is one to understand suffering and sorrow in this world? Is God to be blamed for such calamity? Zwingli engaged this issue directly in his 1525 treatise *Commentary on True and False Religion*. In what was the closest thing for him to a systematic theology, the Reformer used the loci of God proper to dissuade readers from blaming the Lord for human suffering. God's sovereignty and Fatherly care served as an important lens through which to interpret the pain and suffering experienced in this world.

Zwingli employed several prooftexts in conjunction with carefully selected illustrations to highlight his position. Following a lengthy discussion about God's covenantal name, Zwingli contended, "Nothing is hidden from Him, nothing unknown to Him, nothing beyond His reach, nothing disobedient to Him. Hence not even the mosquito has its sharp sting and musical hum without God's wisdom, knowledge, and foresight."[45] This mosquito illustration encouraged others not to think of God as distant or detached from their human plight. Rather, Yahweh was Lord of all, actively engaged with and sovereign over His created order. For Zwingli, this divine governance even extended to the seemingly insignificant affairs of the mosquito. The clever contrast between the pain of a mosquito's sting and the musical harmony of its flight encouraged individuals to look for beauty amid suffering. In a world replete with physical trials and hardships, this was meant to temper hardship with hope.

God's oversight of the mosquito's sting seamlessly led Zwingli to shift attention toward other biblical instruction regarding God's provision through nature. These were themes he brought to life given his familiarity with nature while growing up in rural Wildhaus. For instance, Jesus's words in Matthew 6 set up a helpful literary link between the Lord's feeding birds and clothing flowers with God's provision for His children. Zwingli suggested, that if the Lord took care of nature's necessities, then how much more would the Father care for His covenant people! He deemed this such a simple biblical truth even "a child can explain the meaning of this trope."[46] And when death, the most unnatural of all realities, struck, as it did with Lazarus, Zwingli dissuaded his audience from questioning the origin of such loss: "God is the author even of things which to us seem to happen accidentally."[47] The people were to take comfort in and look for how God was going to glorify Himself through the event, as He did with Lazarus's resurrection.

Zwingli even chided his readers for questioning God's purposes when trying to understand the causes of human pain. He reasoned, "Nothing, therefore, can escape God, nothing can defeat or alter His purpose and ordering. And when we demand of Him a reason for His acts or designs, asking why He made the flea, the fly, the wasp, and the hornet, things that are a plague to humanity and beast," we vainly ascribe to ourselves a level of understanding not warranted.[48] Human curiosity was never to be satiated at the expense of divine fiat.

Over time, Zwingli continued to encourage a proper disposition toward God by employing the potter/vessel illustration we saw earlier. While preaching to introduce the Reformation at Bern, he declared, "If misfortune and sickness come, think always—God is casting you aside just as a metalworker rejects a worn-out tool. Maybe God will take you up again for His purpose; if not, you must not take it wrongly but submit yourself patiently to His will."[49] He deemed this a critical posture, for "if we rightly understood God's providence in these matters, our conscience would enjoy tranquility, peace, joy, and rest."[50] The Reformer suggested passive acceptance, not inquisitive accusation, whenever difficulty or struggle arose.

Zwingli's willing submission to God's sovereignty culminated in his often-maligned statement, "Nothing, therefore, is done or achieved which is not done and achieved by the immediate care and power of God."[51] This "absolute determinism," as some have called it, even extended to human sin, though God remained detached from the moral culpability of such transgressions.[52] For Zwingli, this meant that David's sin with Bathsheba and against Uriah in 2 Samuel was determined by the Lord. The Reformer believed God willed David to commit such atrocities. However, the consequence of this determined sin was to make David "an example of His [God's] bounty and mercy."[53] Drawing especially from Seneca, Zwingli posited that God's righteous glory is amplified and made known specifically in contrast to the unrighteousness of human sin.[54] Therefore, the awfulness of sin became for Zwingli a means to a larger revelatory end, for "how can righteousness be recognized if there is not also unrighteousness?"[55] The Reformer believed this argumentation threaded a theological needle by speaking to the reality of human suffering while also maintaining God's complete sovereignty without making the Lord culpable for evil. Zwingli knew the human temptation to question God's motivations given his painful struggle with plague. Death once nearly took his life. Plague stole his brother away from him. But instead of questioning God for those experiences, Zwingli encouraged the Swiss to look past the particularities of their present struggles toward the providence of God.

From that submissive posture, the Reformer believed one could look with anticipation toward how God might be glorified through times of trouble. And suffering was not always the net outcome of the Lord's will. Through the abolishment of the Roman Mass at Zurich less than a month after penning his *Commentary*, Zwingli witnessed what he believed was

God's kindness through Reformation success. All the personal pain and hardship he had endured since his arrival six years earlier must have felt worth it. The Reformer believed God was faithful and to be trusted in both the good and the bad. The removal of the shackles of the Roman Mass from the Zurich church modeled this important truth.

THE PROVIDENCE OF GOD

Although Zwingli's understanding of providence came more sharply into focus in the early 1520s, his convictions on the topic crystallized into its most mature form amid a painful schism within his own Reformation camp in the mid-1520s.[56] The eventual rise of Swiss Anabaptism, with the movement's embrace of an anthropology similar to that of Erasmus and an emphasis on a theology of holiness that culminated in a believers' church, concerned Zwingli.[57] As a pastor, he was burdened by the thought that some of his sheep were falling prey to what he believed was the idolatry inherent in their synergistic anthropology and over-realized ecclesiology. As Zwingli pushed back against the movement, an expansion and more explicit expression of his covenantal theology coincided with a strengthening of his views on sovereignty. In fact, the emerging convictions were so strong that, as we will soon see, they arguably surpassed the positions held by other contemporary Reformers like Luther and Calvin.

Following years of struggle with the Anabaptists, Zwingli presented the fullest expression of his ideas on sovereignty in a 1530 work titled *Sermon on the Providence of God*. The text that survives was a later expansion of a sermon preached in 1529 at the Marburg Colloquy. Zwingli likely spoke on the matter of God's providence at the behest of the Landgrave, Philip of Hesse, who hoped to engender a unified spirit as the magisterial Reformers sought an accord on Protestant doctrine. The sermon also not-so-subtly suggested that any agreement found during the forthcoming meeting would be a work of God. The text itself was a brilliant piece of humanist rhetoric that showed a mastery of theology and deep philosophical argumentation.

Early in the sermon, Zwingli defines providence as "the enduring and unchangeable rule over and administrator of all things in the universe."[58] Everything was held together by God's power and directed according to His divine will. The scope of the Lord's oversight included humanity. According to Zwingli, no person or thing acted freely. God's dominion extended equally to the natural order and to the crown of His creation, humanity. The designation of Creator is important here, for it became a theme in the sermon that helped maintain a strict demarcation between God and His creation. To blur that line was akin to idolatry.

Despite this important infinite/finite divide, Zwingli quickly pointed out the Lord's Fatherly nature and faithful provision for His children. God's divine support reached down to even the downtrodden of society and extended to ostensibly inconsequential matters. Zwingli contended, "There is now, nothing which is not ruled by God, nothing so high or powerful that it can avoid the sway of our God, nothing so lowly or humble that it is abhorrent to His care."[59] This statement sought to balance the transcendence of a God who was in control of all things with an intimacy that spoke to the nearness of God in Christ through the incarnation. Thus, the great "I AM THAT I AM" was the eternal one who not only desired a relationship with Israel but later secured communion with the elect through His Son, Jesus.[60]

While God's providence is often framed in terms of His activity over creation, Zwingli refused to allow the work of God alone to define providence. Instead, the Reformer looked to a deeper, philosophical foundation based on God's nature. Drawing from late medieval scholastic ideas, Zwingli opened his sermon by arguing that providence demands the existence of a *summum bonum*, or supreme good.[61] The idea of God as the personification of goodness was expanded upon and connected with two related ideas: truthfulness and omnipotence. Zwingli believed this triumvirate of divine attributes spoke to the essence of the divine nature. For the Lord to allow random acts in His creation, whether based on a lack of notice or neglect, was to replace his goodness and truthfulness with "obscurity, darkness, and ignorance."[62] And should God not be able to direct the creation's affairs, then His power and omnipotence were equally in jeopardy.

The Reformer had in view humanity's basic questions about truth and the meaning of life. Understanding who God is, in His nature, was supposed to provide a sense of purpose to the seeming randomness and frequent pain of human history. God was God, and by His very nature He was good. Therefore, He could be trusted. This important supposition helped him make sense of the senseless. It provided purpose and intentionality behind the most ostensibly mundane tasks and events of life. As one historian has argued, for Zwingli, "God is not the life and motion of all things in such a way that he 'blindly' puts breath or motion into them. God's creative power is purposeful, teleological, that is directed toward a specific goal."[63] God's causative power did not merely cast humanity adrift into a sea of uncertainty. God was not some deistic watchmaker. For him, the Lord purposefully charts unique courses for each person, which are maintained through the determinative currents and winds of the divine will.

In 1529, the Protestant Reformers were facing intense opposition from the Roman Catholics and the daunting prospect of division within their camp. Zwingli's reminder about God's providential oversight was meant to encourage them in the work that lay ahead. Once published in 1530, these same notions of God's divine purpose were supposed to minister to the Swiss amid their unique hardships. As Zwingli believed, human experiences such as pain, suffering, adversity, and death could be endured, even welcomed, because of the knowledge that all things were directed by the sovereign hand of a good God. This belief also filled the people's work with meaning and mission, just as the Protestant doctrine of vocation was beginning to develop.

Sovereignty was to be celebrated, not castigated, as Zwingli believed some were mistakenly doing. Discussions related to providence also served as a natural and logical springboard to considerations about the doctrine of election. Zwingli stressed this point in his *Commentary*: "For the whole business of predestination, free will, and merit rests upon this matter of providence."[64] The preacher used the words "predestination" and "election" as synonyms, defining them as "the free disposition of the divine will in regard to those that are to be blessed."[65] He deemed God's eternal decisions to be well beyond human understanding.

Similar to others like Luther and Calvin, Zwingli faced criticisms that his view of election unduly damaged God, making Him a random arbiter of justice. On this point, the Swiss preacher saw no problem. He considered God's providential nature unassailable. Summarizing Paul's sentiments in Romans, Zwingli contended, "God is not unjust simply because He uses His creature according to His will, just as a potter cannot be called unjust by his vessels because he forms out of a lump of clay a vessel for worthy usage and another for a less worthy usage."[66] Instead, "God deals with us without in any way diminishing His justice; for in relation to Him, we are lower than clay is in relation to the potter. Therefore, He makes of His vessels, i.e. us humans, as He wills."[67] The Reformer also rebutted the common view held by many of his contemporaries that this divine choice flowed from God's justice alone. To the contrary, he stressed that justice shaped the divine will, but it was a justice born from God's goodness. In this ethical hierarchy, "goodness is the source of these things [election], as a sort of genus comprehending justice and kindness or mercy, not justice alone, so far as it is a species of goodness."[68] Therefore, election was not to be framed in terms of a human response to the call of the gospel. He framed election as a divine rescue mission initiated by a good Father through Jesus's work and actualized in the elect through the Holy Spirit.

Zwingli's understanding of election was so strong that he later speculated about the salvation of the pious heathen. This was a theme alluded to in his July 1531 work *An Exposition of the Christian Faith*, penned just prior to his unexpected death in October. In this treatise, Zwingli painted a picture of heaven in which pagan figures like Hercules, Theseus, Socrates, Scipio, and others stood alongside biblical heroes like Abraham, Jacob, Isaiah, the Virgin Mary, and Paul.[69] To those aghast at what they perceive to be the Reformer's provocative claim, the exclusivity of Jesus was not really at stake here. Zwingli affirmed that Jesus was the sole mediator between God and humanity.[70] Nor was the point of this creative prose to downplay the need for gospel proclamation. That was a hallmark of his preaching ministry from 1516 onward. Rather, he desired to preserve God's good and powerful will by refusing to relegate salvation to the limited bounds of Christendom.[71] Thus, geography played no part in his view of divine election, as Calvin later argued when considering the reprobate.[72] To limit God in this matter was to assault His very nature and to question His divine purposes.

LORD OF ALL OR NOTHING AT ALL

At the conclusion of his "Sermon on the Providence of God," Zwingli declared, "Either providence cares for all things and is nowhere idle or listless, or there is no providence at all. And if there is no providence, there is no God."[73] The Swiss preacher could not have been clearer when addressing the volatile nature of the human will. The Lord was sovereign over all His creation, or He oversaw none of it. There was no mediating middle ground. To acknowledge the Lord's providential oversight was to submit oneself not only to God's divine hand but to the truth of His existence. The Reformer learned this lesson from Scripture and through his extensive studies of ancient sources. Various life experiences also placed this conviction in Zwingli. Sovereignty was foundational to his biblical, philosophical, and existential understanding of who God was ontologically.[74]

Like many of his age, the Swiss preacher thought deeply about the nature of the human-divine relationship, hoping to more fully understand the human experience. As any humanist might, he drank deeply from the Bible and ancient Christian sources, attempting to find knowledge, meaning, even purpose in life. What he found after all his studies and tireless intellectual pursuits astonished him: "Therefore, it is clear that by ascending in this way from our intelligence we arrive at God, and when we have reached Him, we have searched out providence also."[75] To know God was the noblest of all pursuits. However, one could not know God apart from His providential character. Zwingli concluded that these two realities worked together symbiotically as essential parts of the Divine.

For the Reformer, knowing these truths was crucial to understanding the God of Scripture. And that knowledge was deeply relational in Zwingli's mind, bringing comfort and consolation to humanity. The goodness of God undergirded all the Lord's divine decrees. The Bible and the struggles of life taught Zwingli that God could be trusted. For the people of God, there was more than "an hour's rest and repose" to be found in God's sovereignty.[76] The Lord was in control, and this fact made any circumstance or hardship tolerable, even welcomed. Life was difficult in the early modern world. The appearance of things like disease and war only added privation to daily life. Nevertheless, Zwingli believed this was where divine providence served as a soothing balm covering over the pain and suffering of daily life. For those who "turn often to the contemplation of Providence," Zwingli contended, "there you will find rest and deliverance from all storms and blasts."[77] This theological conviction comforted the Reformer through many seasons and struggles at Zurich.

CONCLUSION

The closing line of William Cowper's famous eighteenth-century hymn "God Moves in a Mysterious Way" reads, "God is his own interpreter, and he will make it plain." The hymnwriter's life offers important context to this powerful statement, given that Cowper struggled most of his life with raging bouts of depression. He even attempted suicide on multiple occasions as a means of escaping his mental health struggles. As Cowper's life reveals, sometimes the torments and challenges of life come from within, not from external adversaries, as they mostly did for Zwingli. Yet amid the hardships of his own personal struggle with sanity, Cowper found comfort in knowing that God's ways were not his own. The Lord's divine perspective was all that mattered, not humanity's limited understanding or experiences. As the preceding stanza from Cowper's hymn explains, "His purposes will ripen fast, unfolding every hour; the bud may have a bitter taste, but sweet will be the flow'r." Cowper believed life was not promised to be free of heartache, pain, and suffering. But through it all, God could be trusted. And at the end of the journey, a beautiful Savior stood waiting to receive His bride, the church.

At the close of his 1530 "Sermon on Providence," Zwingli sternly declared, "Therefore, just as humanity's course and appointment, is so ordained by providence that one tarries a little while in this world like fruit on the trees, and then, when ripe, is gathered and stored away, so is humanity, after the ups and downs of this world stored in the heavenly storehouse."[78] The imagery was similar to Cowper's, the message nearly the same. God was in control of all life's affairs. Zwingli anticipated seasons of serenity alongside seasons of suffering and sorrow. This was a part of the human condition for a people living in a fallen world. But these episodes of life, whether good or bad, were fleeting. Treasured moments and the trials of life were here today and gone tomorrow, never extending beyond that which could be endured, nor lingering beyond their appointed time. God remained good through it all. For Zwingli, the Lord's hands were firmly upon even the seemingly minuscule events in life. Thus, God could be trusted for whatever all that humanity faced. These very experiences were preparing Christians for a future harvest and a stable, unchanging reality, one without tears, pain, or sorrow. The ripening of their Christian character was preparing them for an eschatological partaking, a sweet and succulent meal at the banquet feast of the Lamb.

The endless parades of conflict and struggle throughout Zwingli's life birthed this conviction in him. As a young man, he was scarred by the torments of war. The same plague that nearly took his life also forced him to bury countless parishioners, along with his brother. Zwingli watched as the Catholic Church that he loved and served turned its back on him when he tried to return it back to the prescriptions of Holy Scripture. And he endured what he believed was the stinging pain of betrayal from gospel partners who became his enemies through their embrace of Anabaptism. Still, the sovereign Lord encountered in the Bible seasoned each of these agonizing acts of life with purpose and meaning. Each event taught Zwingli that anything could be suffered with confidence. God was working in and through them all. Thus, he did not lament the struggles from his past, for they were the very things that, when planted in the soil of his own life, helped mature him into a man dependent upon God for all things. Looking back to the sacred Scriptures, he contended that Israel experienced similar hardships along the way to the Promised Land. Because of their bitter suffering, the milk and honey found in the land once promised to them tasted that much sweeter on the other side of the Jordan River. Zwingli believed the same must be true for him and his beloved Zurich church. The promised end was just as sure and certain as the character of a good and sovereign Lord.

The themes of providence and sovereignty were woven throughout the tapestry of Zwingli's theology and threaded through his other doctrinal commitments. These concepts served as two strands of truth that held together the entire fabric of his theology. Both ideas not only provided explanation for why things occurred, but they also served as a constant source of comfort, especially in seasons of uncertainty or difficulty. He did not interpret the Bible based on his experience, as many in modernity have mistakenly done. Instead, he allowed the Bible to interpret his experiences. In the crucible of his exegesis and real-life experience, Zwingli discovered the providential God of Scripture. This was the same Lord he met when standing on death's doorstep in 1519, a God who walked alongside him through the valley of the shadow of death, and a Savior who he believed helped him usher in Reformation and gospel renewal to Zurich.

Chapter 5

Gospel Partnerships

"Therefore, to come to an end at last, it is not the function of one or two to expound passages of Scripture, but of all who believe in Christ."[1]

In Zurich, Switzerland, the famous Lindenhof park resides a short walk north of the Grossmunster Church, alongside the western bank of the Limmat River. This lush greenspace is a popular outdoor destination, sitting high above the old medieval portion of the town. The park's serene location is challenged in beauty by the river below. There, the bubbling rush of the Limmat River's crystal-clear water is as mesmerizing as it is placid. During the summer months, swans often peacefully paddle at this location, adding to its allure. In the middle of this idyllic scene rests a small plaque. The bronze plate is muted in its coloring against the stone wall, leaving most passersby oblivious to the remembrance it inspires. But the story this memorial tells is as jarring as it is unforgettable. Established in 2004, this plaque recounts the chilling events from early 1527 that took place here, and the horrific precedent that was established.

The drama that unfolded on January 5, 1527, tested Zwingli's personal mettle as much as his theological principle. On that day the trial of the Anabaptist leader Felix Manz concluded. The accused faced capital charges stemming from his radical preaching and persistent rebaptisms of Swiss citizens, both of which violated a legal order from 1526.[2] As the criminal proceedings closed, the Zurich Council found Manz guilty of repeatedly breaking his promise to refrain from such activities.[3] Heinrich Bullinger recounted how Manz was immediately taken from the Wellenberg prison to a fishing hut in the middle of the Limmat River for sentencing.[4] The prisoner's hands and feet were trussed to a wooden beam. The executioner then lowered the Anabaptist into the river's chilly waters. Several witnesses were close enough to hear Manz reciting Jesus's famous prayer, "Into your hands I commit my spirit," just before the water silenced him.[5]

Zwingli watched these events with interest as a vested participant. He never defended the accused, nor did he raise opposition to the execution. By then, the Reformer had worked against the Anabaptist movement for more than two years. So, his actions were not surprising. However, Zwingli's silence remains astonishing, given that Manz was once a close friend and co-laborer in the Zurich Reformation. During the early 1520s, Zwingli mentored Manz, the son of a canon at the Grossmunster. The two Reformers shared meals together. They read and discussed Scripture. Zwingli even tutored Manz by helping the young humanist learn the biblical languages.[6] Zwingli sat with Manz when he mastered his Greek parsing tables, just as he stood near when the Anabaptist died uttering words from the New Testament text.

The events from that winter's day in 1527 serve as a reminder of the complexities of gospel partnerships during the Reformation. Zwingli and Manz once shared a love for Scripture and each other. Both yearned for church reform. To this end, they encouraged and supported each other in their shared work at Zurich. But in a letter penned to Johannes Oecolampadius two days before Manz's execution, Zwingli callously said of his former student, "The Anabaptist, who should already have been sent to the devil, disturbs the peace of the pious people. But I believe, the ax will settle it."[7] Discordant visions for what the Reformation should look like and how quickly it was to be realized derailed Zwingli and Manz's gospel work and severed their partnership. Theology was given priority over personal relationships, even if that meant watching a son in the faith executed.

This lamentable drama has proven historically problematic for Zwingli. His participation in the execution of Anabaptists continues to cast a dark shadow over his life and complicates modern reflections related to this important religious figure. Still, this was one encounter among many in which personal gospel relationships colored the narrative of Zwingli's life and ministry at Zurich. Not everyone fought against the Reformer. Many lauded him as a leader. In 1518, Oswald Myconius spoke glowingly of opinions about Zwingli: "You have friends here [at Zurich], and you have carping critics as well, not many of the latter while the former are numerous and good."[8] Detractors were always present, making conflict inevitable. While Zwingli labored to revitalize the community at Zurich, others were always present who offered another way to reformation. At times, their voices were just as loud as or even louder than his. For Zwingli, reformation would be determined in large part based on the people around him and how successful the preacher would be at rallying others around his vision for change amid a sea of competing voices.

ERASMUS

Although a myriad of figures played a part in making Zwingli into the pastor he became, arguably no one person shaped the scope and focus of his ministerial work more than did Erasmus. Despite their limited face-to-face interaction, Erasmus subsumed the young Swiss preacher into his collaborative network of thinkers and young intellectuals.[9] In the Reformer's lone surviving letter to the Dutch humanist, Zwingli spoke of being "frightened by the luster" of Erasmus's intellect, while also "invited by that well-known gentleness" he experienced during their lone encounter.[10] Zwingli was overwhelmed by Erasmus as much as he was drawn to the Dutchman. Affection and respect were mutual. In Erasmus's reply, he congratulated the Swiss on having Zwingli to "finish their education in the arts and the virtues."[11] He also lauded Zwingli's gift of communication, stressing, "if you will but exercise it."[12] The young Reformer heeded Erasmus's words while also mirroring his approach to learning. At Zurich he later instituted the humanist's collaborative pedagogy by building a community of pastors, politicians, and printers to share in his ministry at Zurich.[13] Zwingli learned that ministry was not to be undertaken alone.

Zwingli took from Erasmus not only this communal approach to learning but also his pedagogical approach to reading Scripture. Zwingli first cut his teeth on Renaissance humanism through Erasmus's scholarship. Erasmus mediated the rich and vibrant worlds of Scripture to the young preacher, who was eager to glean truth from antiquity. Zwingli taught himself Greek beginning in 1513. But the wondrous world of Scripture only flowered before him through Erasmus's *Novum Instrumentum*, published in 1516. Zwingli cited an Erasmus poem as the catalyst to his understanding of the gospel and Jesus's place as the "sole Mediator."[14] Through Erasmus, Zwingli learned to view Christ as the locus of Scripture, which imbedded a Christocentrism into the Reformer's reading of the Bible.[15]

Erasmus also instilled in Zwingli an important spirit/flesh dichotomy that became a crucial hermeneutical commitment for the Swiss preacher. Both men lamented how worship practices were being enacted in the church without concern for the inner spiritual motivation undergirding these acts. They feared religion had devolved into external movements disconnected from internal piety. The pursuit of spiritual renewal became part of the Christian's journey for both men. But neither saw this goal exclusively as an eschatological hope. Spiritual vitality could also be realized presently as individuals cast aside worldly, temporal pursuits.[16] Reformation meant more than right doctrine. It also related to a way of being and impacted how the community worshiped. Religion became for Zwingli "more than mere theology: religion was a way of life to him, a total integration of the individual and the community with a higher reality, in the here and now."[17] However, the two figures parted company over the nature of reformation changes and who determined what was proper for the Christian community.

Despite Zwingli's affinity for Erasmus, a forthcoming schism based on disparate theological convictions severed their friendship. As with Luther and Erasmus, this relationship soured over the matter of God's providence and the human will. Zwingli later criticized Erasmus as "a certain genius at word-tinkering" by ascribing to God hyperbolic language regarding His divine providence.[18] Erasmus believed the human will was free, meaning "humanity can apply itself to the things which lead to eternal salvation, or turn away from them."[19] Zwingli found such a view untenable. Not only did it violate God's providential nature, but it spiraled into a works-based righteousness that made humans the masters of their own fates.

More was at play in their falling out than conflicting exegesis. A deeper foundational divide caused the division. Both men vocally criticized the Catholic Church. However, while Erasmus sought to amend forms of religion within the Roman Church, the Zurich Reformer looked to destroy and supplant them with something altogether different.[20] Erasmus later said of this distinction, "When I admonished Zwingli in a friendly way he wrote back disdainfully: 'What you know is of no use to us; what we know is not for you.' "[21] When the two first met, Zwingli was but the learner; now he believed himself to be the master, having moved beyond Erasmus's instruction. The more Zwingli pushed Zurich toward reformation, the more the divide between the erstwhile friends widened until it became a final, irreparable fissure.

HUMANIST SODALITY

From the outset of his ministry at Zurich, Zwingli believed biblical exegesis was a communal endeavor. An individual interpreting the Scriptures in isolation was dangerous to both the cloistered exegete and those who might follow. Hermeneutical solitude must be avoided at all costs. This was a truth taught by countless missteps from history through names like Arius, Apollinarius, and Marcion. Zwingli's humanism also informed this belief. To properly explore the wondrous worlds of the past, one needed intellectual partners willing to share that journey. Zwingli also knew the practical constraints of his ministry. Though his voice was bold and reverberated loudly through his preaching, limitations remained. If he was going to extend and multiply his ministry's reach, then gospel partnerships were required.

These realities were part of the impetus behind Zwingli's gathering of a stable of young, impressionable humanists around him in the early 1520s. Some of those who joined him in exploring Scripture were priests like Simon Stumpf. Others, like Conrad Grebel, were lay patricians. All were educated and eager to drink directly from the Bible. These men pored over the text of Scripture together. Their interaction with Erasmus's *Novum Instrumentum* enriched their studies and helped provide access to the biblical text's deeper meaning. Through their studies they soon became enamored by the Christ of Scripture. A desire to follow Jesus by embracing a biblical ethic and proper forms of worship soon emerged.

This group's shared love for the Bible eventually spilled over and grew into a genuine love for one another. Perhaps the greatest example of this affinity was found in the blossoming relationship between Zwingli and Grebel. From the beginning of their friendship, Grebel effusively praised his master. After all, Zwingli's preaching first led to Grebel's spiritual awakening. Grebel saw Zwingli as an older brother in the faith, a man of impeccable integrity and deep conviction. For his part, Zwingli saw something special in his younger student and regularly made personal investments in the budding young humanist.[22] The two even shared a publication. At the close of his *Archeteles*, Zwingli invited Grebel to offer a short poem to complete the work. Grebel's poem contrasted the Catholic bishops, whom he described as ravenous wolves, with those who faithfully dispensed their biblical duties by allowing the light of the gospel to freely shine forth.[23] Grebel's allusion to Zwingli as the latter of these ministerial types is not easily lost on the reader. To think that these two men would eventually see one another as threats to the faith was unthinkable in 1522. Love and respect characterized their co-labors in those early years.

The theological truths unearthed during their communal examination of Scripture were not for their own personal edification alone. Zwingli later loosed this cadre of learners into the community to help lead others toward a more vibrant Christian faith. This gospel sodality, as the group has been described, created an equality for these men around the Word of God, which also rubbed off on the community.[24] These exerted influence over Zurich through two important avenues. First, their work in the Scriptures supported Zwingli's own pulpit ministry. The biblical truths uncovered by this group bolstered and shaped Zwingli's sermons in the early 1520s.[25] His sermon preparation included their communal discussions about the text's meaning and application. Like multiple tributaries joining to become one powerful river, their collective insights melded into the preacher's one voice. Second, these theological discussions did not remain confined to the group. In the months following their first meetings, several of the participants began mediating their biblical discoveries to others throughout Zurich. This move disseminated Zwingli's ideas to a wider swath of society. It also unintentionally created a powder keg of volatility once those ideas were loosed from Zwingli's direct oversight and linked to the unique ambitions and concerns of others.

THE PEOPLE'S WORD

The underlying belief in the Bible's transformative power that inspired Zwingli's gathering of humanists also led the Reformer to permit the proliferation of Scripture reading among the laity. During the early 1520s, lay Bible study groups sprang up throughout the Zurich community with Zwingli's blessing.[26] The most famous of these Bible schools met in the home of Andreas Castelberger, a local bookseller. Castelberger led a group of lay commoners through a study of several New Testament texts, which Zwingli's preaching focused on at the time. The participants included a local baker, a tailor, and a weaver. Thus, these gatherings embodied a different ethos from Zwingli's more academic reading group. These lay figures set their sights on Scripture, collectively probing the text for meaning and application. Utilizing a vernacular Bible, the group considered God's teachings on theological matters like baptism, social responsibility to the poor, local politics, and questions of personal morality like drinking in pubs. In other words, as one historian summarized, "the New Testament was being read as a practical guide to the Christian life."[27] And that guide was thought to help reform both person and society.

Groups like the Castelberger one proved enticing to a Zurich people eager to receive instruction from the Word, as evidenced by the repeated need to find larger gathering spaces to accommodate their numeric growth and multiplication.[28] At first Zwingli was delighted by the explosive growth of such assemblies. These lay Bible studies embodied an early conviction held by the Reformer that God's people must be granted access to God's Word, for the laity were just as qualified to rightly handle the text as the clergy were. At the close of his *Archeteles*, Zwingli rebutted the notion of exclusive clerical interpretation, citing 1 Corinthians 14:9. Basing his argument on Paul's instruction, Zwingli contended, "The passage, I think, is clear enough to you. You see, therefore, that any one may prophesy, though in a certain order, that all may learn the truth of the Scriptures, and all may be comforted by the Word of God, which alone can give repose unto human longing."[29] When God's people gathered around His Word, those present were of equal value based on their priesthood and all could prophesy, that is, rightly interpret the Scriptures.

For Zwingli, hermeneutical qualification was not based exclusively on one's intellect or formal ordination. Instead, he rooted the right reading of Scripture in the Spirit's work among His people, both clergy and laity alike:

> If it is not lawful for any persons to make definitive proclamations regarding the truth of Scripture, there will arise countless errors. For anyone may mistreat the sacred writings by pursuing one's own lustful will. Country bumpkins! Do you not see that the Spirit of God is everywhere and always the same? The more uneducated a person is in human instruction, yet they are more lovingly devoted to God, the more clearly the Spirit informs that person, as is shown by the Apostles and by the foolish things of this world which God has chosen ... to the degree that they [the reader] are pious, they will understand the Scriptures in the plainest way according to God's purpose.[30]

Proper biblical interpretation was not to be found in the academic skill of exegesis alone. Instead, he linked it with one's piety, pursuit of God, and dependence upon the Spirit-given wisdom of Christ. The inward disposition of the heart was a greater key to understanding God's Word than the cleverness of one's mind. This belief was precisely why Zwingli stressed that ordination was not a prerequisite for proper interpretation. He concluded, "Therefore, to come to an end at last, it is not the function of one or two to expound passages of Scripture, but of all who believe in Christ."[31] A new recasting of the priesthood of all believers guided Zwingli here.[32]

The Holy Spirit was not the only reason the laity were qualified to understand and expound the biblical text. The divine nature of the

Scriptures also provided the laity this access. This theme permeated Zwingli's 1522 sermon "On the Clarity and Certainty of the Word of God." Based upon the experiences of Noah, Abraham, Moses, and Jacob, Zwingli argued, "God's Word can be understood by a person without any human direction."[33] Zwingli believed that just as God spoke directly to the patriarchs in the Old Testament, the Lord was still speaking to His people at Zurich, but now through the sacred Scriptures. He based this epistemological conviction upon a pedagogical principle he called *theodidacti* ("taught by God").[34] According to Zwingli, truth comes from God, not humanity, which was why Jesus declared Himself "the Truth" in John 14:6.

Zwingli's early belief in the laity's ability to interpret the Bible proved invaluable in his battle with Rome in the early 1520s. During the proceedings of the First Zurich Disputation, Zwingli stated, "Even the laymen and women know more of the Scriptures than some priests and clergymen."[35] This was a polemical indictment pertaining to the state of education and Scriptural fluency among the Catholic clergy. The sentiment also spoke to the expansion of biblical literacy and engagement by those in the Bible study groups proliferating around Zurich. Participants in these Bible groups "became proselytizers for increasingly bold reform projects" for Zwingli.[36] These gospel partners helped extend and multiply the Reformer's ministry at Zurich. The Swiss preacher was not alone in his criticisms of Rome, nor was he solely responsible for the Zurich church's reformation. Now a chorus of voices began crying out for change. However, a choir without a director can quickly become a catastrophe. As we will soon see, that became the unintended consequence of these groups.

A HELPMEET IN THE GOSPEL

Sometime in 1522, Zwingli married Anna Reinhart, making him one of the first Reformers to take a bride. While historians have a clearer picture of the marital relationship between Luther and his wife, Katharina von Bora, Zwingli's life with Anna remains veiled. A dearth of sources, likely stemming from the fact that Zwingli was more reserved than Luther on personal matters, limits our understanding. Though a single letter to his beloved Anna is all that remains, evidence of her important participation in Zwingli's reformation efforts can be pieced together. The portrait that emerges suggest her vital role in supporting and walking alongside Zwingli in his ministry, no matter the obstacles faced.

Upon his arrival in Zurich, Zwingli encountered an academically gifted boy, Gerold, who the Reformer began tutoring. Gerold was Anna's son from a previous marriage. She was abruptly widowed when her first husband died in 1517 from the enduring illnesses of war. Anna's son quickly became a point of interest for Zwingli, given the youth's intellectual acumen. The Reformer's affinity for Gerold became so strong that he dedicated a 1523 publication to him.[37] That student-mentor relationship brought Anna into Zwingli's life, and a romantic relationship blossomed. Nearly every historical accounting of Anna cites her stunning beauty. Some claim this was the reason behind Zwingli's infatuation with her. He once spoke of a charitable initiative, citing her financial instability and that of her children "as the reason I also married her."[38] However, Anna's Christian piety and modesty, paired with her attentiveness to his sermons, likely also caught Zwingli's affections as much as her beauty did his eye.[39] That she helped nurse him to health during his battle with plague in 1519 also likely helped kindle their affections for one another. Her educated status, which later proved invaluable for Zwingli's work, undoubtedly also later confirmed the wisdom of this romantic match.[40]

Little is known of their courtship, but a secret marriage certainly occurred by 1522, given Oswald Myconius's salutation "Best wishes to your wife" in a letter from July of that year.[41] The pair delayed their public ceremony, which effectively legalized clerical marriage for Zurich, until April 2, 1524.[42] The Reformation at Zurich had not progressed enough to enact such a bold move. Clergy were still forbidden to marry at this time. Therefore, Huldrych and Anna kept their nuptials initially hidden to avoid inciting scandal. Only a few close friends first knew of their marriage. Nevertheless, due to the typical gossip associated with such liaisons, their nuptials likely became "the worst-kept secret in the city."[43] This illicit union provided the immediate context within which Zwingli's summer 1522 writings about clerical marriage are to be read and understood.[44] Martin Bucer even playfully confessed later to Zwingli, "I never believed you were unmarried," given the tone of his desire for marriage in the 1522 tract.[45] Zwingli could not hide his passion about marriage. His own experience dictated his matrimonial argumentation.

Anna was the primary overseer of the Zwingli home. This meant serving as a supportive and caring wife, while also being a mother to the brood of children in their blended family.[46] Anna's domestic care freed her husband for the daunting work of dispensing his pastoral duties and reforming the Zurich church. As the lone surviving letter between the two reveals, this meant Anna was even left alone to welcome the birth of their child in January 1528 while her husband was dispatched to neighboring Bern. Still, to consider Anna, known affectionately to Zwingli as "his dearest housewife," as one resigned exclusively to the affairs of the home would be a mistake.[47] As she helped shape an early model of the pastor's wife, a deep immersion into her husband's ministerial work became a defining characteristic.

Much like Katie at Wittenberg, Anna served as hostess to religious refugees and visitors to Zurich. She always welcomed these sojourning parties into the Zwingli home. In her husband's absence, Anna provided them access to the intriguing and hopeful world of the Reformation. Her tangible participation in the movement through her marriage, alongside her acumen for theology, proved helpful in these encounters. She also took it upon herself to care for the sick and downtrodden of society. Anna's melding of ethics and predestination, which her husband spoke so passionately about from the pulpit and in print, inspired her to serve as God's vessel to those in need.[48] Anna regularly attended to Zurich's needy, often to her own neglect. Her dedication to service was so commonplace that she became known as "the apostolic Dorcas," a reference to the charitable servant Tabitha from Acts 9.[49]

Perhaps the most intimate and stirring picture of Anna's participation in her husband's ministry related to their shared time together in the Bible. It was a common occurrence for the Zwingli family to gather in the evenings around Scripture. These times became further enriched in 1525 when Zwingli began translating the Bible into their native Swiss German tongue. Each evening, Huldrych and Anna sat together in their home as she perused the daily proofs of her husband's Bible translation work from that day. The invitation from her husband to share in this important work spoke volumes about his trust in and appreciation for Anna. It also suggests her influence in the shaping of the final text. One can imagine the two sitting in their parlor discussing, perhaps even debating, the editorial selection of specific Swiss German terms to best capture the heart of what God conveyed through the biblical text. The visually stunning Zurich Bible of 1531, printed by Christoph Froschauer and replete with Hans Holbein woodcuts, has their impressions all over it.[50] After completing the work, Huldrych gifted Anna a copy of this Bible, which she worked diligently to make accessible to others in the community.

Still, we must not overly romanticize this relationship. The Zwingli marriage undoubtedly looked more like a typical relationship from the early modern period and not like those imagined today by Hollywood. For instance, the Reformer did not even tell his wife about his departure for the Marburg Colloquy in 1529.[51] She also shared the negative fallout from her husband's reforming work. An evening stoning of the Zwingli home in August 1525 was particularly traumatizing to the family. So common spousal pains and frustrations are to be assumed. Still, whether it was behind the scenes guiding her family in the faith, on the streets of Zurich caring for the poor and downtrodden, or sharing in the painstaking task of translating the Bible, Anna proved to be more than just a spouse to her husband. She was an important gospel partner, a strengthening and steadying influence upon him during a turbulent season of ministry at Zurich. In Anna, Zwingli found the priceless wife that King Solomon spoke about in Proverbs. Sadly, of course, this beloved bride had to pick up the devastating pieces of their family once her husband and son were struck down at Kappel in 1531. There was no Hollywood ending for this couple, only a widow's grief, which ultimately bore Anna the name "The Weeping Mother of the Reformation."

PAINFUL BETRAYAL

At the close of July 1523, Zwingli spoke optimistically about the state of the Reformation at Zurich. In the cover letter to his printed sermon "Divine and Human Righteousness," the preacher declared, "For a great deal of friendship and love grows daily among the believers; God be praised. And no one undertakes anything except it be at the bidding of the magistrates and their decision."[52] The steady promotion of Scripture, coupled with carefully measured reforms, was transforming the community. The gospel saturated the community, and people's love for one another was the net result. However, as Zwingli also recounted, there remained "quite a few rebellious spirits who look to other teachings rather than the teaching of Christ; these we must tolerate until God himself chastises them."[53] That tolerance, though driven by Zwingli's pastoral sensibilities, soon changed. What the preacher could not see in July 1523 was that a dissent movement was welling up in his own reformation camp. Despite his words about patient tolerance, both he and the magistrates were about to take judgment into their own hands.

Though Zwingli's model of gospel community helped secure him reformation gains, a flaw in his plan surfaced when figures like Conrad Grebel, Felix Manz, and Simon Stumpf began using this collaborative network to promote radical agendas. Once that shift took place, according to Zwingli, the Radicals departed from the larger hermeneutical community. In truth, they moved away from reading the Bible as Zwingli did. Earlier, in 1522, the Zurich Reformer had said to the Bishop of Constance, "The laity [at Zurich] in general are so well versed in the gospel that they will not listen to any other teaching."[54] Just over a year later, some of these same once-lauded people now refused to listen to Zwingli's instruction from the Bible.

The division between these two camps surfaced at the Second Zurich Disputation in October 1523. The magistrates called for this public debate amid the violent iconoclasm discussed in Chapter 2. The impatience of some who believed Zwingli's reforms were moving too slowly incited discord from the outset of the discussion. But beyond the pace of reform, a more foundational issue threatened to derail the Zurich Reformation into chaos. During discussions about the Roman Mass, Zwingli declared, "My Lords [the Zurich Council] will decide how the Mass should be properly observed in the future."[55] That one statement incensed the Reformer's students. Simon Stumpf immediately snapped, "Master Huldrych!

You have no authority to place the decision in my lords' hands, for the decision is already made: the Spirit of God decides."[56] Zwingli affirmed Stumpf's words and stressed that he too would oppose the magistrates if they detoured from Scriptural instruction. But he still left the final decision on when and how to make biblically prescribed modifications to the Mass in the hands of the Zurich Council. This decision was based on Zwingli's theocratic convictions, pastoral sensibilities regarding those steeped in Catholic beliefs, and enduring desire to maintain an ordered Reformation. But to his students, this concession reeked of compromise and betrayal. Two months later, Grebel called Zwingli's mediating path "diabolical," while also stressing that his now former master was not acting "according to the duty of a shepherd."[57] The two parties shared a commitment to *sola Scriptura*. So there was a shared consensus that the Bible must determine all enacted reforms. However, Zwingli's decision to relegate the final say to the Zurich Council on the enactment of changes was a bridge too far for the Radicals.

Over the next year, the Grebel group pressed for reforms. While their desire to abolish the Mass persisted, hope for even greater changes followed. The establishment of a different kind of church was soon in view. Zwingli later paraphrased the group's plan in December 1523: "According to the Acts of the Apostles those who had believed separated from the others, and then it happened that as others came to believe, they joined those who were now a new church. This is what we must do."[58] Through correspondence with Thomas Müntzer and Andreas Karlstadt, the group began envisioning the gathering of a regenerate body with believers' baptism as its gateway.

Zwingli's territorial church convictions drove his exegesis of Scripture. On the other hand, a lens of political impotence and oppression now increasingly dictated the Radicals' reading of the Bible.[59] And as Zwingli and the magistrates opposed the Radicals' new ecclesiological vision, the more their plan appeared correct, and their former master seemed to be an apostate of the faith. The Radicals believed that the Zurich church's Constantinian ecclesiology mistakenly conflated Christ's eternal Kingdom with a temporal imperial one.[60] The group's failure as magisterial Reformers pushed them to the margins of society. Once persecution ensued, a separatism developed wherein they believed the church and the world were mutually exclusive groups that were not to be intermingled. Their reintroduction of a believers' baptism on January 21, 1525, became the climactic outworking of those beliefs.[61]

Weeks before this baptism, Zwingli made one final appeal, imploring his students to detour from what he believed was a dangerous path.[62] Their establishment of a believers' church in January changed his posture toward them. Writing to Vadian months later, Zwingli called the group "enemies of the gospel," stressing that his previous debates with them "were child's play" compared with the present conditions.[63] By summer 1525, Zwingli's familiarity with Anabaptism amplified his concerns about the movement. In his work *Baptism, Re-Baptism, and Child Baptism*, he addressed "the storm" of Anabaptism that had befallen the St. Gallen community.[64] The Zurich Reformer warned that the Radicals' innovative baptism had an insidious end: to "establish a new church, that is, a community or congregation, a church that would be without sin."[65] Such a church seemed unimaginable to Zwingli, especially given his commitments to the *corpus Christianum* and a Reformed reading of Scripture. Even more, he believed such gatherings were "destroying the Christian peace for the sake of the outward sign of the Lord."[66] Ecclesiastical concerns eventually begat legislative actions. On March 7, 1526, citing Conrad Grebel, Georg Blaurock, and Felix Manz by name, the Reformer worked with the Zurich Council to legally make rebaptism a capital crime.[67] In a letter penned that day to Vadian, he declared, "Patience has endured enough" on the matter. He also said of future infractions, "Whoever is baptized hereafter will be submerged permanently."[68] The chilling nature of the Council's legal decision was only overshadowed by Zwingli's pejorative threat of a second baptism.

Losing his own students to Anabaptism was painful and precipitated a lingering anger in the Reformer toward the group. Later, knowing that Grebel had died from plague, Zwingli callously celebrated that the Radical "doubtlessly burns among the shades [of hell] as much as he froze here through his Anabaptist washings."[69] When describing his ongoing polemic against them, the Reformer even seasoned his posthumous vitriol for the

Anabaptist Radicals with humor, stating, "It seems funny to strive with ghosts."[70] After the leaders of the movement died, Zwingli seemed haunted as much as he was angered by what he perceived to be their betrayal.[71]

Zwingli's animus toward the movement was more than just a man smarting from a loss of friendships. It was rooted in his theology. Their radical beliefs directly threatened his vision for the Zurich Reformation. In October 1524, Martin Bucer, whose Free Imperial City of Strasbourg was awash with Anabaptists and radicals, implored Zwingli to develop a theological justification for infant baptism from the Scriptures.[72] By December 1524 Zwingli had his answer. In his treatise, *Those Who Give Cause for Rebellion*, the reformer looked to the Old Testament for his defense of infant baptism based on patterns of worship for Israel.[73] The preacher also long held to an Augustinian interpretation of the parable of the wheat and tares, stating in a 1524 letter to Jerome Emser, "You see that in the Old Testament as well as in the New the church was composed of the faithful and of those who were unfaithful but pretended [to have] faith."[74] The Reformer's commitment to a territorial church made the Anabaptists' position look like an over-realized ecclesiology. Once Zwingli became aware of the codification of their separatism in the 1527 *Schleitheim Confession*, this belief became further entrenched in the Reformer's thinking.[75] From his perspective, their believers' church appeared presumptuous. Such an assembly was impossible prior to the parousia. Perhaps more dangerously, their beliefs about baptism looked to him like a works-based righteousness. He reasoned, "If it is our choice or power to walk in the resurrection of Christ, or to be buried with Him in death ... then Christ spoke falsely the word, 'No one can come to me except the Father who sent Me to draw him.' "[76] Anabaptism cut against the Reformer's convictions about divine providence and appeared to place eternal decisions into human hands.

The Anabaptists' emphasis on the faith of an individual deviated from Zwingli's corporate understanding of the church, while it also threatened societal cohesion. These realities are why he took issue with the final two articles of the *Schleitheim Confession*, which addressed the sword and oath taking. The Anabaptists' non-resistance (often framed as pacifism) and their refusal to take an oath of allegiance ripped at the fabric of community.

Zwingli believed that "through many schemes they [the Anabaptists] assail the public peace."[77] He perceived Anabaptist separatism to be more than merely bad theology. It left Zurich vulnerable to foreign invasion, while also disintegrating the community's identity as a Christian people. These beliefs provide the contextual frame for Zwingli's cold-hearted disposition toward his former gospel partners, like Grebel and Manz.

THE ZURICH *PROPHEZEI*

In the wake of the Anabaptist controversy, Zwingli purposefully detoured his preaching away from the New Testament toward the Old Testament in 1525.[78] While the former had been especially useful in his battle with Rome, the Anabaptists posed a different challenge. A return to the Hebrew Scriptures allowed him to highlight the continuity he believed existed between Israel and Zurich via a covenantal hermeneutic. To bolster this exegetical work, Zwingli helped found the Zurich *Prophezei* in June 1525 based on 1 Corinthians 14.

Lest we be misguided by this verbiage, it is important to understand how the Reformer used the term "prophecy" as a qualifier. Prophecy did not refer to the forthtelling of future events. Rather, Zwingli connected prophecy to the Hebrew prophets' task of divine truth telling. To be a prophet was to be a faithful interpreter of the Bible. Accordingly, the *Prophezei*, also known as the Zurich Lection, was an assembled body that interpreted the Bible from the original Hebrew for the purpose of providing sound exegesis for the community.[79] The Radicals' misunderstanding and misapplication of the biblical text proved both dangerous and seditious. Therefore, Zwingli gathered a group of thinkers, equipped with the proper tools, to help the Zurich church remain faithful to Scripture through their exegesis.

The prayer offered at the inaugural session of the *Prophezei* provides an important window into the hope for this group:

> Almighty, eternal, and merciful God, whose word is a lamp to our feet and a light to our path [Psalm 119:105], open and enlighten our minds, that we may understand your secrets in a pure and holy

> way, and through that, which we have rightly understood, be transformed, that we may in no way displease your majesty, through Christ Jesus our Lord. Amen.[80]

One can see the importance of the Bible for this group. Scripture was the normative means through which one could know and rightly relate to God. It was also the ultimate authority for determining sound doctrine and church practice. Scripture divided truth from falsehood for a people desperate to maintain doctrinal fidelity. The group believed that intellectual exercises of the mind were the pathway toward knowing God in a meaningful way. Their commitment to humanism was unmistakably imbedded into its methodology. The secret truths of God were also only uncovered as the Lord quickened them to such knowledge through the revelation of Scripture. Therefore, a posture of humility and dependence upon God's revelation like that formerly expressed in Zwingli's "On the Clarity and Certainty of the Word of God" embodied the group.[81] And as any humanist might do, they linked that knowledge with the transformation of the person in both word and deed. Knowing truth ushered in a distinct way of living as a Christian.

Former priests, biblical scholars, and young humanists eager to drink directly from the Bible in the original languages comprised most of the school's participants. These men assembled for two-hour sessions of study in the chancel of the Grossmunster and Fraumunster churches five days a week. The public nature of the school's venue also accommodated inquisitive layfolk, many of whom watched these sessions in wonder. The meetings were structured liturgically, with opening and closing prayers buttressing Scripture readings and an extended time of communal study. The initial Bible reading was in Latin, the more familiar language of Scripture and theology at the time. The same text was subsequently recited in the original Hebrew, followed by the Greek version from the Septuagint. Throughout the session, participants offered explanation and commentary on the text in question. This work was so tightly connected with Scripture it eventually resulted in the publication of a series of biblical commentaries and the 1531 Zurich Bible.[82]

Many of Zwingli's close gospel partners shared in his work through the *Prophezei.* Jakob Ceporin, the famed Hebraist and former student of Johannes Reuchlin, provided the school's opening lecture, which focused on Genesis 1.[83] Zwingli typically followed these Hebrew studies with commentary from the accompanying Greek translations. Leo Jud often completed the day's work by sermonizing the school's doctrinal discoveries into an instructive summary offered in the native Swiss German vernacular. These sermons focused on the practical, contemporary application of the text for the common people. Of course, the work of the *Prophezei* was not strictly defined by its language work. Each person present had ample opportunity to speak, though Zwingli dominated much of what the group concluded. Much like a rug that ties a room together, Zwingli's strong personality helped organize and connect an otherwise eclectic group of scholars. As the Word washed over these men, the Hebrew and Greek studies were philologically focused. The group believed that biblical terms and their accompanying meanings were greatly valuable. Hence, they gave special attention to both. God had inspired the words of Scripture. Therefore, each had meaning that these exegetes needed to mine for theological truth.

Intellectual stimulation alone did not drive these hermeneutical exercises. Nor were they done to satiate the theological curiosity of Zwingli and his compatriots. Rather, this communal interpretation of Scripture had a practical end in sight. The *Prophezei* shaped the sermons that would later be offered from pulpits throughout the community. The school's exegetical work provided a bountiful harvest of gospel preaching intended to feed the spiritually malnourished community.[84] The link between communal exegesis and a unified voice in proclaiming this truth throughout the Zurich State was crucial here. Not only did the *Prophezei* allow Zwingli to uphold his belief in a hermeneutical community of exegetes, which he once championed, but it simultaneously allowed him to reign in rogue Scripture readings, like those of the Anabaptists.[85] Therefore, the timing of this school's founding in 1525 could not have been more important. Their collective instruction came at a crucial moment in the Zurich Reformation, as Zwingli and his fellow Reformers charted a new ecclesial course between what they believed were the dangerous shorelines of Roman Catholicism and radical Anabaptism.

This interpretive school was not merely a medium for doing communal theology and a clever mechanism to shape pulpit proclamation. It was also a strategic means of facilitating a church-state alliance that sought to advance the Reformation without devolving the community into chaos. The instructing prophets guided the other Zurich ministers' biblical exegesis, making certain that the teachings found in the local parishes never seditiously worked against the State magistrates. This model empowered the Zurich Council to assert political independence from Rome, while it also allowed leading Reformers, like Zwingli, to restrain religious radicalism.[86] Gospel partnerships were important not only in the shaping of church reforms, but also in sustaining Reformation viability. Such a balance was always a tenuous reality facing those who sought to see ecclesial change during the early sixteenth century.

In a work published the same month of the school's founding, Zwingli reiterated the above ideas: "In short, it is the primary task of a prophet that he pluck up, tear down and destroy whatever is set up against God and that he build and plant, on the other hand, what God desires."[87] Using the plumb line of Scripture properly interpreted in community, the Zurich preachers were to faithfully guide the Swiss church toward spiritual health and ecclesiastical renewal. The pastors of Zurich spoke prophetically to the church's ills, while simultaneously working through specific reforms to align their parishes with the patterns prescribed in the Bible. Such work required care and a tempered, deft hand. Zwingli's agrarian illustration highlighted the need for the weeds of error to be removed while not upsetting the larger ecclesial ecosystem during seasons of sowing and reaping. According to the Reformer, the Catholics obstinately refused to address the weeds. The Anabaptists, on the other hand, were carelessly destroying the good harvest through their overreaching reforms. Zwingli believed the *Prophezei* would help the Swiss church avoid both errors.

A TRUE SON IN THE FAITH

Sometime in 1521, Heinrich Bullinger met Zwingli on a trip to Zurich.[88] At the time, Bullinger was a young enthusiastic humanist already imbibing Reformation ideas through the writings of Erasmus, Luther, and Melanchthon. By 1523, Bullinger returned from Germany to the Swiss Confederation, having accepted a teaching post at the newly founded Cistercian monastery at Kappel. Zwingli and Bullinger's shared affinity for humanism, their desire to reform the Swiss church according to the patterns of Scripture, and the close geographic proximity of Kappel to Zurich quickly drew them together. A burgeoning partnership in the gospel soon emerged. The location of Bullinger's monastery at Kappel, which is situated a short walk from the sprawling open field where Zwingli would eventually die a decade after their first meeting, foreshadowed a complex and enduring connection between the two.

From the outset of their relationship, shared interests in music, family, community life, and care for religious refugees were but a few of the things that helped solidify their bond with one another. Yet more than anything, it was their unwavering commitment to the gospel and a shared desire to see it rightly preached to their Swiss compatriots that became the cornerstone of their partnership. All their ministerial work and reformation efforts flowed from that shared belief.

Guided by their love for Scripture and a hope to see religious change, the two men supported each other in their reformation work at Kappel and Zurich. Correspondence between the two allowed them to explore how a pathway toward their unique visions for the Swiss church might be realized. Here, they were able to share ministerial successes and frustrations with one another. Words of encouragement became a soothing balm amid the regular hardships of promoting the Reformation. Given this close gospel partnership, it was not surprising that both saw the Mass abolished in their respective locales in 1525. It seems their work was too intertwined for their gospel harvests to arrive at different seasons. Their labors also did not stop at the boundaries of their own ministerial fields. Both men labored alongside each other to help neighboring states like Bern introduce the Reformation in the 1520s and 1530s. The hope of the gospel was not to be confined by political boundaries, hence their shared work outside of the Zurich State.

Although Zwingli was the older brother in the faith, the younger Bullinger helped shape and support his friend's Reformation at Zurich. One of Bullinger's greatest influences on Zwingli came through their dealings with the Anabaptist problem of the mid-1520s. In fact, the Zurich preacher purposefully solicited Bullinger's help. When the opposition group threatened to derail Zwingli's Reformation, Bullinger stood alongside his friend and explored ways to rebut radicalism. Bullinger recounted his presence with Zwingli as a co-debater at each of the three disputations held with the Anabaptists at Zurich in January 1525, which proved to be a crucial moment for the Swiss Reformation.[89] Moreover, Zwingli's founding of the *Prophezei* in 1525, which was aimed in part at rebutting the Anabaptists' radical biblical interpretations, was based on Bullinger's earlier pedagogical model of teaching at Kappel.[90] And as alluded to earlier, Bullinger was present when Zwingli oversaw the execution of the Anabaptist leader Felix Manz in 1527. Through it all, Bullinger stood alongside Zwingli, supporting him in word and deed.

More than just a common enemy engendered a close relationship between the two. Their shared commitment to a developing flavor of Reformed theology facilitated another point of connection between them. As a letter penned by Bullinger in 1525 reveals, the two Reformers shared nearly identical commitments to a covenantal link between the Old and New Testaments, which not only shaped their theological frames but also served as one of their primary arguments against the Anabaptists.[91] The relationship between the old and new covenants as a foundational aspect of God's redemptive work in history was crucial here.[92] This helps explain why Bullinger and Zwingli considered the Anabaptists' synergistic view of salvation a threat to the Swiss church and perceivably more akin to Rome's beliefs. In this regard, each man sharpened the other as they developed their Reformed theologies in concert with one another.

One factor that made Zwingli's relationship with Bullinger fascinating and proved beneficial to the Swiss Reformation over time was their contrasting personas. Zwingli was a firebrand, a man whose life and ministry was surrounded by conflict and volatility.[93] In contrast, Bullinger was a mediating figure whose irenic voice and unifying disposition brought stability and constancy to the Zurich church after decades of religious unrest. Where Zwingli was unyielding, intolerant, and abrasive, Bullinger was conciliatory and temperate, always seeking to unite rather than divide. These contrasting personalities help make Bullinger more desirable to our modern sensibilities, which celebrate diversity, accommodation, and ecumenicism.[94]

The complementary nature of their personalities proved invaluable after the devastating loss of Zwingli in 1531. Reeling in defeat, the Zurich church benefitted from a peaceable shepherd, not an impassioned prophet, to guide them through a season of loss and confusion. Following the Second Kappel War, Bullinger was left to pick up the pieces of their shared work. The Zurich prophet was now gone, and all that the two Reformers had labored toward stood on the precipice of ruin. On December 9, 1531, Bullinger officially succeeded his mentor and friend as the chief priest at the Grossmunster. From that prestigious post, Bullinger continued Zwingli's work overseeing the affairs of the Zurich church. However, because of the long shadow cast by the Kappel disaster, Bullinger did so without the political influence of his mentor on the affairs of the State.[95] According to the Council, the Zurich preachers, including Bullinger, were to be "peaceably and generally oriented toward peace and quiet," and were not to "meddle in any secular matters."[96] The trauma of Zwingli's leadership style, previous interactions with the civil authorities, and the Reformer's death at Kappel demanded as much.

What at first glance might appear to have been a personal limitation may have benefited Bullinger, as he spent the next forty-four years with his attention focused on steadying the Zurich church. That Bullinger continued to promote many of Zwingli's convictions during those years, yet with little mention of his former mentor, remains a fascinating part of this drama. The scandalous nature of Zwingli's death demanded such silence. Nevertheless, the link between the two Reformers was so profound that, as one historian has argued, through Bullinger "many had believed that Zwingli had risen like a phoenix."[97] Zwingli's theological fingerprints can also be found scattered throughout Bullinger's writings, including his *Second Helvetic Confession* of 1566, which was written some three-plus decades after the Swiss Reformer's sudden death.[98] The two men were too theologically and personally linked for this to be otherwise.

Bullinger not only mediated Zwingli's Reformed theology to future generations, but he also helped shape the memory of his beloved friend and mentor to the Swiss people. This was especially true when it came time to rebut the incessant accusations of heresy related to Zwingli's view of the Lord's Supper. Despite the dangers of being associated with a man thought by many to be a failed prophet, Bullinger chose to defend Zwingli when he believed the time was right. That Zwingli's memorialism was not formally deemed a heresy in the Confederation was, in part, due to Bullinger's deft ability to retain aspects of his mentor's theology without the baggage of the Zurich preacher's political and religious failings. In this sense Bullinger never betrayed his beloved friend and gospel partner. Through Bullinger, Zwingli continued to speak to his Swiss compatriots well after his death in 1531.

CONCLUSION

The Zwingli statue that resides on the south side of the Water Church within eyesight of where Manz was executed presents the preacher standing alone. But it would be a mistake to envision the Reformer working in isolation at Zurich. From the very outset of his arrival at the Grossmunster, Zwingli built his ministry around gospel partners. He held an important and influential position as the people's preacher. He also considered himself a unique prophetic voice for the Zurich church. Yet he never believed himself to be the lone voice drawing the Swiss people back to Christ and purer forms of worship. That was a task too large for any one person. The success or failure of his ministry at Zurich would depend on those around him. However, the invitation for others to share in his reformation nearly unraveled all the gospel work he accomplished at Zurich.

In his 1522 sermon "On the Clarity and Certainty of the Word of God," Zwingli confidently declared, "In his Word we can never go astray. We can never be deluded or confounded or destroyed in his Word."[99] The

Reformer believed the Bible would guide the Zurich community toward salvation and true religion. This belief compelled him to place the sacred Scriptures at the center of a textual community at Zurich. Still, these words present a stark contrast to the events surrounding Felix Manz's execution. The rise of Anabaptism, which was born of a strict obedience to the same Bible that Zwingli had taught Manz and others to read, challenged the preacher's theological assumptions.

What made the battle with the Anabaptists so challenging was not just the fact that Zwingli's spiritual children in the faith led the movement. The controversy was exacerbated by the fact that the Bible served as the catalyst to their division. Leo Jud elaborated on this challenge, stating, "The fight is fiercer and the war far more difficult with these people [the Anabaptists] who eclipse the darkness by the light of the Word itself."[100] It was one thing to battle the extrabiblical traditions of Catholicism but quite another to defend against the Anabaptists' text-based biblicism. Ironically, as one historian notes, "The watchword of *sola Scriptura* thus not only united the Reformation's supporters ... it divided them as well."[101] The shared gospel partnership once enjoyed became a curse and challenge to Zwingli's work at Zurich.

Chapter 6

The Broken Body of Christ

"To eat the body of Christ spiritually is nothing else than to trust in spirit and with one's heart upon the mercy and goodness of God through Christ, that is, to be sure with unshakeable faith that God is going to give us pardon for our sins and the joy of everlasting blessedness on account of His Son, who was made wholly ours, offered for us, and reconciled the divine righteousness to us."[1]

NESTLED IN THE HEART OF Hesse, Germany, is the stunning town of Marburg. The word "Marburg" means "frontier fortress." Such a name is an apt designation for a place anchored by an imposing castle that has served as protector to the town since its construction in the eleventh century. For those fortunate enough to visit the castle, a Great Hall can be found tucked deep within the bowels of the impressive building. The space retains its original, fantastic gothic architecture, befitting the room's vintage. This large banquet room is a long rectangular hall buttressed by stone gothic columns staggered throughout the center of the room that carry the weight of the roof. A series of gothic windows are scattered throughout, allowing natural light to create a web of contrasting light and shadows on the stone floor during the day. Today the room serves as a venue for small cultural events hosted by the town. One might catch a Shakespeare play or enjoy a cantata by the famed German composer J.S. Bach at the site. Yet if this room were able to speak, it could also tell a story of heartache from the Reformation era, the effects of which still cast a long shadow on Christianity today.

In fall 1529, several of the most prominent Reformers of the sixteenth century came to Marburg. Figures like Martin Luther, Philipp Melanchthon, Martin Bucer, and Johannes Oecolampadius all came to the castle. Zwingli also made the journey from Zurich. These Reformers did not come to explore the wondrous sites of Marburg or to experience the town's cultural offerings. They came for a discussion over doctrine, a discourse made more daunting given the volatility of the Reformation in the late 1520s. The Landgrave, Philip of Hesse, invited these Reformers to Marburg, hoping that a theological colloquy might help facilitate a Protestant accord. Given Roman Catholicism's strong responses to the Reformation in the 1520s, alongside increasing concerns related to westward-sweeping Muslim advances, Philip longed for the Protestants "to live in Christian agreement and harmony."[2] Religious unity was thought by many, like Philip, to be a political necessity for the Reformation to remain viable.

August Noack later portrayed this gathering at Marburg in a famous nineteenth-century oil painting. In his depiction, a large table resides in the middle of the Great Hall at the Marburg Castle. The venue is framed by numerous observers, witnesses to the event. Some are standing in the back of the room in conversation with one another, presumably discussing the veracity of the various arguments being offered. Other figures are situated closer to the table. A few of those are seated, casually leaning back as passive observers to this Protestant showdown. Others are anxiously leaning forward, hanging on every contested word. At the center of the table rests a gold cross. This icon symbolized Jesus Christ, the one who served not only as the Messiah who unified those present but also as the very person dividing these same Reformers. Philipp Melanchthon and Martin Bucer converse with one another in the background. Bucer is seated, leaning in toward the German Reformer, his hand gesturing to provide further explanation for his theological argument. Melanchthon sits stoic, his hand comfortably resting on a Bible. This positioning highlights the foundation of the Reformer's beliefs and his trust in God's Holy Word. It also implies that he was unconvinced by Bucer's musings. Zwingli and Luther are center stage in the painting, standing at the head of the table debating each other. As the preceding months had demonstrated, these two men served as arguably the loudest and most dominant voices in the Eucharistic controversy that had surfaced. So, Noack's decision to portray them as the focal point of his painting was appropriate. The placement of these two also postulated a historical premise regarding Protestant unity: success or failure would be determined, in large part, based upon their interactions with one another.

Despite admirable hopes for a Protestant alliance, the colloquy proved doomed from the start. No accord was reached at Marburg. Christ's body, the church, would remain broken going forward. However, it would be a mistake to assume that Marburg caused the Protestant fracture that characterized much of the Reformation era. In truth, "the Reformation had never enjoyed an arcadian age of peace and unity," as some mistakenly assume.[3] The church had been divided for centuries, going back to the medieval period.[4] Marburg did not so much mark the genesis of Protestant schism as it embodied and illustrated it. Regarding Huldrych Zwingli, the proceedings from Marburg unveiled his mature Eucharistic theology. These were convictions developed and forged amid a parade of controversies that plagued his ministry at Zurich. They were also ecclesiological beliefs promoted while trying to faithfully navigate the Zurich church toward what he saw as the biblical model for Christ's bride outlined in Scripture. In the end, Zwingli's beliefs precluded agreement with the Wittenbergers. However, this was considered a Eucharistic war worth waging. Not only his own personal beliefs but the very liturgy and practices of the Zurich church were at stake.

EARLY TEACHINGS AND ALLUSIONS

Luther deemed Zwingli's position on the Supper a "poison" as early as November 1524.[5] Although we have no extant writings by Zwingli offering specific instructions to his Zurich flock regarding the Lord's Supper until 1523, several of his preceding publications offer veiled references to convictions that form the basis for his later Eucharistic thinking. One of the earliest such accounts was from his 1522 sermon defending the broken Lenten fast outlined in Chapter 3. While the sermon is not directly focused on the Eucharist, Zwingli adamantly believed that piety was not found through external means, specifically the consumption of foods. Instead, referencing Hebrews 13, the Reformer proclaimed, "The heart is established with grace, not with meats, which have not been useful to them."[6] The humanistic focus on the internal aspect of a person's renewal guided Zwingli's exegesis. Spiritual rebirth for those at Zurich would be based solely on God's initiative and according to His divine power. Only an inner renewal by God's Spirit, not external religious actions or rites undertaken by human hands, could change a person.

Zwingli wanted his Zurich flock to understand that God's grace was not appropriated through a meal, sacramental or otherwise. God firmly established salvation in and through Christ. Accordingly, the internal reality of this new life offered a genuine consolation to the true believer.[7] But the realization of this truth came as a work of God, not via eating or any other human action. According to Zwingli, not only "shall no one reject or consider you [the Zurich people] good on account of any food or holyday," but all festival days were "only symbolic of a Christian holiday."[8] The preacher wanted the Zurich church to understand that feast days were not holy in and of themselves. Such days were mere symbols, public events and actions employed to connote a deeper spiritual reality for the Swiss community. From the outset, the idea of symbolism was embedded in Zwingli's understanding of Christian rites. This belief formed much of the theological basis for the Reformer's later positions on the Supper.

The Christological foundation undergirding Zwingli's Eucharistic views was also well established in this sermon. The preacher rebutted the prevailing assumption by many that certain foods were either pure or unclean depending on unique seasons in the church's liturgical calendar. He maintained a similar line of reasoning in relation to God Himself. The Reformer rejected the notion that anything in our world, or even the Divine nature itself, could shift in essence or ontology. A philosophical constancy of property anchored his theology on this point and subsequently shaped his understanding of the incarnate Lord Jesus. Using Matthew 24:23 to support his argument, the Reformer contended, "The meaning [of the Matthew text] is that God is not revealed more in one place than in another ... the false prophets say that."[9] This important truth related to God's presence, especially in the case of the Incarnate Jesus, situating Him in one geographic locale at any one time according to His humanity. This idea was a key theological premise that later pushed Zwingli to see Jesus seated at the right hand of the Father rather than corporeally present in the elements. That Christ also linked false prophets with signs and wonders undoubtedly colored his reflections on Rome's doctrine of transubstantiation as well.

This same conviction regarding ontological constancy also applied to God's character. Regarding ostensibly contrasting human emotions, like grace and anger, Zwingli stressed that God holds both equally in balance as a part of His nature. This meant that "God is not revealed as merciful or angry more at one time than another but is like these at all times."[10] God balances both attributes equally and perfectly, never losing any portion of one attribute because of the other. This belief was applied to the incarnation. Thus, Zwingli's theology precluded the resurrected Jesus from being in multiple places at the same time because of the limiting attributes of Jesus's humanity. Zwingli refused to allow for God to waffle between emotions, as humans are prone to do. Christ was both the epitome and embodiment of seemingly contradictory attributes always and at the same time. He was fully human and fully divine.

The contours of Zwingli's early views on the Eucharist also surfaced in his 1522 work *Archeteles*. In that writing, Zwingli situated the Lord's Supper alongside other assumed Catholic norms, like clerical celibacy, as part of what needed to be redressed via the Reformation. The Supper, as he decried, had been "mutilated" by the Catholics through their failure to offer the elements in both kinds.[11] His fear here related to the papacy's decision to add restrictions to their ecclesiastical practices, thereby expanding upon the Bible's normative instruction. His rhetorical questions—"Are you mightier than God, that you have ventured to forbid what Christ left free? Or wiser than God, that you complete what God inadvertently left unfinished?"—struck at the heart of his concerns.[12] Late medieval Catholic traditions established Eucharistic practices, like the withholding of the cup from the laity, based upon an authority outside of Scripture. Perhaps more dangerously in Zwingli's mind, adding human laws to God's divine decrees was mistakenly based on an elevation of human revelation. Such a view contradicted *sola Scriptura* and was idolatrous at its core. This stern warning reminds us that Zwingli did not see his proposed liturgical reforms at Zurich, including those related to the Supper, as an innovation. Rather, he viewed them as necessary restorations of earlier biblical and historical patterns of the apostolic church.

Zwingli also took the opportunity in his *Archeteles* to teach the Swiss an important principle about the relationship between God and humanity. The Reformer believed human acts cannot bind or force God to respond in certain ways according to necessary causation. Prayers, for instance, were important to the relationship between Christians and God. However, human intercession was "not a sort of money by which the punishments due our sins could be bought off and as a means of imploring [or begging for] the mercy of God."[13] In his estimation, those who think God is compelled to act based upon human initiatives like prayer or the sale of grace via indulgences could not "be acquitted of blaspheme."[14] To assume any human action necessarily elicits a response from God was as foolish to Zwingli as the notion of the Eucharist functioning medicinally to sanitize the soul of the morally infirm.

There was only a veiled reference to the Lord's Supper in the text, which came via a quotation of Luke 22:19. But the theological point was clear. For Zwingli, the Lord moves and redeems solely at His own good pleasure. His divine hand cannot be coerced. These ideas uncover the Reformer's strong reliance on God's sovereignty, which we outlined in Chapter 4. This was the God Zwingli longed for his people to know and trust. These beliefs also rejected the Augustinian notion of the sacraments functioning *ex opere operato*, based on the act of observance, and detached from a divinely gifted faith. The importance of this rejection became evident as Zwingli began outlining his Eucharistic theology more explicitly.

ONE TRUE SACRIFICE

While shrouded references to the Eucharist were scattered throughout Zwingli's writings from 1522, the issue became more dominant by the time he was trying to stave off heresy charges in early 1523. Given that these discussions took place amid the early advances of the Reformation at Zurich, the Catholic Church's late medieval sacramental theology contextually framed Zwingli's Eucharistic thought during this period. As we saw in Chapter 2, one of the preacher's primary pastoral goals at this time was to reform the Zurich liturgy. Rejecting, as he saw it, the idea of Jesus being viewed as the object of a genuine, real sacrifice during the Mass was a crucial component of his proposed worship alteration. In Article Eighteen of his *Exposition of the Sixty-Seven Articles*, the Reformer contended, "Christ, who offered Himself up once as a sacrifice, is a perpetual and valid payment for the sin of all believers. From this it follows that the Mass is not a sacrifice, but a memorial of the sacrifice and a seal of the redemption which Christ has manifested to us."[15] For Zwingli, what Jesus accomplished at Golgotha could not be repeated. Christ's death on the cross was a one-time reality, thus, "a perfect sacrifice."[16] The elements were an important reminder of the covenantal bond already established between Christ and His bride, the church. There was no need to repeat the act in any real way, since the work had already accomplished the necessary reconciliation.

The Reformer wanted his audience at Zurich to understand that Jesus's once-for-all sacrifice was perdurable in its application. Jesus's death "did not need repeated like the sacrifices of the priests who preceded Him."[17] Citing Hebrews 9, Zwingli emphasized how Christ's perfect sacrifice provided a crucial "distinction between Him [Jesus] and the sacrifice[s] of the ancient priests."[18] Though his Reformed theology posited an enduring theological link between the contemporary Zurich church and the Israelites in the Old Testament, the unique person and work of Jesus also demanded a real sense of discontinuity with Israel's worship traditions. Christ's blood was more powerful than that of bulls and goats. Jesus's sacrifice was of an altogether different, more enduring kind.

Further pressing on this point, Zwingli looked back to the events at Calvary for instruction regarding contemporary church practices at Zurich. Rather than focusing on the connection between the elements and Jesus's body and blood, which was a hallmark of sacramental theology, Zwingli did something different. He harkened to patristic exegetical readings of Scripture that saw "this" in Jesus's institution of the Supper ("this do in remembrance of Me") as corresponding to incarnational action, not substance. Zwingli emphasized Jesus's pouring the wine and breaking the bread, not the actual corporeal blood and body supposedly present in the elements, as that which reminds the communicants of His sacrificial work.

This reading of the institution allowed the Reformer to criticize the common practice of withholding the cup from the laity. As Zwingli reasoned, the breaking of bread and the pouring of wine did not individually connect with Jesus's two separate, distinct accomplishments: his suffering and death. Rather, both sacrificial activities worked in an interconnected and symbiotic way. Together, the pouring and breaking memorialized or mnemonically recalled the already accomplished holistic work of Christ's sacrifice.[19] Jesus "demonstrated the efficacy of His suffering in two forms of the sacrament," not merely in one.[20] Referencing several New Testament texts that spoke of Jesus's shed blood, the preacher subsequently argued, "These words of Christ refer so clearly to his suffering that they become, as we tried to show, a surety, price and payment for our sin, sufficient and inexhaustible for all eternity."[21] Through Rome's misguided administration of the sacraments, Zwingli believed, Zurichers were being robbed of the power behind remembrance. More importantly, Christ's precious blood was mistakenly being forsaken, the power of life contained therein minimized and placed in the hands of priests.

In Zwingli's mind, the Catholic Eucharist created at least three problems for Zurich's worship. First, the practice of withholding the cup from the laity functionally truncated Christ's redemptive work by only allowing the communicants to focus attention on Jesus's suffering, not His death as well. Both aspects of Jesus's work were required for a full and robust picture of the gospel that he wanted the Zurich church to see and experience. Second, the clergy's exclusive access to the wine mistakenly bifurcated Christians into two distinct groups, the clergy and the laity, thereby restricting many from partaking of a full remembrance of Jesus's suffering for all His people. Last, by emphasizing the literal body and blood of Jesus via transubstantiation, Rome's practice minimized the enduring and limitless forgiveness that Jesus's life-giving sacrifice secured on the cross. If Jesus's blood needed to be repeatedly shed and his body continually broken during the Mass, did that not detract from Christ's unique work at Calvary? Each of these issues were a theological offense to the preacher, hence his work to reform Zurich's worship practices. What Zwingli understood to be the abomination of the Roman Eucharist had to be abandoned. But installing a new Mass at Zurich in 1525 soon forced the preacher to defend his Eucharistic theology against not just Catholic opponents but fellow Reformers as well.

THE PEOPLE'S PLEDGE TO REMEMBER

Zwingli believed the sacraments were "sacred and venerable rites, having been instituted and employed by Christ."[22] There was never a question about their inclusion in Zurich's liturgy since God divinely instituted these acts. But if the Zurich community was going to retain a purer form of worship, then they would have to recast these rites in specific forms that remained true to the biblical text. A few key questions rise to the fore of Zwingli's developing Eucharistic theology at this point. If the incarnate Christ was not being re-sacrificed in the Mass, and if God was not infusing a salvific grace into communicants through Jesus's corporeal body and blood, then what was this meal doing? To what end was it undertaken, and how was it of value to the Zurich community? For Zwingli, humanistic readings of Scripture that were rooted in word studies and supported by patristic convictions provided the answers to these queries. It is crucial to remember that the Reformer offered these Eucharistic expressions from the early 1520s, prior to becoming aware of a Protestant schism regarding the Supper. Thus, late medieval Catholic sacramentalism initially framed any sense of a supposed memorialism in Zwingli. In fact, the label "mere memorialist," which is often ascribed to the Reformer, is largely driven by

Lutheran polemics and does not adequately encapsulate his position, as we will soon see.[23]

From the outset, a simple, straightforward reading of Scripture through a humanistic lens guided Zwingli toward an early iteration of his Eucharistic views. Jesus exhorted his disciples in the upper room to reenact the Passover meal, as the synoptics recorded, "in remembrance." Zwingli subsequently reasoned, "Had Christ intended the food of His body and blood to be a sacrifice, He could have easily said, 'This offer up unto Me,' but He didn't."[24] Christ exhorted the disciples to remember, nothing more. Similarly, in 1 Corinthians 11, "Paul underscored the word remembrance," which precluded the meal from being perceived as a real sacrifice.[25] As one committed to mining every word of Scripture for meaning, Zwingli cared greatly about what the text said. What it did not say was equally important. He had no desire to become one "suffering from the disease of 'word-battling.' "[26] God spoke clearly on the matter, hence the Apostle Paul's focus on the word "remembrance." When the Catholics positioned the Supper as a real sacrifice, they mistakenly derailed the meaning behind the rite's institution. Such a reading also literally added to the words of Scripture. For Zwingli, neither of these mistakes could be glossed over if he was going to faithfully shepherd the Zurich community toward true Christian worship.

By November 1524, Zwingli argued for the first time that the word "is" from Matthew 26 and Luke 22 should be understood to mean "signifies" or "represents."[27] It is possible, though contested by some, that this new argumentation surfaced because Zwingli read a letter by Cornelius Hoen in which the Dutch humanist expressed similar sentiments about the verb "to be."[28] However, what is not debatable is the importance of this argumentation for Zwingli. He later called this philological argument a "wonderful pearl."[29] Pointing to biblical examples such as Jesus declaring Himself to be the vine (John 15:1) or Christ's statement that "the seed is the Word of God" (Luke 8:11), the Reformer argued that in many passages of Scripture, "'is' cannot mean 'to be' but must be employed to mean 'signify.' "[30] In such passages, the word "is" served as a literary trope, precluding a rigid, forced, literalistic interpretation of the verb. For Jesus's institution of the Supper, a corporeal interpretation of the Scriptures could not stand, given this hermeneutical literary device.

As one adept at philological studies, Zwingli was also keenly aware that in its original historic usage, the term *sacramentum*, which was synonymous with the Catholic Eucharist, meant "oath."[31] When first employed in a Roman military context centuries earlier, a sacrament was an oath of allegiance offered either to the empire or to a superior officer in the legion.[32] As Zwingli made clear, it was only much later that the definition expanded to include an external means of divine salvific grace. The shift in application from a military to a religious context did not concern the Reformer. The greater issue was both the way the church overstressed God's activity in the meal and how it positioned the Eucharist as a sacrifice of the very thing it was to signify. To what he saw as the Catholic Church's conflation of the *signum* or "sign" and the *res*, the "thing being signified," Zwingli sarcastically declared, "Even a child can tell you that you have not properly explained the word 'sacrament' when you say, 'Yes, it is a sign of a holy thing.' "[33] As one scholar has correctly stated, "Philology governed his [Zwingli's] reading of Scripture."[34] The language of remembrance denoted the people's pledge to recall, not any real sacrifice. In this context, it spoke of the Swiss people's action, not of God's. To memorialize was for the Zurich church to remember Christ's atoning work on the cross and to recommit themselves to Him and to each other in the Christian community.

In 1523, there was still a residual allowance in Zwingli's theology for God's activity in the sacraments, though not in conveying a salvific grace. As he declared, sacraments are those things "God has set up by His own Word which is so firm and certain it is as though He had sworn an oath."[35] The idea of God committing Himself to humanity through the Supper should not come as a surprise. As we outlined in Chapter 3, Zwingli's belief that Christ is the heavenly pledge of God's covenantal promise was a key part of the Reformer's understanding of the gospel.[36] Seeing God's pledge in the Supper as an ongoing reminder to the Swiss people of His everlasting covenant with them made sense and worked symbiotically with the people's subsequent pledge to remember Christ's work, the very event that made reconciliation possible.

By the mid-1520s, such language began to dissipate from Zwingli's Eucharistic lexicon. He now focused almost exclusively on the people's pledge.[37] Some of this shift may have been to elucidate his own convictions on the Supper as the disparate views of others like Luther and Karlstadt became clearer in the early waves of the Eucharistic controversy. Much of this modification was also based on the preacher's desire to see his flock committed to living communally as a renewed people. Referencing 1 Corinthians 10 in his May 1524 work *A Proposal Concerning Images and the Mass*, Zwingli stressed how the Supper connoted an inner and outer union that the communicants have not only to Christ by means of the Spirit but also to one another based on mutual commitment.[38] By observing the rite, the Zurich people were renewing their pledge to one another, while the Spirit knit them together as one people redeemed through Christ. Using powerful Trinitarian language as a model for this union, Zwingli argues, "Christ wills that His own shall be one, just as He is one with the Father, and for this union He has given us this sacrament [the Supper]."[39] The Apostle Paul provided the Corinthians with an illustration of their covenant community, the one loaf, that was applicable for Zurich. The scattered kernels of grain representing each Zuricher were being brought together and united into one body, illustrated by the one loaf of bread. Covenant community was reaffirmed through the Supper's observance, thereby reflecting an ecclesial union perfectly personified in the Triune God.[40]

Further attention on the people's activity also began to crystallize in Zwingli's thought around 1525. This was the same year when Zwingli's covenantal theology began to surface more clearly in his writings. One instance of this is in his 1525 treatise *Subsidiary Tract on the Eucharist*, in which Zwingli made a purposeful link between the Supper and the Passover.[41] This historic connection, which he claimed came to him via a dream, helped highlight the preacher's belief that the Zurich church was a contemporary manifestation of ancient Israel.[42] The association also provided him additional ammunition in the Eucharistic debates. As he pointed out, Israel's repeated observance of the Passover did not literally allow the angel of death to pass over their homes again; rather, "it was the sacrifice or symbol of the Passover!"[43] Similarly, the bread and wine provided a historic metonymy with events from the past. The elements from the Supper were never meant to be conflated with the things signified.

This emphasis on the covenantal and corporate nature of the Eucharist built on Zwingli's beliefs about the sacraments. Therefore, it is beneficial to consider his Eucharistic convictions in relation to his theology of baptism. In his 1525 work *Baptism, Rebaptism, and Child Baptism*, Zwingli illustrated the nature of sacraments as follows:

> If a person sews on a white cross, they proclaim themselves to be Swiss. And if that one makes the pilgrimage to Nähenfels and gives God praise and thanksgiving for the victory awarded to our forebearers, that person testifies that they are Swiss. Similarly, the person who receives the mark of baptism is the one who is resolved to hear what God says to them, to learn the divine precepts, and to live life in accordance with them.[44]

Baptism, just like the Supper, was "a covenant sign or pledge."[45] Through this rite, an external event (the act of sewing or taking a pilgrimage to Nähenfels in the analogy) and an otherwise commonplace image (the white Swiss cross) conveyed a deeper, substantive idea about one's allegiance and identity. Thus, for Zwingli, baptism was a human act of pledging that spoke to community. The act did not cause the recipient's salvation. Zwingli believed strongly that "though the whole world were set against it, it is clear and indisputable that no external element or action can purify the soul."[46] As with his earlier concerns about earthly images being used in worship to direct internal spiritual realities, Zwingli was adamant that the waters of baptism could not change the soul. Only the Spirit of God through the Word of God might usher in an internal disposition of piety. Instead, baptism placed the individual in the covenant community and set them on a redemptive pathway. In a related way, the Lord's Supper was an ongoing pledge and recommitment to the covenant community through the recurring acknowledgement of and thankfulness for Christ's atoning work.[47] Zwingli saw both sacraments as powerful acts of identity for the Zurich church and always framed them in a corporate context.

This focus on remembrance was crucial to Zwingli's developing Eucharistic thought and set an important trajectory for the Reformer. Rather than seeing God as doing something for or to the communicant observing the meal, he highlighted the actions of the Swiss people. The Reformer framed the sacramental nature of the Supper in terms of allegiance or action, as opposed to an external act of divine grace. Even at this early date, Zwingli deviated not only from Catholic sacramental theology but also from that of the Wittenbergers and Martin Luther. It is interesting to note, however, that as late as January 1523, Zwingli did not see his position as being at odds with Luther's. According to him, "Luther called this food [the Lord's Supper] a testament. I gladly concede the point, for he named it after its nature and characteristics. I have named it according to custom and manner of eating the food. There is no real difference in the two names."[48] Zwingli believed the only things that distinguished his view from Luther's were semantics and focus. Time would prove this to be a gross miscalculation.

MORE THAN MERE MEMORIAL

If a parishioner at Zurich walked away from the Lord's Table with only a passing intellectual remembrance of Jesus's work at Calvary, then something was wrong. Their preacher never envisioned memorial to be something commonplace or devoid of passion. Quite the opposite was to be true. For Zwingli, "memory ('to remember'), which was inseparable from 'experience'—hearing and action," embodied memorial.[49] To remember was to encounter. And to encounter was to respond.

For a humanist like Zwingli, to encounter past realities, whether through ancient text or religious rite, was to embark upon a visceral journey, an enlightening odyssey that conveyed not only historical content but life-transforming experiences as well. This was why the Reformer made the changes he did to the Zurich liturgy. Based on the alterations outlined in Chapter 2, Zurich's order of worship became "a brilliant piece of humanist rhetoric in which mind and body were moved, passions aroused, the faithful persuaded and ultimately charged to live according to the truth they had heard."[50] In the case of the new Communion meal, observance promised a "metamorphosis of the faithful, not the elements."[51] This is what Zwingli desired for his Zurich flock in their remembrance. Highlighting this point in January 1523, Zwingli declared, "When in faith they eat his flesh and drink his blood knowing that they [the elements] have been given to them as an assurance that their sins are forgiven, it is as if Christ had only now died on the cross. Christ is so powerful and present at all times, for He is an eternal God. Therefore, His suffering is also eternally fruitful."[52] Here we find Jesus's historic, once-for-all sacrifice in the past made real again in a vibrant and experiential way. And this personal encounter with Christ helped reaffirm faith and provided assurance for the weary soul.

In an activity similar to later forms of Ignatian contemplation, Zwingli believed reflections on the past were to be undertaken experientially and imaginatively, ultimately resulting in action.[53] In much the same way that a familiar song or a family photograph can bring back particular feelings, images, and even scents from the past, as if those distant moments were real again, so too were the details of Christ's sacrifice at Calvary to fill the Zurich people's remembrances. Through a sanctified imagination, communicants were to remember Christ's passion in a way that made these horrific events vibrant and present. Therefore, it was not enough for the Zurich church to merely read about Jesus's suffering in Scripture or hear about the details of his death through a sermon. For Zwingli, his people needed to experience these realities firsthand. For instance, one could be overwhelmed by the loveliness of the crucified Savior even while imagining what His disfigurement beyond that of a man, which Isaiah 52 prophesied, looked like. The stench of death, the splattering of the Savior's blood, or the deafening cries of His suffering on the cross were to become, through the act of one's remembrance, as real as the bread and wine consumed.

This way of remembering followed a pattern found in the Hebrew Scriptures. God never demanded that His people observe empty acts or stale rituals devoid of purpose. Instead, the Lord gave Israel repetitive acts, like the Passover, to remind them of His past works and their standing as His people. In a parallel manner, Zwingli positioned the Supper as a gift to the Zurich church through which the people could reenact a past event for the purpose of assurance and identity. The rite was an accommodating act reminding the Swiss people of their salvation in Christ. The dual themes of faith and assurance marked Zwingli's language about the Supper especially in 1523 and 1524. As he stressed in a letter to Thomas Wyttenbach during the summer of 1523, "This food (the Supper) is given among other things to strengthen weak faith."[54] Yet the recipient's faith, not the independent sacramental actions of the elements, was what generated assurance in the believer. "Everything rests on faith: in faith the recipient feels secure and at peace; if that is not the case then he is no true believer."[55] Without faith there was only a religious act without any real meaning.

In his 1523 work *Advice Concerning the Mass and Images*, Zwingli built on this goal of assurance, emphasizing, "The body and blood of Christ are nothing other than a food of the believing soul."[56] The Reformer's purposeful selection of a unique German term, *fronlychnam*, for "body" in this quotation specifically referenced Christ's glorified humanity. Jesus's presence in the elements was to be assumed, the language possibly even employed to accommodate those with lingering Catholic sensibilities.[57] However, the specific nature of Jesus's presence was not philosophically explained nor conveyed by Zwingli with any theological nuance. There certainly was to be no re-sacrificing of Christ in the Mass. That much was clear. Instead, there was to be a powerful commemoration that strengthened the faith of those partaking. Through Zwingli's understanding of the Supper, the Reformer's Christological and anthropological convictions came crashing together into ecclesial acts intended to bolster the faith of the Zurich community.

Zwingli had offered similar lines of reasoning two months earlier in his 1523 treatise *The Canon of the Mass*. Referencing the broken body and shed blood of Jesus, Zwingli contended that Christ "delivered the same things into the food which we ate by faith, not with teeth, by which God enters into us invisibly and feeds our souls."[58] Once again, faith was a requisite element empowering the consumption of the bread and the wine. God, in Christ, could be encountered in a substantive and real way through partaking of the elements. Still, meeting God was qualified in such a way that a corporeal understanding of this eating was avoided. Feeding on Jesus was for the strengthening of the communicant and the building of community.

THE FLESH IS OF NO AVAIL

In his *Commentary*, Zwingli says of his earlier instructions about the Eucharist, "I wrote rather with a view to the times than to the thing itself."[59] The unveiling of the preacher's views on the Supper, like many of his reforms, should be understood based on his heart for pastoral accommodation. Referencing the importance of plowing and harvesting during the appropriate season, a lesson undoubtedly learned during his upbringing at Wildhaus, he stressed a concern "not to put things forth at a time when no one would receive them."[60] Accordingly, his first instructions on the Supper vehemently opposed seeing Jesus as being sacrificed in the Mass. By the mid-1520s he believed the time was right for him to abolish the Roman Mass, which, as we saw in Chapter 2, the Reformer realized in 1525.

That liturgical accomplishment also coincided with a chance to convey his beliefs more clearly, something that was soon required. Though he had not anticipated it, the swelling of controversy around the Reformers' differing views on the Supper forced a new season of conflict upon Zwingli. The mid-to-late 1520s became for the Zurich preacher a season of strife and division. He was eventually forced to explain his views on the sacrament most linked to the idea of Christian unity. Ironically, Zwingli did this while dialoguing with certain Protestants who increasingly wanted to separate themselves from him precisely because of his Eucharistic beliefs.

As a humanist, Zwingli held the pursuit of the natural or plain sense of the text as one of the chief principles driving his exegesis. Such an approach meant looking for the Bible's inner spiritual instructions as opposed to a rigid surface literalism. Given this hermeneutical principle, the thought of eating literal flesh was forced and unnatural according to Zwingli. It was also a practice common among certain pagans, so this could not be what Jesus meant. Furthermore, the plain meaning of the text was linked with word studies. As he stressed in his 1523 work *The Education of Youth*, only by understanding the original Hebrew and Greek texts could one "draw out the true sense of Scripture," which was "heavenly wisdom."[61] This pedagogy was why understanding the historic usage of the term *sacramentum* was so important to him. Still, another key component to finding the natural sense of Scripture was based on the Reformer's belief in an inner coherence of the Bible. Drawing on convictions derived from Plato and Aristotle, Zwingli contended that the philosophical law of non-contradiction precluded a corporeal reading of Jesus's institution from Matthew 26 and Luke 22 because of other texts.[62]

Regarding this conviction, Zwingli's reading of John 6 shaped his understanding of the Supper from the mid-1520s until the close of his life. This was especially true of verse 63, in which Jesus emphasized the Spirit's role in facilitating life, while also highlighting the flesh's impotence in spiritual matters. As Zwingli once declared to Luther, the John 6:63 passage was "a wall of bronze and an unbroken voice" regarding the growing questions about Jesus's presence in the elements.[63] In his *Commentary* he rhetorically challenged those who believed in a corporeal reading of the institution: "Go now, and bring up all your engines of war, catapults, battering-rams, sheds, and every kind of weapon; far from shattering this wall, you will not even be able to shake it."[64] The preacher's use of war imagery here is fascinating. More than just offering an allusion to his military background, this language also shows him planting a theological flag on this important topic. Such confidence was rooted in his conviction that this passage from John was the hermeneutical key required to unlock the real meaning of Jesus's institution language. This conviction is why John 6 was explained prior to a detailed exegesis of Matthew 26 in his *Commentary* and was always read during Zurich's new Eucharist services beginning in 1525.[65] For Zwingli, John 6 was that clearer text of Scripture that helped shed light on the more challenging and opaque passages.

More than mere proof text, the John 6 passage resonated with Zwingli's spirit/flesh dualism, which was drawn from Erasmus. Like the Dutch humanist, Zwingli believed priority must be given to the spirit over the flesh. The internal realization of divine eternal truths was of greater importance than, and set against, external, physical expressions or activities, even those commanded by Christ. External forms of religion could not mechanically generate Christian piety. Only an internal moral change of the person, wrought by God's Spirit, could do that. In the case of the Eucharist, this meant that an internal appropriation of the Supper, and of the gospel that it represented, was far superior to the external observance of the rite.[66] Zwingli just as easily could have affirmed Erasmus's exhortation from the *Enchiridion* that piety may be realized only when you "try to advance from things visible ... to things invisible."[67] The transforming power of God's Spirit facilitates changes to people that the external word picture of the gospel, via the observance of the elements, simply could not.[68]

Still, Zwingli's views went well beyond a humanistic reading of the text. His Christological convictions demanded that any Eucharistic eating be nothing more than spiritual consumption. While speaking about the glorified Jesus in 1523, the Reformer declared, "Christ sits properly speaking, either in heaven at the right hand of God or on earth in the hearts of the believers."[69] Based on this foundational belief, for Zwingli, the logical reading of all the Eucharistic texts precluded corporeal consumption. Clarifying this point, he explained, "He (Jesus) is our food, ready to be eaten, not taken in hand but through the Spirit who alone is appointed for it."[70] Once again, the internal/external and spirit/flesh interplay characterized much of the Swiss humanist's thought and dictated his reading of Scripture.[71] As Zwingli had stressed earlier about the John 6 passage, "Christ, according to his habit of passing from the things of sense to the inner and spiritual things, very graciously admonished them who sought Him in the hope of food to honor and seek before all things that food which never perishes nor passes away."[72] Zwingli believed the church's rites could not satisfy the otherwise spiritually famished Swiss people. That hunger could only be allayed by Christ alone through faith.

A CRUCIAL ACT OF FAITH

In his 1523–1524 writings, Zwingli frequently spoke about the sacraments strengthening the believer's faith. However, by 1525 that theme vanished from his Eucharistic vocabulary. In fact, in his *Commentary* he made a theological reversal, rejecting this idea in total. Apparently, the formal rise of Anabaptism months earlier precipitated this shift in Zwingli's theology and coincided with the expansion of his covenant theology around that same time. Zwingli chides the Anabaptist Radicals in his *Commentary* for teaching "that the sacraments are signs which make a man sure of the thing that has been accomplished within him."[73] Though he had previously positioned the sacraments as an accommodation to those weak in the faith, now his view appears exactly opposite to such a premise. Zwingli contended, "For if your faith is not so perfect as not to need a ceremonial sign to confirm it, then it is not faith."[74] In other words, to rely upon an external act to corroborate one's salvific standing was to confirm one's place outside the faith community. Just as he had done with infant baptism, the preacher altered his arguments against the Anabaptists as his Reformed convictions surfaced more explicitly in his theology.[75]

Zwingli's rejection of the Anabaptists' regenerate church also coincided with his amplification of the importance of faith within the covenant community. Thus, "to be one who trusts in God and is holy—this was to be a Christian."[76] The Reformer wed together a dependence upon God and a Christian ethic as the standard for participation in Christ's body. Once again, the language of oath and an emphasis on the communicant's action were key elements in this important act of identification. By partaking of the elements, congregants proved their commitment to the covenant body through their confirming pledge and act of renewal.[77] Of course, as it was with Israel, Zurich children had their faith temporarily linked to their parents, who were themselves a part of the covenant community.[78] Zwingli also used this association with Israel as a defense for his mixed-church ecclesiology. Discerning who was elect and who was not, whether child or adult, was not within the purview of the Zurich church, since "He [God] alone knows the hearts of the children of humanity."[79] For the Swiss preacher, a failure to recognize that distinction was a primary catalyst of the Anabaptists' ecclesiological errors. Their supposed regenerate church presumed far too much. It also threatened the unity of Zurich's Christian society, which he refused to tolerate.

Even as Zwingli further divorced himself from the Swiss Radicals, he continued to move further away from what he believed to be Catholicism's abhorrent literal eating of Christ. To accomplish this move, once again he emphasized the importance of faith, something he believed was absent in the Roman Eucharist. Referencing God's provision of manna in the wilderness, alongside reflections from John 6, Zwingli stressed the importance of consuming the elements in faith. "The food He [God] bids us seek," Zwingli argued, "is belief in the Son."[80] Manna came from heaven to sustain physical life. The Son, who is the Bread of Life and Living Water to the believing soul, came to bring eternal life to those given faith. The Christological focus, which permeated Zwingli's theology, was clear but also distinct. As he declared about the incarnation, "The flesh of Christ is of very great profit, indeed, immeasurably and in every way, but as I have said, by being slain, not eaten."[81] Drawing heavily from Augustine, who, one scholar contends, "stressed the spiritual manducation of the faith rather than the corporeal manducation of the sacrament," Zwingli's Neoplatonic dualism took his understanding of the action of eating in a spiritual direction.[82] To consume the elements was to confess a dependence upon Christ's atoning work.

Zwingli later reasoned that to believe one has eaten the flesh of Christ, which is an act perceived via human senses, demonstrates no faith at all. He also believed such an action compelled a dependence upon external things, which his Neoplatonic dualism would not abide. Zwingli decried a corporeal reading of the text, exclaiming, "What an absurd way of speaking this is—I believe I am eating perceptible and physical body. Now if it is bodily, there is no need for faith."[83] But true faith, the faith Zwingli desired for his people, looked beyond what could be experienced, "for things which are perceived when presented to the senses are things of the sense."[84] But, as he continued reasoning, if one's eating is non-corporeal, then it "is a matter of belief, [for] the thing you believe cannot be sensible or bodily."[85] Once again, the relationship between the inner and outer, the spirit and the flesh, was a key to the way the Zurich church was to encounter its Savior in worship. To embrace corporeal eating not only forced his

Zurich flock to remain dependent upon external forms, thereby exacerbating their susceptibility to idolatry, but it also led his people away from true faith. The Zurich shepherd refused to allow his sheep to wander into what he believed was a faithless abyss.

GROWING CONTROVERSY

As mentioned earlier, Zwingli initially thought his views on the Supper accorded with Luther's. Nevertheless, substantive differences between the two men existed from the outset. Eucharistic controversy was inevitable, though the debate that loomed was not incited by Luther. Zwingli attributed that to Karlstadt, who, he believed, "seasonably or unseasonably dragged the matter suddenly before the attention of the public" in 1524.[86] Biblical hermeneutics was at the heart of the divide over the Eucharist. Most of the mainline Reformers affirmed *sola Scriptura*, so fracture was based on different readings of the Bible, not on Scriptural authority.

During the mid-1520s, Zwingli found like minds in figures like the Strasbourgers Martin Bucer and Wolfgang Capito as well as the Basel Reformer Johannes Oecolampadius. While each of these Reformers maintained unique Eucharistic emphases, a common underlying humanistic conviction led them to non-corporeal readings of the institution.[87] The locus of the Eucharistic fissure for Zwingli, therefore, lay mostly outside of the Swiss Confederation. This is where Zwingli faced a daunting challenge. On the one hand, he was keen to find agreement with Luther on the matter. An alliance with the Germans was of strategic importance for the Zurich church, though he increasingly understood the challenges of mediating with Luther. On the other hand, Zwingli had to distance himself from Karlstadt, Luther's former colleague at Wittenberg. Zwingli and the German Radical similarly interpreted "is," from Jesus's institution, to mean "signifies" or "represents." However, Karlstadt's Eucharistic theology was more individualistically focused, while Zwingli framed his convictions against the backdrop of the Zurich covenant community.[88] It was this individualism, which played a key role in the destructive and violent forms of reformation incited by Karlstadt at Wittenberg, that Zwingli was keen to avoid.

The Eucharistic divide widened by 1525. In October, Zwingli felt compelled to defend his Eucharistic views, given recent criticism from the Reformer Johannes Bugenhagen, through his *Open Letter Against the New Error Concerning the Sacrament*.[89] Having initiated a new Reformed Mass at Zurich six months earlier, Zwingli knew it was important that his new liturgy not be perceived as an innovation. Zwingli's rejoinder cited historical precedence as a defense for his views. From the outset, he criticized Bugenhagen for "not know[ing] that the ancients were of our opinion concerning the Eucharist."[90] The contention that Zurich was promoting "a new error" was not applicable, making the title of Bugenhagen's work misguided.[91] This was especially true "because Christ, the apostles, and most ancient Christian people believed" the elements merely signified Jesus's body and blood.[92] Citing a litany of figures from the past, including Cyril, Augustine, and Chrysostom, Zwingli stressed how the word "is" had been understood as a literary trope precluding a corporeal interpretation.[93] Focusing heavily on John 6:63, the Swiss Reformer reminded Bugenhagen, "Just about every cohort of professionals is of the opinion that in this sentence [John 6:63] they may understand ... how they receive Christ's flesh."[94] Thus, any consumption of Christ must be seen as nothing more than a spiritual eating.

Luther eventually waded into the controversy, largely at the request of his friends but also because Bucer translated Bugenhagen's *Commentary on the Psalms*, as he described, sullied with the additions of a Eucharistic memorialism.[95] In *The Sacrament of the Body and Blood of Christ against the Fanatics*, Luther placed Zwingli alongside Karlstadt and Oecolampadius as "fanatics" who "set up these dreams of theirs [their argumentation] without any Scriptural basis."[96] For Luther, Zwingli's reasoning not only failed to ascribe to the Son an omnipresence befitting His divinity but also foolishly tried to make intellectual sense of the incomprehensible. Luther opined during a table talk years later, "Erasmus, Oecolampadius, Zwingli, and Karlstadt want to measure everything by their wisdom and so they become confused. I thank God that I know and believe that God knows more than I do. He can do what is above my ability to comprehend."[97] The importance of *promissio*, or promise, a theme threaded throughout

Luther's theology, meant the language of the Supper's institution had to be understood corporeally.[98]

Despite Luther's refusal to mediate, Zwingli feigned the possibility of an accord with the German Reformer in a fascinating letter penned in 1527. He spoke glowingly of Luther being "of the first rank of the champions of the gospel" and calls him a contemporary David who, through deft argumentation, "chose stones from the river of heaven" before he "stretched his [the Catholic Church's] tremendous limbs over a vast extent of ground."[99] Such lauding was elegant and illustrative. But it also glossed over Zwingli's real intention behind the letter. He wrote to correct what he believed were Luther's errors. Citing 1 Corinthians 14:31, Zwingli declared in his opening remarks to Luther, "For if we are true prophets we shall listen to each other, and if we are in error upon any matter we shall yield the point."[100] Despite the accommodating pleasantries, as one historian has rightly contended, Zwingli's letter "was a carefully measured cup of praise and admonition that belied any real expectation of peace."[101] The Swiss Reformer wrote to clarify and expand upon his Eucharistic convictions. That Zwingli hastily prepared the book for distribution during the famous Frankfurt book fair that spring spoke to the author's real motivation. As with most Reformation disputations, literary sparring partners rarely held out hope of winning an opponent via argumentation. This work was about disseminating and explaining ideas at a time when Zwingli was already thinking of himself as shepherding more than just his beloved Zurich people.

As he had with Bugenhagen, the Reformer cited historical precedent as a defense of his non-corporeal interpretation of the institution. For Zwingli, there was no need to lament if his Zurich flock was to "never eat of the flesh of Christ," for "Noah, Enoch, Abraham, Moses, John the Baptist, and all the thousands of the good and vast numbers of the fathers ... never tasted the flesh of Christ in a bodily sense."[102] Citing Augustine, Zwingli once again stressed that Jesus's body was in heaven.[103] Thus, Christ's use of the verb "to be" was a literary trope never intended to be taken in a rigid literalistic manner.

For years, Zwingli had emphasized the importance of understanding the Supper's institution as a trope. However, in his discourse with Luther, he further developed and expanded on those ideas, employing for the first time the language of alloeosis.[104] Drawing especially from the Greek philosopher Plutarch, Zwingli defined alloeosis as "a trope by which an interchange takes place between members of a category or scheme of things where, namely, on account of some affinity in the grammatical phenomena, a leap or interchange is made from one to the other."[105] This literary device, especially when applied to the incarnation, allowed for "an exchange or interchange of the two natures that are in one person" to further explain Jesus's words of institution in the upper room.[106] Through the grammatical lens of alloeosis, once the bread, which was linked with Christ's flesh, was interchanged for the Son's divine nature, this allowed Jesus to become "the food of the soul."[107] Such a hermeneutic allowed Zwingli to encourage his Zurich flock to feed on Christ as nourishment for their weary souls while avoiding a corporeal reading of the Eucharistic texts, which he thought was a Catholic error.

Luther believed this exegetical "leap or transition," as Zwingli defined alloeosis, was a leap into foolishness and a transition to heresy.[108] For the Wittenberg Reformer, Zwingli's clever humanistic word games veiled the promise Christ made to his disciples regarding His presence in the elements.[109] Luther had already hardened his stance against Zwingli's use of alloeosis prior to Marburg. In his 1527 work *Confession Concerning Christ's Supper*, Luther attacked Zwingli's methodology, stating, "This is the principle of Zwinglian logic called 'proving an uncertain proposition by something more uncertain, and an unknown by one more unknown.' Oh, beautiful learning! The children should pelt it with dung and drive it away!"[110] Luther believed Zwingli's fast and loose word games were not merely academic missteps. Something much more sinister and with far graver consequences was at stake. He concluded, "We condemn and damn alloeosis right down to hell as the devil's own inspiration."[111] For Luther, to follow Zwingli was to believe Satan and to reject the promises of God.

MISHAP AT MARBURG

When accepting Philip's invitation to attend the Marburg Colloquy, Zwingli praised the Landgrave for gathering the famed meeting, even appearing optimistic regarding the assembly.[112] In an age when the Reformers were considering the very nature of the one true church, a charge of Nestorianism echoing against Zwingli stung and required a response. The standing of the Zurich church as Christ's bride was at stake. Therefore, this likely appeared a perfect time to correct any misperceptions about his theology or the Zurich church's liturgy. Alternately, Luther did not share Zwingli's hopeful attitude. He believed the meeting would further validate the misguided opinions of the Swiss, thereby spreading their poison. Knowing the matter was at an impasse, he also feared their failed unity would only add fuel to an already raging fire of controversy at a politically vulnerable time for the German church. However, Luther eventually reneged, and more than a dozen of the most prominent Protestant Reformers descended upon Marburg in fall 1529.

In his 1527 work *A Friendly Exegesis*, Zwingli chastised Luther's ornery temperament, decrying how the Wittenberg Reformer had "treated a difficult subject [the Eucharist] in the heat of your anger."[113] Apparently Zwingli lacked self-awareness regarding growing perceptions about his own stubborn volatility and ill-tempered disposition, for the two men were purposely kept apart at the genesis of the colloquy on Thursday, October 1. This was a strategic move given concerns that the two Reformers, if allowed to immediately spar with one another, might derail the meeting from the outset.[114] Personality and temperament colored the theological discussions at Marburg, which exacerbated the controversy. This divide was never exclusively about theology and exegesis. Given that Zwingli was defending not only his personal views but also the people and practices of his beloved Zurich church, one can assume he maintained an impassioned disposition throughout the event. Much was at stake for him at Marburg.

Sadly, no notary was employed to formally record and publish the event's proceedings. However, several written reports from spectators at Marburg surfaced in the coming days. Some of these sources provided support for Luther, while others were favorably disposed to the Swiss. Despite the polemical ethos of the era, these documents should be considered generally reliable, though they were not verbatim recollections from the event. The arguments contained in these various accounts square with those conveyed by each Reformer in his own extant works; therefore, a level of trustworthiness may be assumed.

While the participants considered various theological matters during the four-day event, the Supper frequently took center stage and epitomized the hermeneutical divide that remained between the camps. At the close of the proceedings, all the signers of the concluding statement acknowledged shared points of agreement on most of the topics discussed. The Reformers present established common ground on basic Trinitarian doctrine derived from the Nicene tradition, the nature of sin, justification by grace through faith, and the role of temporal authority.[115] The Reformers also agreed to the laity's observance of the Supper in both kinds and to a spiritual eating. All parties believed that faith was a crucial requisite for the consumption of the elements to hold any value. However, a major point of contention remained over the nature of Christ's presence in the elements and how to interpret His instituting words. At its core, the contested portion of the debate was Christological in nature, placing biblical hermeneutics center stage.

Early in the Eucharistic discussions, Luther placed the onus on the Swiss to explain their position, citing a "literal meaning" of Jesus's instituting words as a baseline.[116] This was important, for it set Luther on the presumed advantageous high ground of the conflict. It also set Zwingli on the offensive, as he elucidated a humanistic reading of Scripture based on historic context, philological word studies, and patristic precedent. While Luther spoke of a literal sense of Scripture, it would be inaccurate to suggest Zwingli rejected that premise. A literal reading of Scripture can be taken to mean a variety of different things. Humanists like Zwingli affirmed a literal reading of a text. But rather than situating literalism in relation to something like promise, which Luther did with the Matthew 26 and Luke 22 texts, for humanists, the literal sense spoke to reading Scripture in its original historic context.[117]

Knowing of their shared commitment to biblical authority, the Zurich preacher proceeded by stressing the interpretive rule of allowing Scripture to interpret Scripture. Admittedly, there were no passages directly stating that the elements are to represent Christ's body. However, for Zwingli, this was why John 6 was so important, as that text directly "leads away from bodily eating."[118] Moreover, the Old Testament prophets frequently used language in a similar manner to provide analogies teaching Israel crucial truths about the people's shortcomings and God's faithfulness.[119] Luther ceded the latter of these points but also stressed there were many biblical passages "in which 'is' is used demonstrably."[120] Furthermore, according to Luther, the prophets' use of allegory was quite clear and "not to be compared with the words of the Supper unless they have previously proved that here (Matthew 26 and Luke 22) the words must also be understood allegorically."[121] This was not some innovative or reactionary position for Luther. As he stated in a 1515 lecture at Wittenberg, "In the Scriptures, therefore, no allegory, tropology, or anagogy is valid, unless the same truth is expressly stated historically elsewhere."[122] And Jesus did not say that the elements merely signified His body anywhere else in the text of Holy Writ, hence Luther's corporeal reading.

As one might expect with most Reformation debates, the discourse was dense and cumbersome to those present. One observer described Zwingli's explanations as "belabored," his argumentation "long and verbose."[123] These descriptions came from an anonymous person sympathetic to Luther, clouding them with polemical bias. However, that does not mean such chronicles are without value. These reflections help characterize the reception of Zwingli from individuals outside of his own theological camp. Not everyone was as enamored with the Swiss preacher as were those in certain humanist circles and in Zurich.

At times the deliberations became caustic and personal, as the Reformers exchanged demeaning verbal salvos dripping with animus and sarcasm. One such instance took place on the first day of the colloquy. Pressing Zwingli on his interpretation of John 6, Luther pejoratively declared, "Your logic is very poor; it is the kind of logic for which a schoolboy is caned and sent to the corner."[124] Zwingli's response was equally incendiary: "This passage [John 6] is going to break your neck," to which Luther retorted, "Necks do not break that easily here. You are in Hesse, not in Swiss lands."[125] This episode illustrates the debased side of polemical discourse. While hearing pastors speak in such an irreverent manner may seem foreign and offensive to modern ears, it was not uncommon for the era. Reformation rhetoric frequently devolved into name calling and often included veiled threats, as it did here. As one historian aptly argued about moments like this, "Polemic ceased to be a heuristic tool. It became a blunt weapon. Legitimate, discussable differences in opinion developed, in this case, as with so many others, into a confessional fracas between hostile forces."[126] In such an environment, cordial disagreement proved challenging, theological consensus near impossible.

While Zwingli and Luther both spoke German, Zwingli's Swiss dialect made communication between the two Reformers challenging. Yet they were divided by more than mere culture. Given that much of the debate was over a single Greek word, the verb "to be," not surprisingly a controversy over language emerged. As Zwingli referenced the Greek New Testament to defend his interpretation, Luther interrupted, "Read German or Latin, not Greek."[127] Zwingli quickly responded, clarifying that he had been immersed in the original Greek text for years, admittedly having only read the Latin translation once.[128] The moment came and went quickly, making it easy to overlook. However, this was a telling flash point that went beyond any theological discussion about Christology.

Reading different texts of Scripture mattered to this debate. As one scholar eloquently notes, Zwingli "worked from the Greek, with its different connotations and, most importantly, its different constellation of uses within Greek philosophy and the Greek church fathers."[129] As a humanist, Zwingli believed there was no better way of understanding a text than to return to the original sources equipped with a myriad of literary tools to rightly understand what Jesus's words meant. Luther, on the other hand, saw little value in searching out Christ's intention. Only a simple, straightforward obedience to Jesus was required. He makes that point clear in an earlier dialogue with Oecolampadius, stating, "If He [Jesus] should command me to eat dung, I would do it."[130] The scatological reference is classic Luther, as is his point. There was no use for clever speculation here, only trust in and obedience to God's eternal Word.

On the evening of Friday, October 2, a debate about Jesus's location ensued. Almost immediately, Oecolampadius and Luther were at odds over the possible circumscription of Jesus's body. Luther, stressing Jesus's divine nature, had no concerns regarding Christ's ubiquity, believing Jesus could be in multiple places at any one given time. The Messiah's promise to be present during the Supper's institution only amplified that theological reality, for Jesus's words were "clear and sure words from Scripture."[131] Oecolampadius, focusing on Jesus's humanity, rebutted that he "does not know any other God, nor is there another besides Him who was made human."[132] The Basel Reformer also turned Luther's words against him, citing Jesus's earlier statement from Matthew 26:11 about Jesus's absence from his disciples in relation to the poor. For a humanist like Oecolampadius, canonical context was a crucial part of rightly understanding any one biblical verse. Luther acknowledged this was the Swiss's strongest argument. However, it was one easily overcome by faith, trusting in Christ's promise to be both absent and present regardless of an explanation satisfactory to the finite human mind.

Building on Oecolampadius's arguments, Zwingli cited Philippians 2 and Hebrews 4, declaring, "Christ therefore possesses a finite humanity."[133] Since all humans were unable to be everywhere, surely the resurrected Christ was geographically limited because of His humanity. This is where the charge of Nestorianism loomed. As Luther considered Zwingli's argumentation, all he could see was the heretical division of Christ. This was where Zwingli's Christology ran into potential issues. While he relied on the church fathers for much of his Eucharistic argumentation, on this point he strayed dangerously away from the early church's belief in the *communicatio idiomatum*.[134] This patristic doctrine stressed that the divine and human natures related to each other in the one person of the incarnate Jesus without confusion or separation and without either nature violating the unique attributes of the other.[135] Zwingli shrugged off the charge, later stating that Jesus was no more divided in his person given the spatial limitations of his humanity than "the Son's assumption of humanity divides the unity of the divine essence."[136] Luther, however, remained concerned, believing his opponent to be a heretic.

Zwingli pressed Luther again on the point of Jesus in relation to space and time. The German Reformer was ready with his answer. At one point amid the earlier discussions, Luther had scribbled something on the table in chalk. He then casually covered whatever was jotted down with a portion of the velvet tablecloth. Much like in a game of chess, Luther had looked ahead in anticipation, and the moment to spring his trap had arrived. Now, challenged by Zwingli for Scriptural proof regarding Jesus's ubiquity, Luther pulled back the cloth, which uncovered the single word *est*, the verb "is" in Latin. Luther simultaneously stated, "Here is our Scripture passage. You have not wrestled it away from us."[137] Luther remained unpersuaded. Any hope of a Protestant accord died at Marburg because of one simple word.

CONCLUSION

This tense moment between Zwingli and Luther at Marburg takes center stage in the Noack painting mentioned earlier. In that depiction, Luther, eyes fixed on his debate partner, is pointing down to the contested word *est* written in white on a red tablecloth. For him, the truth of Christ's corporeal presence was as sure as the Word of the Lord. Noack portrays Zwingli with his left arm bent, hand extending upward, and fingers pointed to the heavens. Zwingli's position implies a theological rebuttal to Luther's parlor trick. If promise was what Luther wanted, then Jesus's declaration that He was going to heaven to prepare a place for His children was said promise. That guarantee precluded His corporeal presence in the elements.

Perhaps in no other part of the Eucharistic conflict of the 1520s was there a better illustration of the reason for the theological divide between the Lutherans and the Swiss than this moment. Zwingli and Luther were equally dependent upon the Bible for establishing doctrine and church practice. Both trusted that Christ had spoken clearly through the inspired words of Scripture. Yet each Reformer read the same text in different languages based upon disparate hermeneutical convictions. Moreover, their focuses on different Christological aspects of their glorified, resurrected

Lord left them with distinct theological emphases. As one historian states, "All participants in the debate (at Marburg) agreed that Christ was everywhere, and therefore in the sacrament, according to his divine nature, but they disagreed over whether Christ could be everywhere, and specifically in the elements of the sacrament, according to his human nature."[138] The more they talked about the issues dividing them, the more they hardened against one another. In this polemical age, talking past an opponent was far more likely than engaging with the substance of opposing ideas. Personality conflicts facilitated part of the widening divide.

That the sacraments offered a word picture of the gospel only complicated the matter and drove the Reformers further apart on the topic. At Marburg, Luther said, "His [Christ's] words, wherever they are found, are the words of eternal life."[139] Given such convictions it is easy to see why it proved challenging to establish an accord on the matter. The very gospel was presumed to be at stake in the discussions. There was little consideration given to what contemporary theologians describe as theological triage, via which these Eucharistic divisions are often seen as acceptable options within the safe waters of orthodoxy. In a world prior to the age of confessionalism and an era unfamiliar with denominational divides, these lines of theological priority were not so clearly in view. The Reformers believed they were adjudicating their historic positions in relation to the one true Church, which only colored their conflicts.

Looking at Zwingli's later teachings, one cannot help but wonder if some of his battles with the Lutherans and Anabaptists compelled him to say more than he otherwise might have without having experienced these conflicts. For instance, it is tempting to conclude that in debating with Luther, Zwingli was arguing Jesus could be anywhere *except* in the elements. However, that sentiment looked nothing like the one offered by the Zwingli of the early 1530s. In *An Account of the Faith* from July 1530, he stated, "The true body of Christ was present [in the Eucharist] by the contemplation of faith," even as he rejected that Christ's natural body was "chewed with our mouth and teeth."[140] And in the final year of his life he declared, "To eat the body of Christ spiritually is none other than to trust in spirit and heart upon the mercy and goodness of God through Christ, that is, to be sure with an unshakeable faith that God is going to give us pardon for our sins and the joy of everlasting blessedness on account of His Son, who was made wholly ours, was offered for us, and reconciled the divine righteousness to us."[141] The Reformer highlighted a profound and real spiritual presence at that late date. Interestingly, he also reengaged the idea of the Supper offering assurance for one's faith, a theme he had jettisoned during the height of the Eucharistic debates. This shift in Zwingli's theological language may speak as much to the polemical ethos of the era as to his own theological development. Though he was grateful for Luther, even shedding tears while considering his fondness for him, the German Reformer did not bring out the best in Zwingli.[142]

The language of a spiritual, real presence in the Supper that characterized Zwingli's Eucharistic language in the 1530s is important. This was not some mere memorial, as is often assumed about his beliefs. These later ideas highlight theological movement in his thought on the matter. Before his life's abrupt conclusion, Zwingli apparently mediated an understanding of his own earlier views on the Supper prior to when many of the Reformers were negotiating a compromised view on the divisive topic. The spiritual eating Zwingli spoke about in his writings from 1530 and 1531 foreshadowed many of the convictions later outlined in the *Consensus Tigurinus*, a 1549 agreement between the Bullinger-led Zurich church and Calvin's Geneva.[143] One is left wondering if this profoundly important agreement between Zurich and Geneva would have materialized without Zwingli's earlier work. Eucharistic peace, ironic as it may seem for the sacrament most associated with unity, was partially realized for the Swiss church through the conflicts in Zwingli's life. Here, one should remember that humanity's reconciled union with Christ came only after His body, the bread, was broken and His blood, the wine, was poured out as an atoning sacrifice. So, perhaps Zurich's painful path toward unity, which was fraught with heartache and hostility, is to be both expected and appreciated.

Conclusion

The judgment for Huldrych Zwingli at Kappel could hardly have been crueler, though accounts of that day deviate wildly. On October 11, 1531, the preacher accompanied the Zurich army onto the battlefield to stand against the Catholics at Kappel. He went believing the Lord was on his side and would provide victory. The events from later in the day challenged those convictions. That evening the Catholics overwhelmed the Zurich forces in a violent melee. Following Zurich's military failing, the Catholic victors identified Zwingli. One account recorded how Catholic soldiers sarcastically berated him, even subjecting him to scathing charges of heresy.[1] However, through all the accusations the preacher spoke not a word. But this was not some attempt to emulate Jesus before His accusers. The prophet of Zurich was silent because he was dead. His lifeless body faced a mock trial staged by his Catholic foes. After the rendering of a guilty verdict, Zwingli's corpse was beheaded, quartered, and burned.

Alternate reports spoke of the Reformer's wounding and capture by the Catholic forces. These portrayed him defiantly uttering a statement once proclaimed at the outset of his Reformation: "You may kill the body, but you cannot kill the soul."[2] The ruminations of his friend Myconius even provided a sensational account where Zwingli's heart was supposedly recovered from the ashes following his burning, a symbol of his passion and purity amid an otherwise soiled ending.[3] Discerning truth amid the fog of war, where polemical propaganda from

Catholics and lionizing Protestant reflections mired the remembrances of that day, make recounting his death as complex and fascinating as the life he led.

The Chinese military strategist and philosopher Sun Tzu famously warned in his *Art of War* that there was no benefit from prolonged warfare. Zwingli's life and ministry, which were seemingly always devoid of peace, seem to challenge Sun Tzu's rule. In fact, Zwingli realized Reformation through and amid constant warfare. Though a cloud of uncertainty regarding the Reformer's death persists, there is little question about the overall trajectory of his life. Strife always cloaked Reformation both personally and ministerially for him. An endless parade of conflict characterized the preacher's ministry. As a young priest at Glarus and Einsiedeln, he waged war against the despised mercenary industry from the pulpit and in print. The humanist in him also fought to bring the Scriptures to life during this time, only to find a massive disconnect between the biblical text's instruction and the Catholic Church's practices. He took this realization to Zurich, where a life-long struggle with the papacy began. Yet one of Zwingli's first battles at Zurich was not theological, but of flesh and blood. Plague became a unique and unforeseen opponent, one that nearly stole his life. But even a struggle with his mortality taught the preacher important truths about God's providential hand that steadied him in later battles.

The Reformer's ministry at Zurich focused on moving the Swiss Church away from Catholic idolatry toward purer forms of worship. He promoted the evangelical gospel and changed the church's liturgy. With each of these reforms, the preacher had to fight for every inch of Reformation change that the Zurich Council would permit. These moves set him at odds with traditionalists who opposed him at every turn. Charges of heresy from the Bishop of Constance were merely a reminder of what was at stake and just how dangerous Reformation ideas could be during this era. Even beautiful moments of life, like his marriage to Anna Reinhart, forced the preacher to battle with assumed religious and cultural norms like clerical celibacy to make Reformation a reality. The Anabaptists' radical challenge from the mid-1520s also taught him that conflicts could ensue inside an army's barracks. These battles were as personally painful to him as they were dangerous to his Reformation. Nevertheless, the purity of the gospel and the preservation of society compelled him to act, even if it meant opposing—even supporting the execution of—former students. Struggles to promote this same gospel in places like Bern highlighted the Reformer's belief in the gospel's power and his love for the Swiss Confederation. Those two convictions brought him to Kappel in 1531. War with the Catholics became the final struggle concluding a life shrouded in conflict. There was an ironic symmetry to Zwingli's life and ministry.

The recapitulation of Zwingli's combative life in a gruesome death is also what makes placing him in history so challenging. The cascading consequences of his demise forced the Zurich church away from their former pastor in the ensuing years. Even his close gospel ally, Heinrich Bullinger, waited thirty-three years to offer a defense for his former friend's work. But when he did, the summary of Zwingli's ministry was striking and appropriate:

> He [Zwingli] wanted to interpret the Scripture, and not the opinions of others, to the honor of God and His only Son, our Lord Jesus Christ, as well as to the true salvation of souls and the edification of pious and honorable people. ... He praised God the Father, and taught others to trust only in the Son of God, Jesus Christ, as Savior. He vehemently denounced all unbelief, superstition, and hypocrisy. He eagerly strove after repentance, the improvement of life, and Christian love and faith ... He insisted that the government should maintain law and justice, and protect widows and orphans.[4]

Bullinger's words aptly described Zwingli's pastoral labors at Zurich, where his ministry extended to individuals and the whole of society. However, the vibrancy of his ministry at Zurich stands in stark contrast to his remembrance today. In the wee hours of the morning on October 11, 1531, the preacher left his parsonage traveling west. Along the way he passed by the Grossmunster Church for what would be the final time. He crossed over the Limmat River near a location where hundreds of years later a statue was erected to honor him. Today, this statue stands as a reminder that once he left for Kappel, the preacher never returned to his parish or his pulpit. The Zurich shepherd never attended to his beloved flock again.

FIVE THESES ON ZWINGLI

Like other Protestant Reformers of the era, there remains much to appreciate about Huldrych Zwingli's life and ministry. Many of his Reformation successes offer wisdom about how to lead, cast vision, and how to walk patiently alongside a people toward desired changes. There is also great value in the Reformer's theology, even if one does not completely agree with his Reformed convictions. The Swiss preacher's commitment to Scriptural authority, Christological priority, biblical forms of worship, and a host of other convictions are to be lauded. Even his humanistic desire to make the Bible come alive and to instill life-altering change into its readers is commendable. Unfortunately, there were also events from Zwingli's life and convictions he held that are deeply regrettable—even abhorrent. He made statements and enacted reforms that appear unwise and unnecessary, perhaps even unforgivable, from our twenty-first century vantage point. What follows is a series of theses, or summarizing statements, that I hope will guide you in your own remembrances of a vilified and lauded Reformer.

Thesis 1: The Way of the Cross Does No Violence

Thesis 2: Avoid Conflating Kingdom with Christendom

Thesis 3: Distinguish Between Scriptural Authority and Scriptural Interpretation

Thesis 4: Beware the Blind Spots

Thesis 5: Understand the Responsibility of Remembrance

THESIS 1: THE WAY OF THE CROSS DOES NO VIOLENCE

In his novel *The Go-Between*, British novelist L. P. Hartley famously said, "the past is a foreign country. They do things differently there." There is much truth and wisdom in that statement. In fact, only by carefully considering historical context can we better understand disparate and distant worlds from our own. Nevertheless, there are things Zwingli said and did that stretch these maxims to the breaking point. This especially includes his dealings with the Swiss Anabaptists and his willingness to take up arms against the Catholics. These regrettable decisions and a host of other interactions cast a dark cloud of controversy over his life and ministry. How ever one understands those events, there is simply no excusing his culpability in the execution of religious dissenters or his promotion of violence.

As I reflect upon and regret these chapters from Zwingli's life, I cannot help but wonder how he arrived at such a point. Was it a deficiency in his anthropology? Was it his belief that he was a contemporary prophet? Clearly the Reformer believed that he was defending the truth of the gospel and pure religion. But one must ask if the ends justify the means. The Reformer placed a high priority on Scripture and situated Jesus as the axis point for understanding the text. So why did his desire to imitate Christ not lead the Reformer to promote raising the sword of Scripture alone, instead of an actual blade? Or, given that Jesus dined with tax collectors and sinners, why did Zwingli persecute and facilitate the execution of those he thought godless? For a person who believed so strongly in the priority of the inner transformation of a person against purely outer forms of religion, how did he expect external coercion to incite a change that he knew only God could initiate? These lingering questions compel us to ask questions about ourselves and the way of the cross. They force us to consider the means of preserving and promoting biblical truth.

One is not required to affirm a non-resistant pacifism, like the Swiss Anabaptists, to follow Christ. Most traditions coming out of the Reformation era affirm the power of the state to curb evil and protect life. The greater concern is when God's right hand (the church) begins to take up the weapons divinely bestowed upon the left hand (the state). This misappropriation of authority is where Zwingli made decisions that appear not only foreign to us but altogether unbiblical. In the end, I suspect his mistake regarding this matter was based on a misunderstanding and misapplication of Christ's Kingdom.

THESIS 2: AVOID CONFLATING KINGDOM WITH CHRISTENDOM

Zwingli was born into a world where the comingling of the church and state into one confessional body, the *corpus Christianum*, was assumed. Going as far back as Augustine, many considered the notion of a territorial church to be the biblical model. Despite Zwingli's abiding love of Scripture and his deep desire for sound exegesis, a flaw existed in his understanding of the relationship between the church and the state. It is astonishing how an exegete who lauded interpreting Scripture in its context, paying careful attention to every word of Holy Writ, missed Jesus's explanation of the parable of the wheat and tares (Matt 13:38). Zwingli mistakenly thought the regenerate and the reprobate were to remain commingled within the visible church until Jesus's return. However, according to Christ, "the field is the world," meaning the wheat and the chaff were to grow alongside each other in the broader societal community, not within the church. This important distinction made Zwingli's mixed church both unnecessary and overreaching. That reading of the Bible also intertwined Zwingli's eschatological Kingdom concerns with temporal Swiss ones. This mistake led to much of the Reformer's ruin, even contributing to his death.

This is not the place to consider Just War Theory. There are fine treatments of that topic and plenty of disagreement among fair minded brothers and sisters in Christ on the matter. However, what makes Zwingli's understanding of the church's relationship to armed violence so perplexing is how he lamented the loss of life realized by the Swiss mercenary practice but took no issue with the death of professing Christians via holy war. A careful contextual reading of this ostensible paradox may help us to better understand his position. Zwingli refused to tolerate Swiss soldiers dying in foreign wars for temporal gains. But he was also not about to allow the gospel to be distorted and destroyed by Swiss citizens within the Confederation when eternity was at stake. Zwingli waged war against groups like the Catholics and Anabaptists because he saw them as opponents of the gospel.

Framing things contextually may help us better discern the reasons behind the Reformer's motivation for violence. But understanding a position is different than embracing it. To this end, I greatly appreciate my own Baptist heritage, which helped pave the way for modern beliefs regarding the separation of church and state, religious liberty for all people, and freedom of conscience. These beliefs must be maintained and championed, or we risk returning to a world of intolerance and coercion regrettably characterized by Zwingli's Zurich. The church is a unique and divinely established institution. And so, when we conflate it with territorial ambitions, our eschatological hopes can easily become intertwined with temporal pursuits and our coming Messiah viewed as an already present parliament or politician. When this happens Christ's bride is marred and distorted—even made unrecognizable.

THESIS 3: DISTINGUISH BETWEEN SCRIPTURAL AUTHORITY AND SCRIPTURAL INTERPRETATION

When the Alsatian reformer Wolfgang Capito quipped, "Future generations will laugh at the pleasure our age takes in quarrelling when we raise such disturbances about the very signs that should unite us," he was only partially correct.[5] Laughter is only one of the responses elicited by those in modernity who marvel at the theological divide among the Protestant Reformers. Personally, I am not perplexed that Zwingli was unable to resolve differences with other Reformers, whether that be with Luther at Marburg or the Anabaptists at Zurich. In fact, I expect disagreements between them. But what I do lament about such differences is the ends he was willing to go based upon those divides. Even if Zwingli held to orthodox doctrinal views, those were often maintained alongside a disposition and paired with actions that resulted in divisive, even violent ends.

Whether one is looking at Zwingli or other Reformers like Luther, sadly there was often a disconnect in their theological methodology. On the one hand, they were able to discern when late medieval Catholic additions had veiled over and distorted the gospel. However, there was no consensus regarding how, where, or in what way the Catholic Church made those mistakes. There was even disagreement over when the Catholic Church severed its connection with the historic Apostolic Church. Therefore, while the Reformers all desired to strip authority from the papacy and tear down those Catholic practices which they believed were unbiblical, there was not agreement on how to build back and adorn their Reformation churches. This reality was exacerbated by the fact that the Reformers were often unable to recognize when disagreements among themselves were rooted in different interpretations of the Bible, rather than teachings outside of the Scriptures. In short, Reformers like Zwingli utilized a time-honored way of assessing doctrine when looking at the Catholics, but then failed to properly employ that same measure when looking toward each other.

The Reformers benefited from operating based on a "principle of consensus," as one scholar has dubbed the approach.[6] Such a methodology acknowledged a hierarchical tiering of authority, thereby clarifying how the Reformers used the phrase *sola Scriptura*. This model situated the Bible as the supreme and normative authority for the church. However, the Bible's preeminent authority also utilized secondary, interpretive voices from the past, such as the church fathers and ecumenical councils, as a protective hermeneutical scaffolding. Those collective voices helped preserve the foundational truths of the gospel and the one true faith, as recorded in Scripture. This was how the Reformers employed the term "catholic" amid their disdain for the papacy and Catholicism.

While this methodology provided hermeneutical guardrails that helped Zwingli and others avoid heresy and maintain the gospel, they struggled to apply this same principle to different beliefs within the safe waters of orthodoxy. The Protestant Reformers were united in their convictions regarding the location of authority. Whereas early modern Catholics embraced the Bible and church tradition as two equally authoritative taproots of divine revelation, the Reformers believed that the sacred Scriptures exclusively maintained such an authority. Only the Bible was divinely breathed out by God as the Lord's instruction to His people. However, despite the Reformers shared commitment to the Bible's unique authority, they struggled to find consensus on contested issues derived from Scripture. This was especially true on ecclesial matters related to the sacraments. The authority had not changed for the Reformers. But that authority still needed to be interpreted. And therein lay the problem. Convictions and practices relating to baptism and the Lord's Supper, for instance, became firmly codified into unique beliefs by figures like Zwingli during the Reformation. But those beliefs also crystallized without the realization that differing hermeneutics were shaping those convictions.

In short, Zwingli and many of the other Reformers suffered from a lack of epistemic humility. They could not—or refused to—acknowledge limitations to their own understanding of Scripture. As one theologian has rightly argued, "*sola Scriptura* is both a confession of faith that God's word is infallible, and a confession of sin that our human interpretations are, by contrast fallible."[7] Failing to understand and apply this truth in a consistent manner, everything became a "gospel issue" for the Reformers, even those matters of disagreement based on different readings of the text. This failure, for example, is how and why Zwingli was able to persecute the Anabaptists for their beliefs regarding believers' baptism. In this sense, Zwingli and the other Protestant reformers proved Leo X correct. The unseating of papal authority led to a plurality of "popes" and endless divisions. And living in an era devoid of modern sentiments like religious liberty and religious tolerance meant these divisions led to the shedding of Christian blood by the hands of others who confessed Christ.

Reflecting on this reality in an era of confessionalization requires us to seek discernment in identifying gospel matters from differing readings of Scripture. This is where I have found the distinction between working together and worshiping together to be helpful. There are countless Christians from other confessional heritages that I can work together with where theological and ministerial overlap is found. Places like preserving the sanctity of all human life from the womb until natural death, working to overcome the scourge of human trafficking, and maintaining the preservation of religious liberty for all people are fruitful areas of partnership. But different convictions on matters relating to the sacraments and church polity, for example, still exist and matter greatly to me. As a

Baptist living in a post-Vatican II world, I am grateful for and celebrate the labors of Catholic, Lutheran, Anglican, Presbyterian, and Methodist brothers and sisters, but I cannot plant churches with them. My deep and abiding convictions related to a regenerate church and believers' baptism by immersion, for instance, will not allow it. And we should not just accept but also embrace that reality.

THESIS 4: BEWARE THE BLIND SPOTS

We have gone to great lengths to understand the developmental nature of Zwingli's theology. We also saw how a myriad of influences and experiences informed that theology, some of which were discernable to the Reformer, others of which were not. Theology is always contextual. Zwingli benefitted from his culture as much as it hindered him. As we reflect on the Reformer, especially those missteps that we identified during his journey at Zurich, we must do so carefully.

Given the linear nature of history, there are a couple of tendencies that often surface when reflecting on earlier people from history. Scholars have long warned against seeing the ancients as providing more faithful beliefs and patterns of worship given their chronological proximity to Jesus and the apostles. That erroneous methodology is especially tempting when considering ancient sources from the patristic era. However, given our place post-Enlightenment, a greater temptation remains for us in casting judgment upon earlier figures based upon our modern sensibilities. That does not mean that moral standards are pliable or relative. They are not. We should lament the past moral failings of those who have gone before us. Yet we must not succumb to the temptation of believing that we have somehow arrived as enlightened people, for we too are steeped in a context, albeit different from those who came before us. Just as Zwingli could see some of his biases and was blind to some, we too struggle with self-reflection.

This hindsight is one of the great benefits of history. Looking to the past successes and failings of others may serve as a mirror allowing us to reflect upon our own beliefs today. This introspection should challenge theological assumptions and cultural norms that authorities outside of

Scripture may otherwise establish in us. Our beliefs and practices may not only be wrong, but also abhorrent to those in the future and according to God's holy standards. We should always remember that should the Lord tarry, years from now others will stand in judgement over us. Therefore, we should seek to identify our own blind spots and make corrections accordingly.

THESIS 5: UNDERSTAND THE RESPONSIBILITY OF REMEMBRANCE

In a culture heavily focused on cancellation and deconstruction, the presence of the Zwingli statue in Zurich stands out to many people as a great offense. Given the trajectory of modern society, it is easy to see why some would like to blot Zwingli from the landscape of the beautiful city on the Limmat. However, as a historian, I would caution against such an approach, though such concerns are real and warranted.

Try as one might to remove from memory certain people and events that went before us, we simply cannot. Our worlds are forever and inextricably linked, regardless of what we do with bronze statues and patinaed memorials. One prominent historian has rightly framed this reality as follows:

> Like it or not, we are heirs to this host of divergent even contradictory witnesses. Some of their [professing Christians] actions we may find revolting, others inspiring. But all of them form part of our history. All of them, those whose actions we admire as well as those whose actions we despise, brought us to where we are now.[8]

To tear down the Zwingli monument is to remove a part of our story. With such a move, we would not only lose Zwingli but also a window into the people from the late ninetieth century who sought to honor him. And even if the memorial was erected by those seeking to mistakenly link Zwingli's work with their own liberal, social idealism, their remembrances are still a crucial part of human history and connected to our story. In short, such a removal would be a self-inflicted injury.

Of course, not all memorials are alike. And not all remembrances connote the same ideals. Some tributes represent things that our society no longer wants to platform, nor should we. Honest reflection, advancement, and even repentance make such things unnecessary if not altogether unwelcomed. Certain southern states in the US put away the Confederate battle flag, choosing not to celebrate the Civil War. In Germany, concentration camps like Buchenwald and Dachau remain purposefully standing. Yet a visit to those venues offers only somber reminders of past horrors, not veneration. Crematorium ovens and gas chambers remain so that we may never forget and with the hopeful promise that we will never allow the atrocities of the Holocaust to be repeated. So, when considering how to remember the past, much care should be given and wisdom applied.

Rather than abandoning remembrances of Zwingli, perhaps we should seek to tell the complex and sordid story of the Swiss preacher in a more honest way. We can laud him for his passion for truth, even as we lament his intolerance. We may celebrate his desire to unveil and proclaim the gospel, all the while criticizing him for supporting the execution of other Christ-followers. Given the complex and paradoxical nature of his story, perhaps removing this statue from its elevated public perch and placing it in the *Stadtarchiv* Zurich (State Museum) is in order. Or perhaps the statue should remain in public view but somehow respectfully linked geographically to the memorial plaque installed at the shore of the Limmat River that honors the death of the Anabaptist Felix Manz, Zwingli's former friend and student. Many visitors to Zurich are unaware of the Manz plaque and his story. In an act equally ironic as an image of the iconoclast it represents, maybe Zwingli could point people to the leader of a movement he once sought to eradicate. Surely there are respectful and creative ways to remember our past without honoring the barbarous cruelty from it.

In the end, who is worthy of a statue? The truth is all humans are fallen and limited. The life of Zwingli is a reminder of why it is crucial for Christians today to look to Jesus, not others, as our normative and perfect example. Christ, and Christ alone, is the image of the invisible God and the only hope for humanity. He alone can take the brokenness in our world and restore it to the beauty of God's original design. And once that eschatological hope is realized, for those that are in Him, the feast to be partaken of will not be something to remember. Rather, it will be something to enjoy for all eternity.

Abbreviations

HZW	*Huldrych Zwingli Writings*. Translated and edited by H. Wayne Pipkin and E. J. Furcha. 2 vols. Eugene, OR: Pickwick, 1984.
LW	*Luther's Works: American Edition*. Edited by Jaroslav Pelikan, Helmut T. Lehmann, and Christopher Boyd Brown. 78 vols. Philadelphia: Fortress Press; St. Louis: Concordia Publishing House, 1955–.
LWC I	*Ulrich Zwingli: Early Writings*. Edited by Samuel Macauley Jackson. Vol. I of *The Latin Works and the Correspondence of Huldreich Zwingli*. Durham, NC: Labyrinth Press, 1912. Reprint, Eugene, OR: Wipf & Stock, 1999.
LWC II	*Ulrich Zwingli: On Providence and Other Essays*. Edited by Samuel Macauley Jackson and William John Hinke. Vol. 2 of *The Latin Works and the Correspondence of Huldreich Zwingli*. Durham, NC: Labyrinth Press, 1922. Reprint, Eugene, OR: Wipf & Stock, 1999.
LWC III	*Ulrich Zwingli: Commentary on True and False Religion*. Edited by Samuel Macauley Jackson and Clarence Nevin Heller. Vol. 3 of *The Latin Works and Correspondence of Huldreich Zwingli*. Durham, NC: Labyrinth Press, 1929. Reprint, Eugene, OR: Wipf & Stock, 2015.
Z	*Huldreich Zwinglis sämtliche Werke*. Edited by Emil Egli, Georg Finsler, Walther Köhler, et al. Vols. 88–101 of *Corpus Reformatorum*. Leipzig: Heinsius, 1905–.

ZB	*Zwingli and Bullinger*. Translated and edited by G. W. Bromiley, Jr. Vol. 24 of *The Library of Christian Classics*. Philadelphia: Westminster Press, 1953.
ZS	*Huldreich Zwinglis Werke*. Edited by Melchior Schuler and Johannes Schulthess. 8 vols. Zürich: F. Schulthess, 1828–1842.
ZSW	*Ulrich Zwingli (1484–1531): Selected Works*. Edited by Samuel Macauley Jackson. Philadelphia: University of Philadelphia Press, 1972.

Notes

INTRODUCTION

1. Bruce Gordon, *The Swiss Reformation* (Manchester: Manchester University Press, 2002), 1–2, 5.
2. Stephen Brett Eccher, "Huldrych Zwingli: Reformation in Conflict," *Perichoresis* 15, no. 4 (2017): 33–53.
3. Timothy George, "What the Reformers Thought They Were Doing," in *Celebrating the Legacy of the Reformation*, ed. Kevin L. King, Edward E. Hindson, and Benjamin K. Forrest (Nashville: B&H Academic, 2019), 11–12.
4. John Calvin, *Institutes of the Christian Religion*, ed. John T. McNeill (Louisville: Westminster John Knox Press, 1960), I:61, 72, 341.
5. Bruce Gordon, *Zwingli: God's Armed Prophet* (New Haven: Yale University Press, 2021), 8.
6. G. R. Potter, *Zwingli* (Cambridge: Cambridge University Press, 1978), 10.
7. Ulrich Gäbler, *Huldrych Zwingli: His Life and Work*, trans. Ruth C. L. Gritsch (Philadelphia: Fortress Press, 1986), 25.
8. Carlos Eire, *Reformations: The Early Modern World, 1450–1650* (New Haven: Yale University Press, 2018), 223.
9. Alister E. McGrath, *Reformation Thought: An Introduction*, 4th ed. (Oxford: Wiley-Blackwell, 2012), 39.
10. Amy Nelson Burnett, "Revisiting Humanism and the Urban Reformation," *Lutheran Quarterly* 35, no. 4 (2021): 374–81.
11. Charles G. Nauert, *Humanism and the Culture of Renaissance Europe* (Cambridge: Cambridge University Press, 1995), 171.

12. Michael D. Reeve, "Classical Scholarship," in *The Cambridge Companion to Renaissance Humanism*, ed. Jill Kraye (Cambridge: Cambridge University Press, 1995), 25.
13. Bruce Gordon, Luca Baschera, and Christian Moser, "Emulating the Past and Creating the Present: Reformation and the Use of Historical and Theological Models of Zurich in the Sixteenth Century," in *Following Zwingli: Applying the Past in Reformation Zurich*, ed. Luca Baschera, Bruce Gordon, and Christian Moser (Surrey: Ashgate, 2014), 13.
14. Gottfried W. Locher, *Die Zwinglische Reformation im Rahmen der europäischen Kirchengeschichte* (Göttingen: Vandenhoek and Ruprecht, 1979), 42.
15. Martin Davies, "Humanism in Script and Print in the Fifteenth Century," in *The Cambridge Companion to Renaissance Humanism*, 47.
16. *The Fable of the Ox* (1510), in *Z*, I:11–22; *LWC I*, 27–34.
17. Raeget Christoffel, *Zwingli: Or the Rise of the Reformation in Switzerland* (Edinburgh: T&T Clark, 1858), 42.
18. R. J. Schoeck, *Erasmus of Europe: The Prince of the Humanists 1501–1536* (Edinburgh: Edinburgh University Press, 1993).
19. *The Labyrinth* (1516), in *Z*, I:53–60; *LWC I*, 50–54.
20. Gordon, *Zwingli*, 42.
21. G. R. Potter, *Huldrych Zwingli: Documents of Modern History* (London: Edward Arnold, 1978), 10.
22. Rudolf Pfister, *Kirchengeschichte der Schweiz* (Zurich: Theologischer Verlag Zurich), I:24–25.
23. Desiderius Erasmus, *The Correspondence of Erasmus: Letters 842 to 992*, trans. R. A. B. Mynors and D. F. S. Thompson (Toronto: University of Toronto, 1982), 88–136.
24. "Choice and Liberty Regarding Foods" (1522), in *Z*, I:88–136; *LWC I*, 70–112.
25. Later published as *Exposition of the Sixty-Seven Articles* (1523), in *ZS*, I:175–424; *HZW*, I:7–373.
26. Steven Ozment, *The Age of Reform 1250–1550: An Intellectual and Religious History of Late Medieval and Reformation Europe* (New Haven: Yale University Press, 1980), 381.
27. Gordon, *Swiss Reformation*, 96.

28. Irena Backus, "The Disputations of Baden, 1526 and Berne, 1528: Neutralizing the Early Church," *Studies in Reformed Religion* 1 (1993): 46.
29. Potter, *Zwingli*, 358.

CHAPTER 1: THE SWISS PREACHER

1. *Archeteles* (1522), in *ZS*, III:48; *LWC I*, 239.
2. *About Parenthood that They Should Not Hinder Marriage* (1525), in *Z*, III:488; Timothy George, *Theology of the Reformers*, rev. ed. (Nashville: B&H Academic, 2013), 131.
3. Potter, *Zwingli*, 25.
4. *The Fable of the Ox* (1510), in *Z*, I:10–22; *LWC I*, 27–34.
5. Gordon, *Zwingli*, 31.
6. Bruce Gordon, "Huldrych Zwingli," *The Expository Times* 126, no. 4 (2015): 4.
7. Desiderius Erasmus, "*Paraclesis*," in *Christian Humanism and the Reformation: Selected Writings of Erasmus*, 3rd ed., ed. John C. Olin (New York: Fordham University Press, 2000), 108.
8. *Exposition*, *ZS*, I:254; *HZW*, I:117.
9. *LW*, 54:376, no. 5005, "Table Talk."
10. McGrath, *Reformation Thought*, 49.
11. Desiderius Erasmus, *Praise of Folly and Letter to Maarten Van Dorp*, trans. Betty Radice (New York: Penguin Press, 1993), 3–134; Carter Lindberg, *The European Reformations*, 2nd ed. (Oxford: Wiley-Blackwell, 2010), 50–51.
12. Gäbler, *Huldrych Zwingli*, 33.
13. *Exposition*, *ZS*, I:298; *HZW*, I:171. Also, for more details on Zwingli's revulsion of images and his work to remove them from the Zurich worship practices, see Chapter 2.
14. *A Friendly Exegesis* (1527), in *Z*, V:713–14; Urs Leu and Sandra Weidmann, *Huldrych Zwingli's Private Library* (Leiden: Brill, 2018), 39.
15. Gordon, Baschera, and Moser, "Emulating the Past," 6–7.
16. For details on Erasmus's influence on Zwingli, see Chapter 5.
17. Letter from Beatus Rhenanus to Zwingli (December 6, 1518), in *Z*, VII:115; W. Peter Stephens, *The Theology of Huldrych Zwingli* (Oxford: Clarendon Press, 1986), 109.

18. Heinrich Bullinger, *Reformationsgeschichte*, ed. J. J. Hottinger and H. H. Vgeli (Frauenfeld: Druck und Verlag Ch. Beyel, 1838), I:12.
19. Werner O. Packull, *Hutterite Beginnings: Communitarian Experiments during the Reformation* (Baltimore: Johns Hopkins University Press, 1999), 18.
20. Hughes Oliphant Old, *The Reading and Preaching of the Scriptures in the Worship of the Christian Church, Vol. 4: The Age of the Reformation* (Grand Rapids: Eerdmans, 2002), 46.
21. Luther once famously opined during an *Invocavit* sermon from 1522, "I opposed indulgences and all the papists, but never with force. I simply taught, preached, and wrote God's Word; otherwise, I did nothing. And while I slept, or drank Wittenberg beer with my friends Philip and Amsdorf, the Word so greatly weakened the papacy that no prince or emperor ever inflicted such losses upon it. I did nothing; the Word did everything." *LW*, 51, 77.
22. *Archeteles*, *ZS*, III:48; *LWC I*, 238.
23. Gordon, *Zwingli*, 180.
24. For details on these and other gospel partners, see Chapter 5.
25. *Exposition*, *ZS*, I:253; *HZW*, I:116.
26. *Archeteles*, *ZS*, III:27–28; *LWC I*, 198.
27. For details on Zwingli's understanding of the gospel at Zurich, see Chapter 3.
28. *Archeteles*, *ZS*, III:48; *LWC I*, 239.
29. *Exposition*, *ZS*, I:253; *HZW*, I:116.
30. "The Shepherd" (1524), in *Z*, III:50; *HZW*, II:111.
31. *Archeteles*, *ZS*, III:29; *LWC I*, 201.
32. Oskar Farner, *Huldrych Zwingli: seine Verkündigung und ihre ersten Früchte 1520–1525* (Zürich: Zwingli-Verlag, 1954), III:114–20.
33. His greatest concern was the mercenary business that saw Swiss soldiers as one of the chief exports of the Confederation. "The Ox" (1510) and "The Labyrinth" (1516), in *Z*, I:10–22 and 53–60; *LWC I*, 27–34 and 50–54.
34. Gordon, *Swiss Reformation*, 52.
35. Thomas Platter, *The Autobiography of Thomas Platter: A Schoolmaster of the Sixteenth Century*, 2nd ed., trans. Mrs. Finn (London: B. Wertheim, Aldine Chambers, Paternoster Row, 1847), 39.
36. Lina Hug and Richard Stead, *Switzerland*, rev. and enl. ed. (New York: G.P. Putnam's Sons, 1920), 259.

37. "Letter from Caspar Heido to Huldrych Zwingli (November 6, 1519)," in *ZS*, VII:89–90; Samuel Macauley Jackson, *Huldreich Zwingli: The Reformer of German Switzerland, 1484–1531* (New York: The Knickerbocker Press, 1903), 108.
38. Erasmus attacked many sectors of society, including schoolmasters, lawyers, philosophers, theologians, monks, priests, and even the Pope. Erasmus, *Praise of Folly*, 78ff. Gäbler, *Huldrych Zwingli*, 49.
39. Potter, *Zwingli*, 10.
40. Joe Mock, "Huldrych Zwingli: A Truly Quintessential Reformer," in *Celebrating the Reformation: Its Legacy and Continuing Relevance*, ed. Mark D. Thompson (London: Apollos, 2017), 33.
41. "The Shepherd," *Z*, III:13; *HZW*, II:86.
42. "On the Clarity and Certainty of the Word of God" (1522), in *Z*, I:360; *ZB*, 74.
43. "Clarity and Certainty," *Z*, I:361; *ZB*, 75.
44. Bernhard Wyss, "Die Chronik Bernhard Wyss 1519–1530," in *Quellen zur Schweizerischen Reformationsgeschichte*, ed. Georg Finsler (Basel: Verlag der Basler Buch- und Antiquariatshandlung, 1901), I:10–12; Lee Palmer Wandel, *Always Among Us: Images of the Poor in Zwingli's Zurich* (Cambridge: Cambridge University Press, 1990), 32.
45. Potter, *Zwingli*, 7.
46. The details of this scandalous event are outlined in Chapter 3.
47. "Choice and Liberty Regarding Foods," *Z*, I:88–136; *LWC I*, 70–112.
48. Christopher Kissane, *Food, Religion and Communities in Early Modern Europe* (London: Bloomsbury Academic, 2018), 63.
49. "Choice and Liberty Regarding Foods," *Z*, I:110–11; *LWC I*, 89.
50. *Archeteles*, *ZS*, III:48; *LWC I*, 239.
51. Gordon, *Swiss Reformation*, 54–55.
52. "Clarity and Certainty," *Z*, I:338–84; *ZB*, 59–95.
53. "Clarity and Certainty," *Z*, I:342; *ZB*, 60.
54. "Clarity and Certainty," *Z*, I:356; *ZB*, 71.
55. "Clarity and Certainty," *Z*, I:361; *ZB*, 75.

56. Heiko A. Oberman, *Forerunners of the Reformation: The Shape of Late Medieval Thought*, trans. Paul L. Nyhus (London: Lutterworth, 1967), 60.
57. Heiko A. Oberman, *The Dawn of the Reformation: Essays in Late Medieval and Early Reformation Thought* (Edinburgh: T&T Clark, 1986), 281.
58. "Clarity and Certainty," *Z*, I:375; *ZB*, 87. See also Martin Brecht, *Martin Luther: His Road to Reformation, 1483–1521*, trans. James L. Schaff (Philadelphia: Fortress, 1985), 320–21.
59. "Clarity and Certainty," *Z*, I:375; *ZB*, 87.
60. "Clarity and Certainty," *Z*, I:370; *ZB*, 82.
61. See Chapter 3.
62. "Clarity and Certainty," *Z*, I:383; *ZB*, 94.
63. See Chapter 5.
64. "Sermon on the Eternal Purity of the Virgin Mary" (1522), in *Z*, I:391–428.
65. "Sermon on the Eternal Purity of the Virgin Mary," *Z*, I:395; Gottfried W. Locher, *Zwingli's Thought: New Perspectives* (Leiden: Brill, 1981), 84.
66. Gordon, *Swiss Reformation*, 56.
67. Locher, *Zwingli's Thought*, 84–85.
68. Gordon, Baschera, and Moser, "Emulating the Past," 21.
69. Iren L. Snavely, Jr., "Huldrych Zwingli and the Preaching Office in German Switzerland," *Fides et Historia* 25 (1993): 33–45.
70. Randolph C. Head, "The Swiss Reformations: Movements, Settlements, and Reimagination, 1520–1720," in *The Oxford Handbook of the Protestant Reformations* (Oxford: Oxford University Press, 2017), 170.
71. Hans-Jürgen Goertz, *The Anabaptists* (London: Routledge, 1996), 8–9.
72. Kaspar von Greyerz, *Religion and Culture in Early Modern Europe, 1500–1800*, trans. Thomas Dunlap (Oxford: Oxford University Press, 2008), 160.
73. "Divine and Human Righteousness" (1523), in *Z*, II:471–525; *HZW*, II:3–40.
74. "Divine and Human Righteousness," *Z*, II:476–78; *HZW*, II:6–7.
75. "Divine and Human Righteousness," *Z*, II:478; *HZW*, II:7.
76. This was especially present in Books 4–7 of Erasmus' *Enchiridion*. See Desiderius Erasmus, *The Enchiridion of Erasmus*, ed. Raymond Himelick (Gloucester: Indiana University Press, 1970), 59–78. Darren M. Provost, "Erasmus, Christian Humanism, and Spiritual Warfare," in *Re-Envisioning*

Christian Humanism: Education and the Restoration of Humanity, ed. Jens Zimmermann (Oxford: Oxford University Press, 2019), 49ff.

77. Stephens, *Theology of Zwingli*, 296–97.
78. "Divine and Human Righteousness," *Z*, II:497–98; *HZW*, II:21–22.
79. W. Peter Stephens, "The Theology of Zwingli," in *The Cambridge Companion to Reformation Theology*, ed. David Bagchi and David C. Steinmetz (Cambridge: Cambridge University Press, 2004), 95.
80. "Divine and Human Righteousness," *Z*, II:500; *HZW*, II:23.
81. McGrath, *Reformation Thought*, 105.
82. I. L. Snavely, Jr., "Ulrich Zwingli (1484–1531)," in *Historical Handbook of Major Biblical Interpreters*, ed. Donald K. McKim (Downers Grove, IL: InterVarsity Press, 1998), 254.
83. Peter Opitz, "The Exegetical and Hermeneutical Work of John Oecolampadius, Huldrych Zwingli, and John Calvin," in *From the Renaissance to the Enlightenment*, ed. Magne Sæbø, Vol. II of *Hebrew Bible / Old Testament: The History of Its Interpretation* (Göttingen: Vandenhoeck & Ruprecht, 2008), 416.
84. Locher, *Zwingli's Thought*, 245–46.
85. "Reply to Balthasar Hubmaier" (1525), in *Z*, IV:637–38.
86. "Reply to Balthasar Hubmaier," *Z*, IV:618.
87. J. Wayne Baker, *Heinrich Bullinger and the Covenant: The Other Reformed Tradition* (Athens: Ohio University Press, 1980), 2.
88. Opitz, "Exegetical and Hermeneutical Work," 416.
89. Hilmar M. Pabel, *Erasmus' Vision of the Church* (Kirksville, MO: Truman State University Press, 1994), 58.
90. "Letter to Franz Lambert (December 16, 1524)," in *Z*, VIII:269; Leland Harder, ed., *The Sources of Swiss Anabaptism* (Scottdale: Herald Press, 1985), 304.
91. John H. Yoder, *Anabaptism and Reformation in Switzerland: An Historical and Theological Analysis of the Dialogues Between Anabaptists and Reformers* (Kitchener: Pandora Press, 2004), 177.
92. Joachim Vadian, *Die Vadienische Briefsammlung der Stadtbibliothek St. Gallen*, Vol. III, no. 437 (St. Gallen: Fehr'sche Buchhandlung, 1888), 127.
93. H. Wayne Pipkin and John H. Yoder, eds., *Balthasar Hubmaier: Theologian of Anabaptism* (Scottdale: Herald Press, 1989), 151.

94. George Huntston Williams, *The Radical Reformation* (Philadelphia: Westminster Press, 1964), 593–94.
95. "The Shepherd," *Z*, III:5–68; *HZW*, II:81–124.
96. "The Shepherd," *Z*, III:13; *HZW*, II:86.
97. "The Shepherd," *Z*, III:13, 18, and 22; *HZW*, II:86, 90, and 92–93.
98. Stephens, "Theology of Zwingli," 94.
99. "The Shepherd," *Z*, III:19–20; *HZW*, II:90–91.
100. "The Shepherd," *Z*, III:43; *HZW*, II:106.
101. Andrew Allan Chibi, *The Wheat and the Tares: Doctrines of the Church in the Reformation, 1500–1590* (Eugene, OR: Pickwick, 2015), 108.
102. This biblical connection was reiterated in both the preface and main body of the 1524 published version. "The Shepherd," *Z*, III:9, 27; *HZW*, II:83, 95.
103. *On the Preaching Office* (1525), in *Z*, IV:382–433; *HZW*, II:150–84.
104. *On the Preaching Office*, *Z*, IV:390–93, 398; *HZW*, II:155–58, 161. G. Sujin Pak, *The Reformation of Prophecy: Early Modern Interpretations of the Prophet and Old Testament Prophecy* (Oxford: Oxford University Press, 2018), 94.
105. *On the Preaching Office*, *Z*, IV:383; *HZW*, II:150–51.
106. *On the Preaching Office*, *Z*, IV:393–94; *HZW*, II:158.
107. *On the Preaching Office*, *Z*, IV:394, 417–18; *HZW*, II:159, 173–74. For details on the *Prophezei*, see Chapter 5.
108. Malcolm B. Yarnell. "Anabaptist Spirituality," in *The Pure Flame of Devotion: The History of Christian Spirituality*, ed. G. Stephen Weaver Jr. and Ian Hugh Clary (Kitchener: Joshua Press, 2013), 163–64.
109. "Divine and Human Righteousness," *Z*, II:495; *HZW*, II:20.
110. *A Short Christian Instruction* (1523), in *Z*, II:656; *HZW*, II:69.
111. "Divine and Human Righteousness," *Z*, II:503; *HZW*, II:25.
112. "Divine and Human Righteousness," *Z*, II:494; *HZW*, II:19.
113. *A Faithful and Earnest Exhortation to the Swiss* (1524), *Z*, III:112–13; *HZW*, VI:121; Locher, *Zwingli's Thought*, 4.
114. *A Faithful and Earnest Exhortation*, *Z*, III:112; *HZW*, VI:121. Locher, *Zwingli's Thought*, 4.
115. *The Acts of the First Zurich Disputation* (1523), in *Z*, I:497.

CHAPTER 2: THE REFORMATION OF WORSHIP

1. *Subsidiary Tract on the Eucharist* (1525), in *Z*, IV:460; *HZW*, II:189.
2. "An Order of Mass and Communion for the Church at Wittenberg" (1523), *LW*, 53, 20.
3. "An Order of Mass and Communion for the Church at Wittenberg" (1523), *LW*, 53, 21.
4. For a detailed assessment of Zwingli's understanding of the doctrine of priesthood, see Chapter 5.
5. *Archeteles*, *ZS*, III:31; *LWC I*, 204.
6. *Archeteles*, *ZS*, III:31; *LWC I*, 204.
7. Mark U. Edwards, *Printing, Propaganda, and Martin Luther* (Minneapolis: Fortress Press, 2005), 37.
8. *Exposition*, *ZS*, IV:74; *LWC*, II:287.
9. *Exposition*, *ZS*, IV:77; *LWC*, II:291.
10. Bruce Gordon, "Transcendence and Community in Zwinglian Worship: The Liturgy of 1525 in Zurich," in *Continuity and Change in Christian Worship*, ed. R. N. Swanson (Suffolk: The Boydell Press, 1999), 138.
11. *Archeteles*, *ZS*, III:31; *LWC I*, 204.
12. Bullinger, *Reformationsgeschichte*, I:12.
13. Packull, *Hutterite Beginnings*, 18.
14. Old, *Reading and Preaching*, 46.
15. For the standard medieval lectionary, see Martin Luther, *Deutsche Bibel*, Band 7 of *D. Martin Luthers Werke* (Weimar: H. Böhlaus Nachfolger, 1968), 536–44.
16. Snavely, "Ulrich Zwingli," 250.
17. Emidio Campi, "The Reformation in Zurich," in *A Companion to the Swiss Reformation*, ed. Amy Nelson Burnett and Emidio Campi (Leiden: Brill, 2016), 69; Peter Opitz, "The Authority of Scripture in the Early Zurich Reformation (1522–1540)," *Journal of Reformed Theology* 5 (2011): 298.
18. *Archeteles*, *Z*, I:257; *LWC*, I:200.
19. Gordon, *Swiss Reformation*, 52.
20. For a detailed account of this broken fast, see Chapter 3.
21. Jean Rilliet, *Zwingli: Third Man of the Reformation*, trans. Harold Knight (Philadelphia: Westminster, 1964), 83.

22. J. P. Whitney, "The Helvetic Reformation," in Vol. 2 of *The Cambridge Modern History*, ed. A. W. Ward, G. W. Prothero, and Stanley Leathes (The Macmillan Company, 1904), 318.
23. *An Attempt Regarding the Canon of the Mass* (1523), in *Z*, II:556–608.
24. Yoder, *Anabaptism and Reformation*, 10.
25. *Zwingli's Apology of His Canon of the Mass* (1523) in *Z*, II:620; *Sources of Swiss Anabaptism*, 227.
26. *Zwingli's Apology of His Canon of the Mass*, *Z*, II:620; *Sources of Swiss Anabaptism*, 228.
27. Charles Garside, Jr., "Ludwig Haetzer's Pamphlet Against Images: A Critical Study," *Mennonite Quarterly Review* 34, no. 1 (1960): 20–36.
28. Gordon, *Swiss Reformation*, 63.
29. Lee Palmer Wandel, *Voracious Idols & Violent Hands: Iconoclasm in Reformation Zurich, Strasbourg, and Basel* (Cambridge: Cambridge University Press, 1999), 73, 79.
30. John of Damascus, *On the Images of the Divine: Three Apologies against Those Who Attack the Divine Images*, trans. David Anderson (Crestwood, NY: St. Vladimir's Seminary Press, 1980), 25.
31. Wandel, *Voracious Idols & Violent Hands*, 39.
32. Karen Maag, *Worshiping with the Reformers* (Downers Grove, IL: InterVarsity Press, 2021), 192.
33. *Commentary on True and False Religion* (1525) in *Z*, III:900; *LWC*, II:331.
34. Mary G. Winkler, "A Divided Heart: Idolatry and the Portraiture of Hans Asper," *The Sixteenth Century Journal* 18 (1987): 214.
35. "Reply to Valentin Compar" (1525), in *Z*, IV:108; Wandel, *Always Among Us*, 61.
36. "Reply to Valentin Compar," *Z*, IV:146; Wandel, *Always Among Us*, 63.
37. "Zwingli's Final Sermon at Bern" (1528), in *ZS*, II:227; Maag, *Worshiping with the Reformers*, 193.
38. Brecht, *Martin Luther, Volume 2: Shaping and Defining the Reformation*, trans. James L. Schaaf (Philadelphia: Fortress Press, 1994), 34.
39. These especially involved congregations withholding their tithes and the demand that the Mass be abolished. See Goertz, *The Anabaptists*, 10–11.
40. The details related to this debate will be covered more comprehensively in Chapter 5.

41. *The Second Zurich Disputation* (1523), in *Z*, II:707; *Sources of Swiss Anabaptism*, 236.
42. *The Second Zurich Disputation*, *Z*, II:708; *Sources of Swiss Anabaptism*, 237.
43. *A Short Christian Instruction* (1523), in *Z*, II:628; *HZW*, II:48.
44. *A Short Christian Instruction*, *Z*, II:655; *HZW*, II:68.
45. *A Short Christian Instruction*, *Z*, II:655; *HZW*, II:68.
46. See Chapter 6 on the Lord's Supper.
47. *A Short Christian Instruction*, *Z*, II:655; *HZW*, II:69.
48. *A Short Christian Instruction*, *Z*, II:655; *HZW*, II:69.
49. *A Short Christian Instruction*, *Z*, II:656; *HZW*, II:69.
50. *A Short Christian Instruction*, *Z*, II:657; *HZW*, II:70.
51. *Exposition*, *ZS*, I:372; *HZW*, I:284.
52. *Exposition*, *ZS*, I:374; *HZW*, I:287.
53. *Exposition*, *ZS*, I:373; *HZW*, I:286.
54. *Exposition*, *ZS*, I:373, 375; *HZW*, I:286, 288.
55. *Exposition*, *ZS*, I:373; *HZW*, I:285.
56. Maag, *Worshiping with the Reformers*, 177.
57. *Exposition*, *ZS*, I:372; *HZW*, I:284.
58. *Exposition*, *ZS*, I:374; *HZW*, I:287.
59. *Exposition*, *ZS*, I:373; *HZW*, I:285.
60. *Exposition*, *ZS*, I:374; *HZW*, I:287.
61. Charles Garside, Jr., *Zwingli and the Arts* (New Haven: Yale University Press, 1966), 47.
62. Wandel, *Voracious Idols & Violent Hands*, 90–92.
63. Emil Egli, *Actensammlung zur Geschichte der Zürcher Reformation in den Jahren 1519–1533* (Zurich: Druck von J. Schabelitz, 1879), 234.
64. Wandel, *Voracious Idols & Violent Hands*, 94–95.
65. *Commentary on True and False Religion*, *Z*, III:774; *LWC*, II:198–99.
66. *Commentary on True and False Religion*, *Z*, III:774; *LWC*, II:198.
67. Gordon, Baschera, and Moser, "Emulating the Past," 4.
68. *Subsidiary Tract on the Eucharist* (1525), in *Z*, IV: 480–81; *HZW*, II:209–10.

69. Fritz Büsser, *Das katholische Zwinglibild: Von der Reformation bis zur Gegenwart* (Zurich: Zwingli-Verlag, 1968), 197ff.

70. *Act or Custom of the Supper* (1525), in *Z*, IV:13–24; Jonathan Gibson and Mark Earngey, eds., *Reformation Worship: Liturgies from the Past for the Present* (Greensboro, NC: New Growth Press, 2018), 180–92; *An Exposition of the Christian Faith* (1531), in *ZS*, IV:42–78; *LWC*, II:287–90.

71. Norman P. Tanner, *Decrees of the Ecumenical Councils* (Washington, DC: Georgetown University Press, 1990), I:245.

72. Carrie Euler, "Huldrych Zwingli and Heinrich Bullinger," in *A Companion to the Eucharist in the Reformation*, ed. Lee Palmer Wandel (Leiden: Brill, 2014), 63.

73. Gordon, "Transcendence and Community," 133.

74. James F. White, *Protestant Worship: Traditions in Transition* (Louisville: Westminster John Knox, 1989), 61.

75. Bruno Bürki, "The Reformed Tradition in Continental Europe, Switzerland, France, and Germany," in *The Oxford History of Christian Worship*, ed. Geoffrey Wainwright and Karen B. Westerfield Tucker (Oxford: Oxford University Press, 2006), 439.

76. *Order of the Christian Church at Zurich* (1525), in *Z*, IV:686; Gibson and Earngey, *Reformation Worship*, 193.

77. *Order of the Christian Church at Zurich*, *Z*, IV:686; Gibson and Earngey, *Reformation Worship*, 193.

78. *Order of the Christian Church at Zurich*, *Z*, IV:687; Gibson and Earngey, *Reformation Worship*, 194.

79. *Order of the Christian Church at Zurich*, *Z*, IV:686; Gibson and Earngey, *Reformation Worship*, 193.

80. For details on this encounter, see Chapter 4.

81. *Commentary on True and False Religion*, *Z*, III:820; *LWC II*, 253.

82. *An Exposition of the Christian Faith*, *ZS*, IV:74; *LWC II*, 287.

83. This is how Zwingli described the content of all Eucharist sermons. See *An Exposition of the Christian Faith*, *ZS*, IV:74; *LWC II*, 287.

84. *An Exposition of the Christian Faith*, *ZS*, IV:78; *LWC II*, 292.

85. Luther had similarly invited the people to a greater active participation in the faith as a part of the priesthood of all believers. See Hans-Joachim Köhler, "Erste Schritte zu einem Meinungsprofil der frühen Reformationszeit," in

Martin Luther: Probleme seiner Zeit, ed. Volker Press and Dieter Stievermann (Stuttgart: Klett-Cotta, 1986), 246.

86. Much of this drama was outlined by Zwingli in 1531. See *An Exposition of the Christian Faith*, *ZS*, IV:74–777; *LWC II*, 287ff.
87. *Commentary on True and False Religion*, *Z*, III:776; *LWC II*, 201.
88. Gordon, "Transcendence and Community," 138.
89. Campi, "The Reformation in Zurich," 78.
90. *Act or Custom of the Supper*, *Z*, IV:17; Gibson and Earngey, *Reformation Worship*, 185.
91. *An Exposition of the Christian Faith* (1531) in ZS, IV, 77; *LWC*, II, 290.
92. For more details on Zwingli's belief in these two related focuses of the Supper see Chapter 6.
93. *Act or Custom of the Supper*, *Z*, IV:19; Gibson and Earngey, *Reformation Worship*, 186–87.
94. This was rooted in a new vision for priesthood among the Reformers. Elsie McKee, ed., *Katharina Schütz Zell: Church Mother* (Chicago: University of Chicago Press, 2006), 84–85.
95. *Act or Custom of the Supper*, *Z*, IV:19–20; Gibson and Earngey, *Reformation Worship*, 187–88.
96. Lee Palmer Wandel, *The Eucharist in the Reformation: Incarnation and Liturgy* (Cambridge: Cambridge University Press, 2006), 23.
97. *An Exposition of the Christian Faith*, *ZS*, IV:78; *LWC II*, 292.
98. *Act or Custom of the Supper*, *Z*, IV:13; Gibson and Earngey, *Reformation Worship*, 182.
99. Euler, "Zwingli and Bullinger," 63.
100. *Exposition*, *ZS*, I:234, *HZW*, I:94.
101. *An Exposition of the Christian Faith*, *ZS*, IV:76; *LWC II*, 289.
102. *An Exposition of the Christian Faith*, *ZS*, IV:77; *LWC II*, 290.
103. *An Exposition of the Christian Faith*, *ZS*, IV:78; *LWC II*, 292.
104. *Commentary on True and False Religion*, *Z*, III:777; *LWC II*, 202.
105. *Commentary on True and False Religion*, *Z*, III:777; *LWC II*, 202.
106. Gordon, "Transcendence and Community," 130.
107. Gordon, Baschera, and Moser, "Emulating the Past," 19.

108. Gibson and Earngey, *Reformation Worship*, 176.
109. *Act or Custom of the Supper*, *Z*, IV:13; Gibson and Earngey, *Reformation Worship*, 182.

CHAPTER 3: UNVEILING THE GOSPEL

1. "Divine and Human Righteousness," *Z*, II:478; *HZW*, II:7.
2. Caroline Walker Bynum, *Holy Feast & Holy Fast: The Religious Significance of Food to Medieval Women* (Berkeley: University of California Press, 1987), 33.
3. John F. Romano, "Priests and the Eucharist in the Middle Ages," in *A Companion to Priesthood: Priesthood and Holy Orders in the Middle Ages*, ed. Greg Peters and C. Colt Anderson (Leiden: Brill, 2016), 188.
4. *Exposition*, *ZS*, I:298; *HZW*, I:171.
5. *Exposition*, *ZS*, I:261; *HZW*, I:128.
6. *Exposition*, *ZS*, I:261; *HZW*, I:129.
7. *A Short Christian Instruction* (1523), in *Z*, II:645; *HZW*, II:61.
8. *Exposition*, *ZS*, I:261; *HZW*, I:128.
9. Janet Gordon Hardy, *Story of a Noble Life or Zurich and its Reformer, Ulric Zwingli* (Edinburgh: Wiam P. Nimmo & Co., 1884), 30.
10. Jean Henry Merle D'Aubigné, *History of the Reformation in the Sixteenth Century*, part 1 (London: Whittaker & Company, 1842), 229.
11. *Exposition*, *ZS*, I:261; *HZW*, I:128.
12. *Exposition*, *ZS*, I:261; *HZW*, I:128.
13. *Exposition*, *ZS*, I:180, 379–81; *HZW*, I:17, 298–300.
14. W. Peter Stephens, *Zwingli: An Introduction to His Thought* (Oxford: Clarendon, 1994), 68.
15. *Exposition*, *ZS*, I:261; *HZW*, I:129.
16. *Exposition*, *ZS*, I:269; *HZW*, I:138.
17. *Exposition*, *ZS*, I:269; *HZW*, I:138.
18. *Exposition*, *ZS*, I:175; *HZW*, I:7.
19. *Exposition*, *ZS*, I:175; *HZW*, I:7.
20. *Exposition*, *ZS*, I:205; *HZW*, I:52.
21. *Exposition*, *ZS*, I:205; *HZW*, I:52–53.
22. Locher, *Zwingli's Thought*, 72–86.

23. *Third Writing Against Johann Faber* (1526), in *Z*, V:307; Locher, *Zwingli's Thought*, 72.
24. *Exposition*, *ZS*, I:195; *HZW*, I:37.
25. *Third Writing Against Johann Faber*, *Z*, V:307; Locher, *Zwingli's Thought*, 78.
26. Locher, *Zwingli's Thought*, 72.
27. George, *Theology of the Reformers*, 82.
28. *A Friendly Exegesis* (1527), in *Z*, V:609; *HZW*, II:270.
29. *A Friendly Exegesis*, *Z*, V:609; *HZW*, II:270.
30. *A Friendly Exegesis*, *Z*, V:713–14; *HZW*, II:344.
31. *Exposition*, *ZS*, I:257; *HZW*, I:121.
32. Bruce Gordon, "For If We Are True Prophets: Huldrych Zwingli on Martin Luther," *Reformation* 22, no. 2 (2017): 107.
33. See Chapter 1.
34. "Letter to Matthew Alber" (1524), in *Z*, III:340; *HZW*, II:135.
35. Erasmus, "*Paraclesis*," 108.
36. Kissane, *Food, Religion and Communities*, 56.
37. Gäbler, *Huldrych Zwingli*, 52.
38. Gibson and Earngey, *Reformation Worship*, 177.
39. Gordon, *Zwingli*, 63.
40. Kissane, *Food, Religion and Communities*, 60–61.
41. "Choice and Liberty Regarding Foods," *Z*, I:89; *LWC I*, 71.
42. "Choice and Liberty Regarding Foods," *Z*, I:89; *LWC I*, 71.
43. "Choice and Liberty Regarding Foods," *Z*, I:91–92; *LWC I*, 73.
44. "Choice and Liberty Regarding Foods," *Z*, I:94; *LWC I*, 76.
45. "Choice and Liberty Regarding Foods," *Z*, I:89; *LWC I*, 71–72.
46. Gordon, Baschera, and Moser, "Emulating the Past," 5.
47. Peter A. Lillback, "The Relationship of Church and State," in *Reformation Theology: A Systematic Introduction*, ed. Matthew Barrett (Wheaton: Crossway, 2017), 689.
48. "The Shepherd," *Z*, III:36; *HZW*, II:102.
49. *Commentary on True and False Religion*, *Z*, III:691; *LWC III*, 119.
50. *A Friendly Exegesis*, *Z*, V:719; *HZW*, II:345.

51. *Commentary on True and False Religion*, *Z*, III:678–79; *LWC III*, 103.
52. Alister E. McGrath, *Iustitia Dei: A History of the Christian Doctrine of Justification*, 3rd ed. (Cambridge: Cambridge University Press, 2005), 107–17.
53. *Commentary on True and False Religion*, *Z*, III:708; *LWC III*, 138–39.
54. See Chapter 4.
55. "Divine and Human Righteousness," *Z*, II:483; *HZW*, II:11.
56. Stephens, *Zwingli: An Introduction*, 68.
57. "Divine and Human Righteousness," *Z*, II:478; *HZW*, II:7.
58. Stephens, *Theology of Zwingli*, 118–20.
59. *Commentary on True and False Religion*, *Z*, III:676; *LWC III*, 100.
60. *Commentary on True and False Religion*, *Z*, III:681; *LWC III*, 106.
61. *Exposition*, *ZS*, I:242; *HZW*, I:104.
62. *Commentary on True and False Religion*, *Z*, III:695, *LWC III*, 123.
63. *Commentary on True and False Religion*, *Z*, III:784; *LWC III*, 211.
64. *Commentary on True and False Religion*, *Z*, III:695, *LWC III*, 123.
65. *An Exposition of the Christian Faith*, *ZS*, IV:45; *LWC II*, 243.
66. *An Exposition of the Christian Faith*, *ZS*, IV:54, *LWC II*, 253.
67. *Commentary on Exodus*, *Z*, XIII:389.
68. *Commentary on True and False Religion*, *Z*, III:695, *LWC III*, 123.
69. *Exposition*, *ZS*, I:249; *HZW*, I:112.
70. *Exposition*, *ZS*, I:179; *HZW*, I:14.
71. *Exposition*, *ZS*, I:330; *HZW*, I:267.
72. Aurelio A. García, "'Summum Bonum' in the Zurich Reformation," *Zwingliana* 44, (2017): 179–97.
73. *Exposition*, *ZS*, I:56, 58; *HZW*, I:42–43. Also see "The Shepherd," *Z*, III:47–48; *HZW*, II:110.
74. Jaques Courvoisier, *Zwingli: A Reformed Theologian* (Richmond: John Knox, 1963), 51.
75. *An Account of the Faith* (1530), in *Die Bekenntnisscriften der Reformierten Kirche*, ed. E. F. Karl Müller (Leipzig: A. Deichert'sche Verlagsbuchhandlung Nachfolge), 85; *LWC II*, 44.
76. Calvin, *Institutes*, II:1021–22.
77. *An Exposition of the Christian Faith*, *ZS*, IV:58; *LWC II*, 260.

78. *An Exposition of the Christian Faith*, *ZS*, IV:58; *LWC II*, 261
79. "Letter to Ambrosius Blaurer" (1528), in *Z*, IX:452.
80. James M. Stayer, *Anabaptists and the Sword* (Lawrence: Coronado Press, 1972), 49.
81. McGrath, *Reformation Thought*, 129.
82. Mock, "Quintessential Reformer," 33.
83. "Divine and Human Righteousness," *Z*, II:473; *HZW*, II:6.
84. "Divine and Human Righteousness," *Z*, II:500; *HZW*, II:23.
85. *Commentary on True and False Religion*, *Z*, III:636; *LWC III*, 53.
86. "The Shepherd," *Z*, III:57; *HZW*, II:116.
87. *Commentary on True and False Religion*, *Z*, III:692; *LWC III*, 119.
88. *A Short Christian Instruction*, *Z*, II:640; *HZW*, II:57.
89. *Commentary on True and False Religion*, *Z*, III:692; *LWC III*, 120.
90. *Commentary on True and False Religion*, *Z*, III:692; *LWC III*, 119.
91. Also see *Commentary on True and False Religion*, *Z*, III:640; *LWC III*, 58. The opening of Book One, Chapter One of Calvin's *Institutes* declares, "Nearly all the wisdom we possess, that is to say, true and sound wisdom, consists in two parts: the knowledge of God and ourselves." Calvin, *Institutes*, I:35.
92. *A Short Christian Instruction*, *Z*, II:640; *HZW*, II:57.
93. *A Short Christian Instruction*, *Z*, II:639; *HZW*, II:56–57.
94. *Commentary on True and False Religion*, *Z*, III:821; *LWC III*, 254.
95. See Chapter 6.
96. *Exposition*, *ZS*, I:185; *HZW*, I:25. In his *Commentary*, Zwingli connected this second part of the gospel with repentance. *Commentary on True and False Religion*, *Z*, III:702; *LWC III*, 131.
97. "Divine and Human Righteousness," *Z*, II:478; *HZW*, II:7.
98. Stephens, *Theology of Zwingli*, 160.
99. *Exposition*, *ZS*, I:209; *HZW*, I:62.
100. *Exposition*, *ZS*, I:211; *HZW*, I:64.
101. "Letter to Franz Lambert" (1524), in *Z*, VIII:264; Stephens, *Theology of Zwingli*, 164.
102. *A Short Christian Instruction*, *Z*, II:640; *HZW*, II:57.
103. *Commentary on True and False Religion*, *Z*, III:705; *LWC III*, 137.

104. "Reply to Jerome Emser" (1524), in *Z*, III:253; *LWC III*, 367.
105. "Reply to Jerome Emser," *Z*, III:253; *LWC III*, 367.
106. *An Account of the Faith*, *Z*, VI:800; *LWC II*, 43.
107. "Reply to Emser," *Z*, III:254; *LWC III*, 367.
108. *Refutation of the Catabaptist Tricks* (1527), in *Z*, VI.1:113; Samuel Macauley Jackson, *Ulrich Zwingli (1484–1531): Selected Works*, (Philadelphia: University of Pennsylvania Press, 1972), 182.
109. In a July 2, 1522, letter, he suggested that the Bishop of Constance "wink" at the marriages of certain Swiss clergy as a practical concession, despite what might have been best, especially if the bishop was not going to formally grant priests permission to marry. See *Petition to Allow the Priests to Marry* (1522), in *Z*, I:197; *LWC I*, 150.
110. *Baptism, Rebaptism, and Infant Baptism* (1525), in *Z*, IV:207.
111. *Refutation of the Catabaptist Tricks*, *Z*, VI.1:113; Jackson, *Zwingli: Selected Works*, 182.
112. Stephen Brett Eccher, "A Return to Christ's Kingdom," *Southeastern Theological Review* 5, no. 2 (2014): 231.
113. "Letter to Franz Lambert," *Z*, VIII:265; Stephens, *Theology of Zwingli*, 164.
114. *Refutation of the Catabaptist Tricks*, *Z*, VI.1:31; Jackson, *Zwingli: Selected Works*, 132.
115. See Chapter 5.

CHAPTER 4: THE SOVEREIGN LORD OF ZURICH

1. "Plague Song" (1519), in *ZS*, II.2:270; *LWC I*, 56.
2. *A Faithful and Earnest Exhortation*, *Z*, III:106; Potter, *Huldrych Zwingli: Documents*, 2.
3. *A Faithful and Earnest Exhortation*, *Z*, III:106; Potter, *Huldrych Zwingli: Documents*, 2.
4. *A Faithful and Earnest Exhortation*, *Z*, III:106; Potter, *Huldrych Zwingli: Documents*, 2.
5. *A Godly Exhortation to the Swiss Confederates* (1522), in *ZS*, II.2:315; *LWC I*, 135.
6. *A Godly Exhortation*, *ZS*, II.2:289; *LWC I*, 135.
7. *A Godly Exhortation*, *ZS*, II.2:290; *LWC I*, 136.
8. *A Godly Exhortation*, *ZS*, II.2:290–91; *LWC II*, 137.

9. *A Godly Exhortation*, *ZS*, II.2:297–98; *LWC II*, 147–48.
10. *A Godly Exhortation*, *ZS*, II.2:297; *LWC II*, 148; quoting Romans 8:31.
11. *A Godly Exhortation*, *ZS*, II.2:297–98; *LWC II*, 148.
12. Hunt Janin and Ursula Carlson, *Mercenaries in Medieval and Renaissance Europe* (Jefferson: McFarland & Company, 2013), 178–80.
13. *A Godly Exhortation*, *ZS*, II.2:297–98; *LWC II*, 148.
14. "Sermon on the Providence of God" (1530), in *ZS*, IV:113; *LWC II*, 184.
15. McGrath, *Iustitia Dei*, 250–51.
16. Arthur Rich, *Die Anfänge der Theologie Huldrych Zwinglis* (Zürich: Zwingli-Verlag, 1949), 67–70.
17. Lindberg, *The European Reformations*, 26.
18. Potter, *Zwingli*, 57.
19. *LW*, 43, 120.
20. Gordon, "Huldrych Zwingli," 161.
21. "Plague Song," *ZS*, II.2:270; *LWC I*, 56.
22. "Plague Song," *ZS*, II.2:270; *LWC I*, 56.
23. "Plague Song," *ZS*, II.2:271; *LWC I*, 57.
24. "Plague Song," *ZS*, II.2:270; *LWC I*, 56.
25. "Plague Song," *ZS*, II.2:271; *LWC I*, 57.
26. Jean Grob, *Ulrich Zwingli: Second Jubilee Gift for the Fourth Centenary of His Birthday* (Reading: Daniel Miller, 1885), 67.
27. McGrath, *Reformation Thought*, 194–95.
28. "Letter to Oswald Myconius" (1520), in *ZS*, VII:144; Jackson, *Huldreich Zwingli*, 148.
29. "Letter to Oswald Myconius," *ZS*, VII:144.
30. *Exposition*, *ZS*, I:278; *HZW*, I:148.
31. *Exposition*, *ZS*, I:273; *HZW*, I:142.
32. *Exposition*, *ZS*, I:261; *HZW*, I:128.
33. *Exposition*, *ZS*, I:274; *HZW*, I:144.
34. *Exposition*, *ZS*, I:275; *HZW*, I:145.
35. *Exposition*, *ZS*, I:275; *HZW*, I:145.
36. "Letter to Joachim Vadian" (March 28, 1528), in *ZS*, VII:333–34; Stephens, *Zwingli: An Introduction*, 47.

37. Stephens, *Zwingli: An Introduction*, 47.
38. Jackson, *Huldreich Zwingli*, 148.
39. "Letter to Oswald Myconius," *ZS*, VII:155.
40. "Letter to Oswald Myconius," *ZS*, VII:155.
41. "Letter to Oswald Myconius," *ZS*, VII:104.
42. Alister E. McGrath, *The Intellectual Origins of the European Reformation* (Oxford: Basil Blackwell, 1987), 49.
43. Rich, *Anfänge der Theologie*, 75–77.
44. *Archeteles*, *ZS*, III:47–48; *LWC*, I:239.
45. *Commentary on True and False Religion*, *Z*, III:647; *LWC III*, 66.
46. *Commentary on True and False Religion*, *Z*, III:649; *LWC III*, 69.
47. *Commentary on True and False Religion*, *Z*, III:649, *LWC III*, 70.
48. *Commentary on True and False Religion*, *Z*, III:647; *LWC III*, 67.
49. "Zwingli's Two Sermons in Bern" (1528), in *Z*, VI.1:455; Potter, *Huldrych Zwingli: Documents*, 82.
50. "Zwingli's Two Sermons in Bern," *Z*, VI.1:455; Potter, *Huldrych Zwingli: Documents*, 82.
51. "Sermon on the Providence of God," *ZS*, IV:134; *LWC II*, 218.
52. Mark A. Blackwelder, "A Comparison of Aquinas and Zwingli on the Providence of God," in *Reformation Faith: Exegesis and Theology in the Protestant Reformations*, ed. Michael Parsons (Eugene, OR: Wipf & Stock, 2014), 8.
53. "Sermon on the Providence of God," *ZS*, IV:134; *LWC II*, 219.
54. "Sermon on the Providence of God," *ZS*, IV:108; *LWC II*, 175–76.
55. "Sermon on the Providence of God," *ZS*, IV:108–9; *LWC II*, 175.
56. Stephens, "The Theology of Zwingli," 86.
57. Kenneth Ronald Davis, *Anabaptism and Asceticism: A Study in Intellectual Origins* (Scottdale: Herald Press, 1974), 129ff; Goertz, *The Anabaptists*, 62–64.
58. "Sermon on the Providence of God," *ZS*, IV:84; *LWC II*, 136.
59. "Sermon on the Providence of God," *ZS*, IV:86; *LWC II*, 138.
60. "Sermon on the Providence of God," *ZS*, IV:91; *LWC II*, 147.

61. "Sermon on the Providence of God," *ZS*, IV:81; *LWC II*, 130–31; García, "'Summum Bonum,'" 183–88.
62. "Sermon on the Providence of God," *ZS*, IV:83; *LWC II*, 133.
63. George, *Theology of the Reformers*, 126–27.
64. *Commentary on True and False Religion*, *Z*, III:650; *LWC II*, 70.
65. "Sermon on the Providence of God," *ZS*, IV:113; *LWC II*, 184.
66. *Exposition*, *ZS*, I:275; *HZW*, I:145.
67. *Exposition*, *ZS*, I: 275; *HZW*, I:145.
68. "Sermon on the Providence of God," *ZS*, IV:111; *LWC II*, 181.
69. *An Exposition of the Christian Faith*, *ZS*, IV:65; *LWC III*, 271–72.
70. See Chapter 3.
71. George, *Theology of the Reformers*, 128–29.
72. On this matter, Calvin argued that "He [God] sometimes deprives them [the reprobate] of the capacity to hear His word" and that "He leaves in blindness those whom He has once condemned and deprived of participation in His light." Calvin, *Institutes*, II:978–79.
73. "Sermon on the Providence of God," *ZS*, IV:143; *LWC II*, 233.
74. Stephens, "The Theology of Zwingli," 85.
75. "Sermon on the Providence of God," *ZS*, IV:143; *LWC II*, 233.
76. "Plague Song," *ZS*, II.2:270; *LWC I*, 56.
77. "Sermon on the Providence of God," *ZS*, IV:143; *LWC II*, 233.
78. "Sermon on the Providence of God," *ZS*, IV:143; *LWC II*, 232.

CHAPTER 5: GOSPEL PARTNERSHIPS

1. *Archeteles*, *Z*, I:323; *LWC I*, 286.
2. This order was ratified by the Council on March 7. *Mandat des Rates* (7 March 1526) in *Quellen Zur Geschichte Der Täufer in Der Schweiz*, ed. Leonhard von Muralt and Walter Schmid (Zürich: Theologischer Verlag Zürich, 1974), I:180–81.
3. This was Manz's third arrest and imprisonment. Edmund Pries, "Oath Refusal in Zurich from 1525 to 1527: The Erratic Emergence of Anabaptist Practice," in *Anabaptism Revisited*, ed. Walter Klaassen (Scottdale: Herald Press, 1992), 70–71.

4. Bullinger, *Reformationsgeschichte*, II:382.
5. Williams, *Radical Reformation*, 145–46.
6. Ekklehard Krajewski, *Leben und Sterben des Zürcher Täuferführers Felix Manz: Über die Anfänge der Täuferbewegung und des Freikirchentums in der Reformationszeit* (Kassel: Kassel Oncken Verlag, 1957), 22ff.
7. Ruth A. Tucker, *Parade of Faith: A Biographical History of the Christian Church* (Grand Rapids: Zondervan, 2015), 267.
8. "Letter from Oswald Myconius to Zwingli" (1518), in *Z*, VII:107; Potter, *Zwingli: Documents*, 10.
9. Lisa Jardine, *Erasmus: Man of Letters* (New Jersey: Princeton University Press, 1993), 24.
10. "Letter to Erasmus of Rotterdam" (1516), in *Z*, VII:35–36.
11. "Letter to Zwingli" (1516), in *The Correspondence of Erasmus: Letters 298 to 445*, trans. R. A. B. Mynors and D. F. S. Thompson (Toronto: University of Toronto Press, 1976), 281.
12. "Letter from Erasmus to Zwingli" (1516), in *Correspondence of Erasmus: 298 to 445*, 281.
13. Gordon, *Swiss Reformation*, 40.
14. See Chapter 3 and *Exposition*, *ZS*, I:261; *HZW*, I:128.
15. Stephens, *Theology of Zwingli*, 10.
16. Gäbler, *Huldrych Zwingli*, 40.
17. Eire, *Reformations*, 232.
18. "Sermon on the Providence of God," *ZS*, IV:124; *LWC III*, 202–3.
19. Desiderius Erasmus, *Freedom of the Will* (1524), in *Luther and Erasmus: Free Will and Salvation*, ed. E. G. Rupp and P. S. Watson (Philadelphia: Westminster, 1969), 47.
20. Bruce Mansfield, *Erasmus in the Twentieth Century: Interpretations, 1920–2000* (Toronto: University of Toronto Press, 2003), 102.
21. Margaret Mann Phillips, *Erasmus and the Northern Renaissance* (London: Hodder & Stoughton, 1949), 210.
22. After their relationship dissolved, Zwingli lamented Grebel's ingratitude and disloyalty for all that he had done for him. "Letter to Joachim Vadian (31 March 1525)" in *Sources of Swiss Anabaptism*, 356.
23. *Archeteles*, *ZS*, III:76; *LWC I*, 292.

24. Andrea Strübind, *Eifriger als Zwingli: Die frühe Täuferbewegung in der Schweiz* (Berlin: Duncker & Humblot, 2003), 131–47.
25. C. Arnold Snyder, "Swiss Anabaptism: The Beginnings, 1523–1525," in *A Companion to Anabaptism and Spiritualism, 1521–1700*, ed. John D. Roth and James M. Stayer (Leiden: Brill, 2007), 49.
26. Arnold Snyder, "Word and Power in Reformation Zurich," *Archiv für Reformationsgeschichte* 81 (1990): 269.
27. Packull, *Hutterite Beginnings*, 19.
28. Heine Aberli, a founding member of this Castelberger group, testified about a repeated need to secure larger venues because of the group's numerical growth. *Sources of Swiss Anabaptism*, 204–5.
29. *Archeteles*, *Z*, I:321–22; *LWC I*, 284.
30. *Archeteles*, *Z*, I:321–22; *LWC I*, 284–85.
31. *Archeteles*, *Z*, I:323; *LWC I*, 286.
32. Stephen Brett Eccher, "The Priesthood of All Believers: Theological Intent and Subsequent Practice," in *Celebrating the Legacy of the Reformation*, ed. Kevin L. King, Edward E. Hindson, and Benjamin K. Forrest (Nashville: B&H Academic, 2019), 50–52.
33. "Clarity and Certainty," *Z*, I:365; *ZB*, 78.
34. "Clarity and Certainty," *Z*, I:377; *ZB*, 89.
35. *The First Zurich Disputation* (1523) in *ZS*, I:151; *Sources of Swiss Anabaptism*, 203.
36. Head, "The Swiss Reformation," 170–71.
37. *The Christian Education of Youth* (1523), in *Z*, II:536–51; *ZB*, 102–18.
38. *On the Preaching Office* (1525), in *Z*, IV:407; *HZW*, II:166.
39. Jean Henri Merle D'Aubigné, *For God and His People: Ulrich Zwingli and the Swiss Reformation*, trans. Henry White (Greenville, SC: BJU Press, 2000), 89.
40. Edward J. Furcha, "Women in Zwingli's World," *Zwingliana* XIX (1992): 137–38.
41. "Letter from Oswald Myconius to Zwingli, 22 July 1522," in *ZS*, VII:210.
42. Marjorie Elizabeth Plummer, *From Priest's Whore to Pastor's Wife: Clerical Marriage and the Process of Reform in the Early German Reformation* (Surrey: Ashgate, 2012), 115; Christoffel, *Zwingli: Or the Rise*, 123.
43. Gordon, *Swiss Reformation*, 55.

44. This includes a July 2, 1522, petition to the Bishop of Constance and a July 13, 1522, open letter to his Swiss compatriots requesting that priests be allowed to marry. "Petition to Hugo Bishop of Constance" (1522), in *Z*, I:197–209; *LWC*, 150–95; *A Friendly Request and Admonition* (1522), in *Z*, I:214–48.
45. Martin Bucer, "Letter from Martin Bucer to Zwingli, 14 April 1524," in *ZS*, VII:335.
46. Anna had three children from her former marriage to Hans Meyer von Knonau named Margaret, Gerold, and Agatha. She subsequently bore Zwingli four children: William, Ulrich, Regula, and Anna.
47. Raymond Potgieter, "Anna Reinhard Zwingli—'Apostolic Dorcas,' 'Dearest Housewife,' 'Angel-wife,' 'Ziel van Mijn' and 'Mater Dolorosa of the Reformation': From Woman to Valued Citizen," *In die Skriflig / In Luce Verbi* 50, no. 3 (2016): 5.
48. Locher, *Zwingli's Thought*, 139–40.
49. James I. Good, *Women of the Reformed Church*, 1st ed. (Reading: The Sunday School Board of the Reformed Church, 1901), 11.
50. Gordon, *Swiss Reformation*, 242–43.
51. Gordon, *Zwingli*, 177.
52. "Divine and Human Righteousness," *Z*, II:472; *HZW*, II:4.
53. "Divine and Human Righteousness," *Z*, II:472; *HZW*, II:4.
54. *Archeteles*, *ZS*, III:28; *LWC I*, 200.
55. *The Acts of the Second Disputation*, 26–28 (1523), in *Z*, II:784; *Sources of Swiss Anabaptism*, 242.
56. *The Acts of the Second Disputation*, *Z*, II:784; *Sources of Swiss Anabaptism*, 242.
57. Conrad Grebel, "Letter from Grebel to *Vadian* (18 December 1523)," in *Sources of Swiss Anabaptism*, 276.
58. *Refutation of the Catabaptist Tricks*, *ZS*, III:362; *ZSW*, 132.
59. Goertz, *The Anabaptists*, 16.
60. Neal Blough, "Introduction," in Yoder, *Anabaptism and the Reformation*, liii.
61. Williams, *Radical Reformation*, 122–23.
62. *Those Who Give Cause for Rebellion* (1524), in *Z*, III:355–469.
63. "Letter from Zwingli to Vadian (28 May 1525)," *Z*, VIII:332; *Sources of Swiss Anabaptism*, 375.
64. *Baptism, Re-Baptism, and Child Baptism*, *Z*, IV:206.

65. *Baptism, Re-Baptism, and Child Baptism*, *Z*, IV:206.
66. *Baptism, Re-Baptism, and Child Baptism*, *Z*, IV:206.
67. *Judgment of the Council* (7 March 1526), in *Quellen Zur Geschichte der Täufer*, 178.
68. "Letter to Joachim Vadian (7 March 1526)," in *Z*, VIII:542; *Sources of Swiss Anabaptism*, 449.
69. *Refutation of the Catabaptist Tricks*, *ZS*, III:376; *ZSW*, 158.
70. *Refutation of the Catabaptist Tricks*, *ZS*, III:374; *ZSW*, 155.
71. Leland Harder, "Zwingli's Reaction to the Schleitheim Confession of Faith of the Anabaptists," *Sixteenth Century Journal* 11, no. 4 (1980): 53.
72. Peter A. Lillback, *The Binding of God: Calvin's Role in the Development of Covenant Theology* (Grand Rapids: Baker Academic, 2001), 89.
73. *Those Who Give Cause for Rebellion* (1524) in *Z*, III, 368-469 and John D. Roth, "Harmonizing the Scriptures: Swiss Brethren Understandings of the Relationship Between the Old and New Testament During the Last Half of the Sixteenth Century," in *Radical Reformation Studies: Essays Presented to James M. Stayer*, ed. by Werner O. Packull and Geoffrey L. Dipple (Aldershot: Ashgate, 1999), 37
74. "Reply to Jerome Emser" (1524), in *Z*, III:254; *LWC III*, 367.
75. Michael Sattler, *Schleitheim Confession* (1527), in *The Legacy of Michael Sattler*, ed. John H. Yoder (Scottdale: Herald Press, 1973), 27–43.
76. *Refutation of the Catabaptist Tricks*, *ZS*, III:389; *ZSW*, 179.
77. *Refutation of the Catabaptist Tricks*, *ZS*, III:401; *ZSW*, 199.
78. Packull, *Hutterite Beginnings*, 22.
79. Bullinger, *Reformationsgeschichte*, I:289–90.
80. *Regulations Concerning the School* (1525), in *Z*, IV:365; Opitz, "Exegetical and Hermeneutical Work," 421.
81. See Chapter 1.
82. Mock, "Huldrych Zwingli," 35.
83. Following Ceporin's death, another of Zwingli's close gospel partners, Conrad Pellican, took over those duties. Locher, *Die Zwinglische Reformation*, 581, 605.
84. Eccher, "Priesthood," 58.

85. Roland Diethelm, "Bullinger and Worship: 'Thereby Does One Plant and Sow the True Faith,' " in *Architect of Reformation: An Introduction to Heinrich Bullinger, 1504–1575*, ed. Bruce Gordon and Emidio Campi (Grand Rapids: Baker, 2004), 139–40.
86. Packull, *Hutterite Beginnings*, 23.
87. *On the Preaching Office*, *Z*, IV:394; *HZW*, II:158.
88. D'Aubigné, *For God and His People*, 68.
89. Heinrich Bullinger, *Diarium*, vol. 2 of *Quellen zur Schweizerischen Reformationsgeschichte*, ed. Emil Egli (Basel: Basler Buch und Antiquariatshandlung, 1904), 9.
90. Bruce Gordon, "Introduction: Architect of Reformation," in *Architect of Reformation*, 18.
91. Johann Jakob Simler, *Sammlung alter und neuer Urkunden zur Beleuchtung der Kirchen-Geschichte vornehmlich des Schweizer-Landes*, (Zürich: Ben Drell, Gessner, and Comp., 1767), II:90ff. For Bullinger's use of this as a foundational argument against the Anabaptists, see Heinrich Bullinger, "How to Deal with Anabaptists: An Unpublished Letter of Heinrich Bullinger," trans. and ed. Heinold Fast and John H. Yoder, *Mennonite Quarterly Review* 33 (1959): 84–88.
92. Heinold Fast, *Heinrich Bullinger und die Täufer: Ein Beitrag zur Historiographie und Theologie im 16. Jahrhundert* (Weierhof: Mennonite Geschichtsvereine e. V., 1959), 156.
93. Eccher, "Reformation in Conflict," 33–53.
94. Gordon, "Huldrych Zwingli," 2.
95. Andreas Mühling, "Heinrich Bullinger as Church Politician," in *Architect of Reformation*, 247–49.
96. Campi, "Reformation in Zurich," 95.
97. Gordon, *Zwingli*, 252.
98. Heinrich Bullinger, "The Second Helvetic Confession," in *Reformed Confessions of the 16th and 17th Centuries in English Translation*, ed. James T. Dennison, Jr. (Grand Rapids: Reformation Heritage Books, 2010), II:810–81.
99. "Clarity and Certainty," *Z*, I:372; *ZB*, 84.
100. "Letter from Leo Jud to Vadian (8 August 1525)," in *Vadianische Briefsammlung der Stadtbibliothek St. Gallen*, III, ed. Emil Arbenz and Hermann Wartmann

(St. Gallen: Vormals Huber & Co., 1897), 118; Harder, "Zwingli's Reaction," 52.

101. Goertz, "Scriptural Interpretation among Radical Reformers," in *From the Renaissance to the Enlightenment*, 587.

CHAPTER 6: THE BROKEN BODY OF CHRIST

1. *An Exposition of the Christian Faith*, *ZS*, IV:53; *LWC II*, 252.
2. "Philip of Hesse's Invitation to Zwingli," in *Z*, X:108; Potter, *Zwingli: Documents*, 102.
3. Gordon, *Zwingli*, 164.
4. George, "What the Reformers Thought They Were Doing," 11–12.
5. *LW*, 49, 88.
6. "Choice and Liberty Regarding Foods," *Z*, I:97; *LWC I*, 78–79.
7. "Choice and Liberty Regarding Foods," *Z*, I:97; *LWC I*, 79.
8. "Choice and Liberty Regarding Foods," *Z*, I:129; *LWC I*, 107.
9. "Choice and Liberty Regarding Foods," *Z*, I:100; *LWC I*, 81.
10. "Choice and Liberty Regarding Foods," *Z*, I:100; *LWC I*, 81.
11. *Archeteles*, *ZS*, III:70; *LWC I*, 282.
12. *Archeteles*, *ZS*, III:71; *LWC I*, 282.
13. *Archeteles*, *ZS*, III:73; *LWC I*, 286.
14. *Archeteles*, *ZS*, III:73; *LWC I*, 287.
15. *Exposition*, *ZS*, I:232; *HZW*, I:92.
16. *Exposition*, *ZS*, I:233; *HZW*, I:92.
17. *Exposition*, *ZS*, I:233; *HZW*, I:92.
18. *Exposition*, *ZS*, I:233; *HZW*, I:93.
19. *Exposition*, *ZS*, I:234–35; *HZW*, I:95.
20. *Exposition*, *ZS*, I:235; *HZW*, I:95.
21. *Exposition*, *ZS*, I:235; *HZW*, I:95.
22. *An Exposition of the Christian Faith*, *ZS*, IV:56; *LWC II*, 257.
23. Euler, "Zwingli and Bullinger," 57–58.
24. *Exposition*, *ZS*, I:248; *HZW*, I:110.

25. *Exposition*, *ZS*, I:248; *HZW*, I:110.
26. *Subsidiary Tract on the Eucharist*, *Z*, IV:501; *HZW*, II:225.
27. "Letter to Matthew Alber" (1524), in Z, III:345; Potter, *Zwingli: Documents*, 98.
28. Oberman, *Forerunners of the Reformation*, 252–53; Joe Mock, "Bullinger and the Lord's Holy Supper," in *From Zwingli to Amyraut: Exploring the Growth of European Reformed Traditions*, ed. Jon Balserak and Jim West (Göttingen: V&R Academic, 2017), 61.
29. "Reply to Johannes Bugenhagen" (1525), in *Z*, IV:560; Potter, *Zwingli: Documents*, 100.
30. "Letter to Matthew Alber," *Z*, III:345; Potter, *Zwingli: Documents*, 98.
31. *Exposition*, *ZS*, I:238; *HZW*, I:98.
32. Jonathan Michael Gray, *Oaths and the English Reformation* (Cambridge: Cambridge University Press, 2013), 23.
33. *Exposition*, *ZS*, I:238; *HZW*, I:99.
34. Wandel, *The Eucharist*, 71.
35. *Exposition*, *ZS*, I:238; *HZW*, I:98.
36. See Chapter 3.
37. McGrath, *Reformation Thought*, 175.
38. *A Proposal Concerning Images and the Mass*, *Z*, III:124.
39. *A Proposal Concerning Images and the Mass*, *Z*, III:125–26; Stephens, *Theology of Zwingli*, 225.
40. *Commentary on True and False Religion*, *Z*, III:801–2; *LWC III*, 231–32.
41. *Subsidiary Tract on the Eucharist*, *Z*, IV:468; *HZW*, II:198.
42. *Subsidiary Tract on the Eucharist*, *Z*, IV:480–81; *HZW*, II:209–10; Bruce Gordon, "Huldrych Zwingli's Dream of the Lord's Supper," in *Crossing Traditions: Essays on the Reformation in Intellectual History*, ed. Maria-Christina Pitassi and Daniela Solfaroli Camillocci (Leiden: Brill, 2017), 296–310.
43. *Subsidiary Tract on the Eucharist*, *Z*, IV:486; *HZW*, II:212.
44. *Baptism, Rebaptism, and Child Baptism*, *Z*, IV:218; *ZB*, 131.
45. *Baptism, Rebaptism, and Child Baptism*, *Z*, IV:218; *ZB*, 131.
46. *Baptism, Rebaptism, and Child Baptism*, *Z*, IV:252; *ZB*, 156.
47. *Baptism Rebaptism, and Child Baptism*, *Z*, IV:218; *ZB*, 131.

48. *Exposition*, *ZS*, I:249; *HZW*, I:111.
49. Gordon, Baschera, and Moser, "Emulating the Past," 19.
50. Gordon, Baschera, and Moser, "Emulating the Past," 19.
51. Gordon, *Zwingli*, 169.
52. *Exposition*, *ZS*, I:242; *HZW*, I:103.
53. Timothy M. Gallagher, *Mediation and Contemplation: An Ignatian Guide to Praying with Scripture* (New York: Crossroad, 2008); Helmut Gabel, "Ignatian Contemplation and Modern Biblical Studies," *The Way* 44, no. 2 (2005): 38.
54. "Letter to Thomas Wyttenbach" (1523), in *Z*, VIII:85; Potter, *Zwingli: Documents*, 94.
55. "Letter to Thomas Wyttenbach," *Z*, VIII:85; Potter, *Zwingli: Documents*, 94.
56. *Advice Concerning the Mass and Images*, *Z*, II:812.
57. Stephens, *Theology of Zwingli*, 226.
58. *The Canon of the Mass*, *Z*, II:592.
59. *Commentary on True and False Religion*, *Z*, III:774; *LWC III*, 198.
60. *Commentary on True and False Religion*, *Z*, III:774; *LWC III*, 198.
61. *The Christian Education of Youth*, *Z*, II:543; *ZB*, 109.
62. E. M. Henning, "The Architectonics of Faith: Metalogic and Metaphor in Zwingli's Doctrine of the Eucharist," *Renaissance and Reformation* 10, no. 4 (1986): 319.
63. *A Friendly Exegesis*, *Z*, V:616; *HZW*, II:274.
64. *Commentary on True and False Religion*, *Z*, III:785–86; *LWC III*, 212.
65. See Chapter 3 and Euler, "Zwingli and Bullinger," 61.
66. Erika Rummel, "The Theology of Erasmus," in *The Cambridge Companion to Reformation Theology*, ed. David Bagchi and David C. Steinmetz (Cambridge: Cambridge University Press, 2004), 36.
67. Erasmus, *Enchiridion*, 101.
68. Stephens, "Theology of Zwingli," 87.
69. "Letter to Thomas Wyttenbach," *Z*, VIII:85; Potter, *Zwingli: Documents*, 96.
70. "Letter to Thomas Wyttenbach," *Z*, VIII:85; Potter, *Zwingli: Documents*, 96.
71. *Commentary on True and False Religion*, *Z*, III:698; *LWC III*, 126.
72. "Letter to Matthew Alber," *Z*, III:337; *HZW*, II:132.

73. *Commentary on True and False Religion*, *Z*, III:761; *LWC III*, 183.
74. *Commentary on True and False Religion*, *Z*, III:761; *LWC III*, 184.
75. Peter A. Lillback, *The Binding of God, Calvin's Role in the Development of Covenant Theology* (Grand Rapids: Baker Academic, 2001), 90.
76. *Commentary on True and False Religion*, *Z*, III:775; *LWC III*, 199.
77. *Commentary on True and False Religion*, *Z*, III:775; *LWC III*, 200.
78. *An Account of the Faith*, *Z*, 802; *LWC II*, 45.
79. *An Account of the Faith*, *Z*, 800; *LWC II*, 43.
80. *Commentary on True and False Religion*, *Z*, III:776; *LWC III*, 201.
81. *Commentary on True and False Religion*, *Z*, III:782; *LWC III*, 209.
82. Amy Nelson Burnett, *Karlstadt and the Origins of the Eucharistic Controversy: A Study in the Circulation of Ideas* (Oxford: Oxford University Press, 2011), 93.
83. *Commentary on True and False Religion*, *Z*, III:786; *LWC III*, 213.
84. *Commentary on True and False Religion*, *Z*, III:786; *LWC III*, 213.
85. *Commentary on True and False Religion*, *Z*, III:786; *LWC III*, 214.
86. "Letter to Matthew Alber," *Z*, III:335; *HZW*, II:131.
87. Brecht, *Martin Luther: Shaping and Defining the Reformation,* 295.
88. Amy Nelson Burnett, "Zwingli, Erasmus, and the Roots of Reformed Sacramental Theology," *Calvin Theological Journal* 55, no. 2 (2020): 247.
89. Brecht, *Martin Luther: Shaping and Defining the Reformation*, 295.
90. "Reply to Johannes Bugenhagen," *Z*, I:558.
91. "Reply to Johannes Bugenhagen," *Z*, I:558.
92. "Reply to Johannes Bugenhagen," *Z*, I:558.
93. "Reply to Johannes Bugenhagen," *Z*, I:561–62.
94. "Reply to Johannes Bugenhagen," *Z*, I:562.
95. Brecht, *Martin Luther: Shaping and Defining the Reformation*, 304–5.
96. *LW*, 36, 346.
97. *LW*, 54, 147.
98. Lindberg, *The European Reformations*, 184.
99. *A Friendly Exegesis*, *Z*, V:613, 722; HZW, II:272, 346.
100. *A Friendly Exegesis*, *Z*, V:563; *HZW*, II:238.
101. Gordon, "True Prophets," 114.

102. *A Friendly Exegesis*, *Z*, V:570; *HZW*, II:243.
103. *A Friendly Exegesis*, *Z*, V:617; *HZW*, II:275.
104. *A Friendly Exegesis*, *Z*, V:654; *HZW*, II:303.
105. *A Friendly Exegesis*, *Z*, V:679; *HZW*, II:318.
106. "That These Words: This Is My Body" (1527), in *Z*, V:925–26.
107. *A Friendly Exegesis*, *Z*, V:681; *HZW*, II:320.
108. *A Friendly Exegesis*, *Z*, V:680; *HZW*, II:320.
109. Ryan Tafilowski, "Marburg Colloquy," in *Encyclopedia of Martin Luther and the Reformation*, ed. Mark A. Lamport (New York: Rowman & Littlefield, 2017), 499.
110. *LW*, 37, 212.
111. *LW*, 37, 212.
112. "Reply to Philip of Hesse" (1529), in *Z*, X:117–18.
113. *A Friendly Exegesis*, *Z*, V:566; *HZW*, II:240.
114. Brecht, *Martin Luther: Shaping and Defining the Reformation*, 328.
115. *The Marburg Articles* (1529) in *Z*, VI.2:521–23.
116. *LW*, 38, 37.
117. McGrath, *Reformation Thought*, 104.
118. *LW*, 38, 20.
119. *LW*, 38, 22.
120. *LW*, 38, 24.
121. *LW*, 38, 40.
122. *LW*, 10, 4.
123. *LW*, 38, 41.
124. *LW*, 38, 25.
125. *LW*, 38, 26.
126. Peter Matheson, *The Rhetoric of the Reformation* (Edinburgh: T&T Clark, 1998), 187.
127. *LW*, 38, 32 and 60.
128. *LW*, 38, 19 and 60.
129. Wandel, *Eucharist*, 71.
130. *LW*, 38, 19.

131. *LW*, 38, 45.
132. *LW*, 38, 46.
133. *LW*, 38, 31.
134. Euler, "Zwingli and Bullinger," 61.
135. J. M. Drickamer, "Communication of Attributes, Communicatio Idiomatum," in *Evangelical Dictionary of Theology*, ed. Walter A. Elwell (Grand Rapids: Baker Books, 1999), 257.
136. *An Account of the Faith*, *Z*, VI.2:807; *LWC II*, 50.
137. *LW*, 38, 67.
138. Burnett, "Zwingli, Erasmus, and the Roots," 238.
139. *LW*, 38, 39.
140. *An Account of the Faith*, *Z*, VI.2:806; *LWC II*, 49.
141. *An Exposition of the Christian Faith*, *ZS*, IV:53; *LWC II*, 252.
142. *LW*, 38, 35.
143. *Consensus Tigurinus*, in *Reformed Confessions of the 16th and 17th Centuries*, ed. by James T. Dennison, Jr. (Grand Rapids: Reformation Heritage Books, 2008), 537–45.

CONCLUSION

1. Johannes Stumpf, *Schweizer-und Reformationschronik*, II (Basel: Birkhäuser, 1955), 136–37.
2. *Sermon on the Eternal Purity of the Virgin Mary* (1522) in *Z*, I, 394.
3. Gordon, *Zwingli: God's Armed Prophet*, 249.
4. Hans J. Hillerbrand, *The Reformation in Its Own Words* (New York: SCM, 1964), 118.
5. George, *Theology of the Reformers*, 148.
6. Scott H. Hendrix, *Luther and the Papacy: Stages in a Reformation Conflict* (Philadelphia: Fortress, 1981), 40–41, 51.
7. Kevin J. Vanhoozer, "Sola Scriptura, Tradition, and Catholicity," in *Worship, Tradition, and Engagement: Essays in Honor of Timothy George*, ed. David S. Dockery, James Early Massey, and Robert Smith, Jr. (Eugene: Pickwick, 2018), 126.
8. Justo L. Gonzalez, *The Story of Christianity: The Early Church to the Dawn of the Reformation*, vol. 1 (New York: Harper Collins, 2010), 3.

Bibliography

PRIMARY SOURCES

Bullinger, Heinrich. *Diarium.* Vol. 2 of *Quellen zur Schweizerischen Reformationsgeschichte.* Edited by Emil Egli. Basel: Basler Buch und Antiquariatshandlung, 1904.

———. "How to Deal with Anabaptists: An Unpublished Letter of Heinrich Bullinger." Translated and edited by Heinold Fast and John H. Yoder. *Mennonite Quarterly Review* 33 (1959): 83–95.

———. *Reformationsgeschichte,* Bands 1 and 2. Edited by J. J. Hottinger and H. H. Vögeli. Frauenfeld: Druck und Verlag Ch. Beyel, 1838.

———. "The Second Helvetic Confession." Pages 809–81 in vol. 2 of *Reformed Confessions of the 16th and 17th Centuries in English Translation.* Edited by James T. Dennison, Jr. Grand Rapids: Reformation Heritage Books, 2010.

Calvin, John. *Institutes of the Christian Religion.* Edited by John T. McNeill. Louisville: Westminster John Knox, 1960.

Dennison, James T., Jr., ed. *Reformed Confessions of the 16th and 17th Centuries.* Grand Rapids: Reformation Heritage Books, 2010.

Erasmus, Desiderius. *The Correspondence of Erasmus: Letters 298 to 445.* Translated by R. A. B. Mynors and D. F .S. Thompson. Toronto: University of Toronto, 1976.

———. *The Correspondence of Erasmus: Letters 842 to 992.* Translated by R. A .B. Mynors and D. F. S. Thompson. Toronto: University of Toronto, 1982.

———. *The Enchiridion of Erasmus.* Edited by Raymond Himelick. Gloucester: Indiana University Press, 1970.

———. *Freedom of the Will*. Pages 35–97 in *Luther and Erasmus: Free Will and Salvation*. Edited by E. G. Rupp and P. S. Watson. Philadelphia: Westminster Press, 1969.

———. "*Paraclesis*." Pages 97–108 in *Christian Humanism and the Reformation: Selected Writings of Erasmus*. 3rd ed. Edited by John C. Olin. New York: Fordham University Press, 2000.

———. *Praise of Folly and Letter to Maarten Van Dorp*. Translated by Betty Radice. New York: Penguin Press, 1993.

Grebel, Conrad. "Letter from Grebel to Vadian, 18 December 1523." Pages 275–76 in *The Sources of Swiss Anabaptism*. Edited by Leland Harder. Scottdale: Herald Press, 1985.

Harder, Leland, ed. *The Sources of Swiss Anabaptism*. Scottdale: Herald Press, 1985.

John of Damascus. *On the Images of the Divine: Three Apologies against Those Who Attack the Divine Images*. Translated by David Anderson. Crestwood, NY: St. Vladimir's Seminary Press, 1980.

Jud, Leo. "Letter from Leo Jud to Vadian (8 August 1525)." Pages 118–19 in vol. 3 of *Vadianische Briefsammlung der Stadtbibliothek St. Gallen*. Edited by Emil Arbenz and Hermann Wartmann. St. Gallen: Vormals Huber & Company, 1897.

Luther, Martin. *Deutsche Bibel*. Band 7 of *D. Martin Luthers Werke*. Weimar: H. Böhlaus Nachfolger, 1968.

———. *Luther's Works: American Edition*. Edited by Jaroslav Pelikan, Helmut T. Lehmann, and Christopher Boyd Brown. 78 vols. Philadelphia: Fortress; St. Louis: Concordia, 1955–.

Muralt, Leonhard von, and Walter Schmid, eds. *Quellen Zur Geschichte Der Täufer In Der Schweiz*, Band I. Zurich: Theologischer Verlag Zürich, 1952.

Pipkin, H. Wayne, and John H. Yoder. *Balthasar Hubmaier: Theologian of Anabaptism*. Scottdale: Herald Press, 1989.

Platter, Thomas. *The Autobiography of Thomas Platter: A Schoolmaster of the Sixteenth Century*. 2nd ed. Translated by Mrs. Finn. London: B. Wertheim, Aldine Chambers, Paternoster Row, 1847.

Potter, G. R. *Huldrych Zwingli: Documents of Modern History*. London: Edward Arnold, 1978.

Sattler, Michael. *Schleitheim Confession*. Pages 24–43 in *The Legacy of Michael Sattler*. Edited by John H. Yoder. Scottdale: Herald Press, 1973.

Simler, Johann Jakob. *Sammlung alter und neuer Urkunden zur Beleuchtung der Kirchen-Geschichte vornehmlich des Schweizer-Landes*, Band 2. Zürich: Ben Drell, Gessner, and Company, 1767.

Stumpf, Johannes. *Schweizer-und Reformationschronik*, Band II. Basel: Birkhäuser, 1955.

Vadian, Joachim. *Die Vadienische Briefsammlung der Stadtbibliothek St. Gallen*, vol. 3, no. 437. St. Gallen: Fehr'sche Buchhandlung, 1888.

Wyss, Bernhard. "Die Chronik Bernhard Wyss 1519–1530." Pages 1–152 in vol. 1 of *Quellen zur Schweizerischen Reformationsgeschichte*. Edited by Georg Finsler. Basel: Verlag der Basler Buch- und Antiquariatshandlung, 1901.

Zwingli, Huldrych. *Act or Custom of the Supper*. Pages 175–94 in *Reformation Worship: Liturgies from the Past for the Present*. Edited by Jonathan Gibson and Mark Earngey. Greensboro, NC: New Growth Press, 2018.

———. *An Account of the Faith*. Pages 79–94 in *Die Bekenntnisscriften der Reformierten Kirche*. Edited by E. F. Karl Müller. Leipzig: A. Deichert'sche Verlagsbuchhandlung Nachfolge.

———. *Huldreich Zwinglis sämtliche Werke*. Vols. 88–101 of *Corpus Reformatorum*. Edited by Emil Egli, Georg Finsler, Walther Köhler, et al. Leipzig: Heinsius, 1905–.

———. *Huldreich Zwinglis Werke*. 8 Bands. Edited by Melchior Schuler and Johannes Schulthess. Zürich: F. Schulthess, 1828–1842.

———. *Huldrych Zwingli Writings*. Translated and edited by H. Wayne Pipkin and E. J. Furcha. 2 vols. Eugene, OR: Pickwick, 1984.

———. *Ulrich Zwingli: Commentary on True and False Religion*. Vol. 3 of *The Latin Works and Correspondence of Huldreich Zwingli*. Edited by Samuel Macauley Jackson and Clarence Nevin Heller. Eugene, OR: Wipf & Stock, 2015.

———. *Ulrich Zwingli: Early Writings*. Vol. I of *The Latin Works and the Correspondence of Huldreich Zwingli*. Edited by Samuel Macauley Jackson. Eugene, OR: Wipf & Stock, 1999.

———. *Ulrich Zwingli: On Providence and Other Essays*. Vol. 2 of *The Latin Works and the Correspondence of Huldreich Zwingli*. Edited by Samuel Macauley Jackson and William John Hinke. Eugene, OR: Wipf & Stock, 1999.

———. *Ulrich Zwingli: Selected Works*. Edited by Samuel Macauley Jackson. Philadelphia: University of Philadelphia Press, 1972.

———. *Zwingli and Bullinger*. Vol. 24 of *The Library of Christian Classics*. Translated and edited by G. W. Bromiley, Jr. Philadelphia: Westminster Press, 1953.

SECONDARY SOURCES

Backus, Irena. *The Disputations of Baden, 1526 and Berne, 1528: Neutralizing the Early Church. Studies in Reformed Religion* 1. Princeton: Princeton Theological Seminary, 1993.

Baker, J. Wayne. *Heinrich Bullinger and the Covenant: The Other Reformed Tradition*. Athens: Ohio University Press, 1980.

Blackwelder, Mark A. "A Comparison of Aquinas and Zwingli on the Providence of God." Pages 1–11 in *Reformation Faith: Exegesis and Theology in the Protestant Reformations*. Edited by Michael Parsons. Eugene, OR: Wipf & Stock, 2014.

Blough, Neal. "Introduction." Pages xli–lx in *Anabaptism and Reformation in Switzerland: An Historical and Theological Analysis of the Dialogues between Anabaptists and Reformers*. Edited by John H. Yoder. Kitchener: Pandora Press, 2004.

Brecht, Martin. *Martin Luther, Volume 1: His Road to Reformation, 1483–1521*. Translated by James L. Schaaf. Philadelphia: Fortress 1985.

———. *Martin Luther, Volume 2: Shaping and Defining the Reformation, 1521–1532*. Translated by James L. Shaaf. Philadelphia: Fortress, 1991.

Bürki, Bruno. "The Reformed Tradition in Continental Europe, Switzerland, France, and Germany." Pages 436–52 in *The Oxford History of Christian Worship*. Edited by Geoffrey Wainwright and Karen B. Westerfield Tucker. Oxford: Oxford University Press, 2006.

Burnett, Amy Nelson. *Karlstadt and the Origins of the Eucharistic Controversy: A Study in the Circulation of Ideas*. Oxford: Oxford University Press, 2011.

———. "Revisiting Humanism and the Urban Reformation." *Lutheran Quarterly* 35, no. 4 (2021): 373–400.

———. "Zwingli, Erasmus, and the Roots of Reformed Sacramental Theology." *Calvin Theological Journal* 55, no. 2 (2020): 235–54.

Büsser, Fritz. *Das katholische Zwinglibild: Von der Reformation bis zur Gegenwart*. Zurich: Zwingli-Verlag, 1968.

Bynum, Caroline Walker. *Holy Feast & Holy Fast: The Religious Significance of Food to Medieval Women*. Berkeley: University of California Press, 1987.

Campi, Emidio. "The Reformation in Zurich." Pages 59–125 in *A Companion to the Swiss Reformation*. Edited by Amy Nelson Burnett and Emidio Campi. Leiden: Brill, 2016.

Chibi, Andrew Allan. *The Wheat and the Tares: Doctrines of the Church in the Reformation, 1500–1590*. Eugene, OR: Pickwick, 2015.

Christoffel, Raeget. *Zwingli: Or the Rise of the Reformation in Switzerland*. Edinburgh: T&T Clark, 1858.

Courvoisier, Jaques. *Zwingli: A Reformed Theologian*. Richmond: John Knox, 1963.

D'Aubigné, Jean Henri Merle. *For God and His People: Ulrich Zwingli and the Swiss Reformation*. Translated by Henry White. Greenville: BJU Press, 2000.

———. *History of the Reformation in the Sixteenth Century*. Part 1. London: Whittaker & Company, 1842.

Davies, Martin. "Humanism in Script and Print in the Fifteenth Century." Pages 47–62 in *The Cambridge Companion to Renaissance Humanism*. Edited by Jill Kraye. Cambridge: Cambridge University Press, 1995.

Davis, Kenneth Ronald. *Anabaptism and Asceticism: A Study in Intellectual Origins*. Scottdale: Herald Press, 1974.

Diethelm, Roland. "Bullinger and Worship: 'Thereby Does One Plant and Sow the True Faith.'" Pages 135–57 in *Architect of Reformation: An Introduction to Heinrich Bullinger, 1504–1575*. Edited by Bruce Gordon and Emidio Campi. Grand Rapids: Baker, 2004.

Drickamer, J. M. "Communication of Attributes, Communicatio Idiomatum." Page 257 in *Evangelical Dictionary of Theology*. Edited by Walter A. Elwell. Grand Rapids: Baker Books, 1999.

Eccher, Stephen Brett. "Huldrych Zwingli: Reformation in Conflict." *Perichoresis* 15, no. 4 (2017): 33–53.

———. "The Priesthood of All Believers: Theological Intent and Subsequent Practice." Pages 45–64 in *Celebrating the Legacy of the Reformation*. Edited by Kevin L. King, Edward E. Hindson, and Benjamin K. Forrest. Nashville: B&H Academic, 2019.

———. "A Return to Christ's Kingdom." *Southeastern Theological Review* 5, no. 2 (2014): 203–31.

Edwards, Mark U. *Printing, Propaganda, and Martin Luther*. Minneapolis: Fortress, 2005.

Egli, Emil. *Actensammlung zur Geschichte der Zürcher Reformation in den Jahren 1519–1533*. Zurich: Druck von J. Schabelitz, 1879.

Eire, Carlos. *Reformations: The Early Modern World, 1450–1650*. New Haven: Yale University Press, 2018.

Euler, Carrie. "Huldrych Zwingli and Heinrich Bullinger." Pages 57–74 in *A Companion to the Eucharist in the Reformation*. Edited by Lee Palmer Wandel. Leiden: Brill, 2014.

Farner, Oskar. *Huldrych Zwingli: seine Verkündigung und ihre ersten Früchte 1520–1525*, Band 3. Zürich: Zwingli-Verlag, 1954.

Fast, Heinold. *Heinrich Bullinger und die Täufer: Ein Beitrag zur Historiographie und Theologie im 16. Jahrhundert*. Weierhof: Mennonite Geschichtsvereine e. V., 1959.

Furcha, Edward J. "Women in Zwingli's World." *Zwingliana* 14 (1992): 131–42.

Gabel, Helmut. "Ignatian Contemplation and Modern Biblical Studies." *The Way* 44, no. 2 (2005): 37–49.

Gäbler, Ulrich. *Huldrych Zwingli: His Life and Work*. Translated by Ruth C. L. Gritsch. Philadelphia: Fortress, 1986.

Gallagher, Timothy M. *Mediation and Contemplation: An Ignatian Guide to Praying with Scripture*. New York: Crossroad, 2008.

García, Aurelio A. "'Summum Bonum' in the Zurich Reformation." *Zwingliana* 44 (2017): 179–97.

Garside, Charles, Jr. "Ludwig Haetzer's Pamphlet against Images: A Critical Study." *Mennonite Quarterly Review* 34, no. 1 (1960): 20–36.

———. *Zwingli and the Arts*. New Haven: Yale University Press, 1966.

George, Timothy. *Theology of the Reformers*. Rev. ed. Nashville: B&H Academic, 2013.

———. "What the Reformers Thought They Were Doing." Pages 9–25 in *Celebrating the Legacy of the Reformation*. Edited by Kevin L. King, Edward E. Hindson, and Benjamin K. Forrest. Nashville: B&H Academic, 2019.

Gibson, Jonathan, and Mark Earngey, eds. *Reformation Worship: Liturgies from the Past for the Present*. Greensboro, NC: New Growth Press, 2018.

Goertz, Hans-Jürgen. *The Anabaptists*. London: Routledge, 1996.

———. "Scriptural Interpretation among Radical Reformers." Pages 576–601 in *From the Renaissance to the Enlightenment*. Edited by Magne Sæbø. Vol. 2 of *Hebrew Bible / Old Testament: The History of Its Interpretation*. Edited by Magne Sæbø. Göttingen: Vandenhoeck & Ruprecht, 2008.

Gonzalez, Justo L. *The Story of Christianity: The Early Church to the Dawn of the Reformation*, vol. 1. New York: Harper Collins, 2010.

Good, James I. *Women of the Reformed Church*. 1st ed. Reading: The Sunday School Board of the Reformed Church, 1901.

Gordon, Bruce. "For If We Are True Prophets: Huldrych Zwingli on Martin Luther." *Reformation* 22, no. 2 (2017): 102–19.

———. "Huldrych Zwingli." *The Expository Times* 126, no. 4 (2015): 152–74.

———. "Huldrych Zwingli's Dream of the Lord's Supper." Pages 296–310 in *Crossing Traditions: Essays on the Reformation in Intellectual History*. Edited by Maria-Christina Pitassi and Daniela Solfaroli Camillocci. Leiden: Brill, 2017.

———. "Introduction: Architect of Reformation." Pages 17–32 in *Architect of Reformation: An Introduction to Heinrich Bullinger, 1504–1575*. Edited by Bruce Gordon and Emidio Campi. Grand Rapids: Baker, 2004.

———. *The Swiss Reformation*. Manchester: Manchester University Press, 2002.

———. "Transcendence and Community in Zwinglian Worship: The Liturgy of 1525 in Zurich." Pages 128–50 in *Continuity and Change in Christian Worship*. Edited by R. N. Swanson. Suffolk: The Boydell Press, 1999.

———. *Zwingli: God's Armed Prophet*. New Haven: Yale University Press, 2021.

Gordon, Bruce, Luca Baschera, and Christian Moser. "Emulating the Past and Creating the Present: Reformation and the Use of Historical and Theological Models of Zurich in the Sixteenth Century." Pages 1–39 in *Following Zwingli: Applying the Past in Reformation Zurich*. Edited by Luca Baschera, Bruce Gordon, and Christian Moser. Surrey: Ashgate, 2014.

Gray, Jonathan Michael. *Oaths and the English Reformation*. Cambridge: Cambridge University Press, 2013.

Greyerz, Kaspar von. *Religion and Culture in Early Modern Europe, 1500–1800*. Translated by Thomas Dunlap. Oxford: Oxford University Press, 2008.

Grob, Jean. *Ulrich Zwingli: Second Jubilee Gift for the Fourth Centenary of His Birthday*. Reading: Daniel Miller, 1885.

Harder, Leland. "Zwingli's Reaction to the Schleitheim Confession of Faith of the Anabaptists." *Sixteenth Century Journal* 2, no. 4 (1980): 51–66.

Hardy, Janet Gordon. *Story of a Noble Life or Zurich and Its Reformer, Ulric Zwingli*. Edinburgh: William P. Nimmo & Company, 1884.

Head, Randolph C. "The Swiss Reformations: Movements, Settlements, and Reimagination, 1520–1720." Pages 167–89 in *The Oxford Handbook of the Protestant Reformations*. Oxford: Oxford University Press, 2017.

Hendrix, Scott H. *Luther and the Papacy: Stages in a Reformation Conflict*. Philadelphia: Fortress, 1981.

Henning, E. M. "The Architectonics of Faith: Metalogic and Metaphor in Zwingli's Doctrine of the Eucharist." *Renaissance and Reformation* 10, no. 4 (1986): 316–65.

Hillerbrand, Hans J. *The Reformation in Its Own Words*. New York: SCM, 1964.

Hug, Lina, and Richard Stead. *Switzerland*. Rev. and enl. ed. New York: G. P. Putnam's Sons, 1920.

Jackson, Samuel Macauley. *Huldreich Zwingli: The Reformer of German Switzerland, 1484–1531*. New York: The Knickerbocker Press, 1903.

Janin, Hunt, and Ursula Carlson. *Mercenaries in Medieval and Renaissance Europe*. Jefferson: McFarland & Company, 2013.

Jardine, Lisa. *Erasmus: Man of Letters*. Princeton: Princeton University Press, 1993.

Kissane, Christopher. *Food, Religion and Communities in Early Modern Europe.* London: Bloomsbury Academic, 2018.

Köhler, Hans-Joachim. "Erste Schritte zu einem Meinungsprofil der frühen Reformationszeit." Pages 244–81 in *Martin Luther: Probleme seiner Zeit*, edited by Volker Press and Dieter Stievermann. Stuttgart: Klett-Cotta, 1986.

Krajewski, Ekklehard. *Leben und Sterben des Zürcher Täuferführers Felix Manz: Über die Anfänge der Täuferbewegung und des Freikirchentums in der Reformationszeit.* Kassel: Kassel Oncken Verlag, 1957.

Leu, Urs, and Sandra Weidmann. *Huldrych Zwingli's Private Library.* Leiden: Brill, 2018.

Lillback, Peter A. *The Binding of God: Calvin's Role in the Development of Covenant Theology.* Grand Rapids: Baker Academic, 2001.

———. "The Relationship of Church and State." Pages 675–719 in *Reformation Theology: A Systematic Introduction.* Edited by Matthew Barrett. Wheaton: Crossway. 2017.

Lindberg, Carter. *The European Reformations.* 2nd ed. Oxford: Wiley-Blackwell, 2009.

Locher, Gottfried W. *Die Zwinglische Reformation im Rahmen der europäischen Kirchengeschichte.* Göttingen: Vandenhoek and Ruprecht, 1979.

———. *Zwingli's Thought: New Perspectives.* Leiden: Brill, 1981.

Maag, Karen. *Worshiping with the Reformers.* Downers Grove, IL: InterVarsity Press, 2021.

Mansfield, Bruce. *Erasmus in the Twentieth Century: Interpretations, 1920–2000.* Toronto: University of Toronto Press, 2003.

Matheson, Peter. *The Rhetoric of the Reformation.* Edinburgh: T&T Clark, 1998.

McGrath, Alister E. *The Intellectual Origins of the European Reformation.* Oxford: Basil Blackwell, 1987.

———. *Iustitia Dei: A History of the Christian Doctrine of Justification.* 3rd ed. Cambridge: Cambridge University Press, 2005.

———. *Reformation Thought: An Introduction.* 4th ed. Oxford: Wiley-Blackwell, 2012.

McKee, Elsie, ed. *Katharina Schütz Zell: Church Mother.* Chicago: University of Chicago Press, 2006.

Mock, Joe. "Bullinger and the Lord's Holy Supper." Pages 57–78 in *From Zwingli to Amyraut: Exploring the Growth of European Reformed Traditions*. Edited by Jon Balserak and Jim West. Göttingen: V&R Academic, 2017.

———. "Huldrych Zwingli: A Truly Quintessential Reformer." Pages 30–39 in *Celebrating the Reformation: Its Legacy and Continuing Relevance*. Edited by Mark D. Thompson. London: Apollos, 2017.

Mühling, Andreas. "Heinrich Bullinger as Church Politician." Pages 243–53 in *Architect of Reformation: An Introduction to Heinrich Bullinger, 1504–1575*. Edited by Bruce Gordon and Emidio Campi. Grand Rapids: Baker, 2004.

Nauert, Charles G. *Humanism and the Culture of Renaissance Europe*. Cambridge: Cambridge University Press, 1995.

Oberman, Heiko A. *The Dawn of the Reformation: Essays in Late Medieval and Early Reformation Thought*. Edinburgh: T&T Clark, 1986.

———. *Forerunners of the Reformation: The Shape of Late Medieval Thought*. Translated by Paul L. Nyhus. London: Lutterworth, 1967.

Old, Hughes Oliphant. *The Reading and Preaching of the Scriptures in the Worship of the Christian Church, Volume 4: The Age of the Reformation*. Grand Rapids: Eerdmans, 2002.

Opitz, Peter. "The Authority of Scripture in the Early Zurich Reformation (1522–1540)." *Journal of Reformed Theology* 5 (2011): 296–309.

———. "The Exegetical and Hermeneutical Work of John Oecolampadius, Huldrych Zwingli, and John Calvin." Pages 407–51 in *From the Renaissance to the Enlightenment* of *Hebrew Bible / Old Testament: The History of Its Interpretation*. Edited by Magne Sæbø. Göttingen: Vandenhoeck & Ruprecht, 2008.

Ozment, Steven. *The Age of Reform 1250–1550: An Intellectual and Religious History of Late Medieval and Reformation Europe*. New Haven: Yale University Press, 1980.

Pabel, Hilmar M. *Erasmus' Vision of the Church*. Kirksville, MO: Truman State University Press, 1994.

Packull, Werner O. *Hutterite Beginnings: Communitarian Experiments during the Reformation*. Baltimore: Johns Hopkins University Press, 1999.

Pak, G. Sujin. *The Reformation of Prophecy: Early Modern Interpretations of the Prophet and Old Testament Prophecy*. Oxford: Oxford University Press, 2018.

Pfister, Rudolf. *Kirchengeschichte der Schweiz*. Vol. 1. Zurich: Theologischer Verlag Zurich, 1974.

Phillips, Margaret Mann. *Erasmus and the Northern Renaissance*. London: Hodder & Stoughton, 1949.

Plummer, Marjorie Elizabeth. *From Priest's Whore to Pastor's Wife: Clerical Marriage and the Process of Reform in the Early German Reformation*. Surrey: Ashgate, 2012.

Potgieter, Raymond. "Anna Reinhard Zwingli—'Apostolic Dorcas,' 'Dearest Housewife,' 'Angel-wife,' 'Ziel van Mijn' and 'Mater Dolorosa of the Reformation': From Woman to Valued Citizen." *In die Skriflig / In Luce Verbi* 50, no. 3 (2016): 1–8.

Potter, G. R. *Zwingli*. Cambridge: Cambridge University Press, 1978.

Pries, Edmund. "Oath Refusal in Zurich from 1525 to 1527: The Erratic Emergence of Anabaptist Practice." Pages 65–84 in *Anabaptism Revisited*. Edited by Walter Klaassen. Scottdale: Herald Press, 1992.

Provost, Darren M. "Erasmus, Christian Humanism, and Spiritual Warfare." Pages 119–34 in *Re-Envisioning Christian Humanism: Education and the Restoration of Humanity*. Edited by Jens Zimmermann. Oxford: Oxford University Press, 2019.

Reeve, Michael D. "Classical Scholarship." Pages 20–46 in *The Cambridge Companion to Renaissance Humanism*. Edited by Jill Kraye. Cambridge: Cambridge University Press, 1995.

Rich, Arthur. *Die Anfänge der Theologie Huldrych Zwinglis*. Zürich: Zwingli-Verlag, 1949.

Rilliet, Jean. *Zwingli: Third Man of the Reformation*. Translated by Harold Knight. Philadelphia: Westminster, 1964.

Romano, John F. "Priests and the Eucharist in the Middle Ages." Pages 188–216 in *A Companion to Priesthood: Priesthood and Holy Orders in the Middle Ages*. Edited by Greg Peters and C. Colt Anderson. Leiden: Brill, 2016.

Rummel, Erika. "The Theology of Erasmus." Pages 28–38 in *The Cambridge Companion to Reformation Theology*. Edited by David Bagchi and David C. Steinmetz. Cambridge: Cambridge University Press, 2004.

Schoeck, R. J. *Erasmus of Europe: The Prince of the Humanists 1501–1536*. Edinburgh: Edinburgh University Press, 1993.

Snavely, Iren L., Jr. "Huldrych Zwingli and the Preaching Office in German Switzerland." *Fides et Historia* 25 (1993): 33–45.

———. "Ulrich Zwingli (1484–1531)." Pages 249–55 in *Historical Handbook of Major Biblical Interpreters*. Edited by Donald K. McKim. Downers Grove, IL: InterVarsity Press, 1998.

Snyder, C. Arnold. "Swiss Anabaptism: The Beginnings, 1523–1525." Pages 45–81 in *A Companion to Anabaptism and Spiritualism, 1521–1700*. Edited by John D. Roth and James M. Stayer. Leiden: Brill, 2007.

———. "Word and Power in Reformation Zurich." *Archiv für Reformationsgeschichte* 81 (1990): 263–85.

Stayer, James M. *Anabaptists and the Sword*. Lawrence: Coronado Press, 1972.

Stephens, W. Peter. *The Theology of Huldrych Zwingli*. Oxford: Clarendon, 1986.

———. "The Theology of Zwingli." Pages 80–99 in *The Cambridge Companion to Reformation Theology*. Edited by David Bagchi and David C. Steinmetz. Cambridge: Cambridge University Press, 2004.

———. *Zwingli: An Introduction to His Thought*. Oxford: Clarendon, 1994.

Strübind, Andrea. *Eifriger als Zwingli: Die frühe Täuferbewegung in der Schweiz*. Berlin: Duncker & Humblot, 2003.

Tafilowski, Ryan. "Marburg Colloquy." Pages 498–500 in *Encyclopedia of Martin Luther and the Reformation*. Edited by Mark A. Lamport. New York: Rowman & Littlefield, 2017.

Tanner, Norman P. *Decrees of the Ecumenical Councils*. Vol. 1. Washington, DC: Georgetown University Press, 1990.

Tucker, Ruth A. *Parade of Faith: A Biographical History of the Christian Church*. Grand Rapids: Zondervan, 2015.

Vanhoozer, Kevin J. "Sola Scriptura, Tradition, and Catholicity." Pages 109–28 in *Worship, Tradition, and Engagement: Essays in Honor of Timothy George*. Edited by David S. Dockery, James Early Masey, and Romert Smith, Jr. Eugene, OR: Pickwick, 2018.

Wandel, Lee Palmer. *Always Among Us: Images of the Poor in Zwingli's Zurich*. Cambridge: Cambridge University Press, 1990.

———. *The Eucharist in the Reformation: Incarnation and Liturgy*. Cambridge: Cambridge University Press, 2006.

———. *Voracious Idols & Violent Hands: Iconoclasm in Reformation Zurich, Strasbourg, and Basel*. Cambridge: Cambridge University Press, 1999.

White, James F. *Protestant Worship: Traditions in Transition*. Louisville: Westminster John Knox, 1989.

Whitney, J. P. "The Helvetic Reformation." Pages 305–41 in vol. 2 of *The Cambridge Modern History*. Edited by A. W. Ward, G. W. Prothero, and Stanley Leathes. The Macmillan Company, 1907.

Williams, George Huntston. *The Radical Reformation*. Philadelphia: Westminster, 1962.

Winkler, Mary G. "A Divided Heart: Idolatry and the Portraiture of Hans Asper." *The Sixteenth Century Journal* 18 (1987): 213–30.

Yarnell, Malcolm B. "Anabaptist Spirituality." Pages 151–75 in *The Pure Flame of Devotion: The History of Christian Spirituality*. Edited by G. Stephen Weaver Jr. and Ian Hugh Clary. Kitchener: Joshua Press, 2013.

Yoder, John H. *Anabaptism and Reformation in Switzerland: An Historical and Theological Analysis of the Dialogues Between Anabaptists and Reformers*. Kitchener: Pandora Press, 2004.

Subject & Author Index

Scripture Index

Old Testament

New Testament